WORDS

of

WISDOM

Four Minutes a Day to
A Richer and More Powerful Vocabulary
by
Stan Dunlap

This is a book you just have to put down –
every day after you spend four minutes with it

www.MorePowerfulWords.com

Why **Words of Wisdom**?

One third of students who start 9th grade do not complete high school.

One-Third of a Nation: Rising Dropout Rates and Declining Opportunities

Educational Testing Service

http://www.ets.org/Media/Education_Topics/pdf/onethird.pdf

"California and the nation are facing a dropout crisis. About one-quarter of all students who enter the ninth grade fail to earn a diploma four years later. … Higher English language proficiency also lowers the odds of dropping out."

The California Dropout Research Project

http://www.slocounty.ca.gov/Assets/CSN/PDF/Flyer++Why+students+drop+out.pdf

"Of the two ways students acquire vocabulary, direct study is the more efficient, particularly for high-risk students with poor vocabularies. There are several reasons that students may fail to learn new vocabulary on their own: high-risk students often have a history of reading difficulties. As a result, these students generally read less— and with less comprehension—than students with strong reading skills and rich vocabularies. The less students read, the fewer the opportunities to acquire new vocabulary."

Helping Students Learn Vocabulary-Acquisition Skills

http://www.glencoe.com/sec/teachingtoday/subject/vocab_acquisition.phtml

"Many English Language Learners [ELLs] lack content area vocabulary & have limited comprehension skills in English. Although they may be able to sound out words phonetically, they may not be able to ascertain meaning from the context. English contains many idioms and figurative expressions that may be overwhelming to ELLs. Furthermore, the cultural background depicted in the text may be unfamiliar."

Teaching English Language Learners Across the Content Areas   **by Judie Haynes**

[Our recent] "study also noted significant gaps between proficiency levels among English language learners and other students: Of the 35 states examined, 11 had differences of more than 30 percentage points between English-learner students and their non-ELL counterparts. … The findings come as the English language learner population continues to grow: In 2007, 20% of U.S. children ages 5 to 17 spoke a language other than English at home, up from nine percent in 1979."

Center for Education Policy   http://www.cep-dc.org/

We must address and resolve the incredible challenges facing students and all people learning English if we are to save our future.

Bob Girard

WORDS of WISDOM

Four Minutes a Day to
A Richer and More Powerful
Vocabulary

by

Stan Dunlap

www.MorePowerfulWords.com

Fresh Perspectives

Alternate forms: The content of this book is also available in PowerPoint Show format on DVD.
Contact Fresh Perspectives or go to the www.MorePowerfulWords.com website for details.
Some of the content available in that format is not available in this book format and vice versa.
The author is available for further training related to the content, face to face or on-line.
Coursework based on this text is available, including the option of graduate credit.
Using "Words of Wisdom" to Enhance Writing and Technology Skills
Contact Fresh Perspectives for details. freshper@gmail.com

The fact that an organization or website is referred to in this work as a citation or possible
source of additional information does not mean that the author or the publisher endorses that
source. Neither the publisher nor the author shall be liable for damages arising herefrom.
Further the reader should be aware that Internet websites listed in this work may have changed
or disappeared between when this work was written and when it is read.

Cover art: Stan Dunlap

Trademarks: The Fresh Perspectives logo, the "Words of Wisdom: Four Minutes a Day to a
Richer and More Powerful Vocabulary" logo, the cover and background art and the
www.MorePowerfulWords.com website are registered trademarks of Fresh Perspectives.

Library of Congress Cataloging-in-Publication Data:
Dunlap, Stan
   "Words of Wisdom: Four Minutes a Day to a Richer and More Powerful Vocabulary" /
      By Stan Dunlap
   ISBN 978-0-615-36469-8

Acknowledgements

The author would like to thank all his teachers over the years, as well as the thousands of his students who have all taught him so much.

Thaves -- creator of "Frank & Ernest" who continue to bring new meaning to double entendre

Jonathon Hartsell, creator of "Let's Have a Word or Two"

Thanks also to Mary for her patience and support.

Dedication

The author would like to dedicate this book to:

Family – Stanley & Martha and my brothers and sisters who helped me learn to love language – and to all our children, grandchildren and great grandchild who symbolize the future

Readers & Learners – in hopes that your literacy and love of language will be enhanced through this effort

Words of Wisdom

Four minutes a day to a richer and more powerful vocabulary

by
Stan Dunlap

Foreword

Welcome to "***Words of Wisdom***".

This book is intended to help you expand your vocabulary by understanding families of words – roots, stems, affixes (both prefixes and suffixes). Rather than just providing isolated words without context, this book is designed to help you see how words in our American English language evolved – where they came from and where they are as of now.

Starting with a root word – frequently a Latin verb or noun – we will add prefixes and suffixes to that stem and help you build your vocabulary from that context.

The chances are very good that you will be seeing some words that you already know. ***Words of Wisdom*** will show you some words that may have been right next to those and that can easily be added to your <u>active vocabulary</u>.

Understand that vocabulary exists on many levels. There are words that you have never seen or heard before. These words are total strangers. What you do when you encounter them is critical. I hope that you will want to learn more about them. ***Words of Wisdom*** will teach you to do that.

There are words that you may have seen or heard before, but perhaps you really hadn't paid any attention to them or come to understand what they mean. More importantly, you may not be able to explain what the word means. These words are "on this planet", but not a close acquaintance for you.

Next there are words that you recognize because you have seen or heard them before and remember the context. You may be able to use the word, but cannot clearly explain it. Sadly, recognition and even occasional usage does not make it a successful part of your <u>active vocabulary</u>.

There are words you use when you write and speak.

If a working definition of vocabulary could be "all the words known and used by a particular person", then vocabulary ownership needs to be defined by this quality:

A person is <u>fluent</u> with the word – knows how to <u>explain</u> and <u>use</u> it.

Words of Wisdom offers you the tools to make over 2,500 words part of your active vocabulary.

It's great to watch children acquire language, because vocabulary growth requires no effort. Babies hear words and mimic them. Eventually, they associate them with specific objects and actions. This is how they build their listening vocabulary.

As the child grows, the smattering of "almost words" comes into focus and the speaking vocabulary develops. They are learning that the sounds they are making mean something to the big people in their lives. This is truly a joyous time for the big people, as well as for the little ones.

When students go to school, both the listening and speaking vocabularies grow. Next they learn to associate their sounds with these squiggly little lines that big people like to write on paper and classroom boards. This establishes the oral/visual connection required for reading. Then teachers work on helping students acquire hundreds of basic words.

By the time an English-speaking child from a middle class family enters first grade, the child will *know* about 2,500–5,000 words. The higher the level of "advantage" the student has, the richer the vocabulary. This means that some first graders already have twice as many words in their vocabulary as some of their classmates. Ask any first grade teacher about the range they see. A typical student learns some 2,000-3,000 words per year, or approximately five to eight words per day. Elementary teachers frequently concentrate on the 570 words in the Academic Word List (AWL) or the 850 families from the University Word List (UWL).

Words of Wisdom is designed to build on that foundation. The basic premise is to help readers carefully OBSERVE words and learn to analyze them. Knowing the multiple options offered by several dozen prefixes and suffixes can provide great insights into new words that readers encounter. Knowing the origin of dozens of Latin verbs and multiple nouns and adjectives provides a powerful base of knowledge. By the time you finish this book, I hope that you can look at a word and analyze it – find its root, understand what the affixes may tell you

By knowing the 2000 most frequent word families of English, readers can understand approximately 80% of the words in any text. Unfortunately, recent studies indicate that approximately one third of college freshmen require remedial work, so there are some gaps in this knowledge base.

Words of Wisdom targets the "passive" vocabulary that people hear and helps you make that "active" – words that come to mind immediately when you need to use them in a sentence, either orally or in writing.

How to use this book
This is not a book that you "can't put down".
This is a book you can and should put down – every day – <u>after</u> you have invested four minutes in it. It is designed to be chewed on in small bites, roughly four minutes a day, one lesson at a time.

OK, I must warn you that you may spend more than four minutes on some of the lessons. Consider the time an investment in <u>YOU</u>.

Key words will be in bold with the root underlined and prefixes in italics. At the back (p.215-227) is an Index containing the 2690 words referenced in the book identified by Unit-lesson (e.g. "acrimonious 7-80" tells you that you can find more details in Unit 7, lesson 80). Feel free to use this approach when you find a new word and wish to learn more about it.

If you find additional words in the sample sentences with which you are not familiar, check them out and add them to your vocabulary.

The key is for you to be able to look at and analyze a word. Identify the root word or stem and affixes (pre- and suf-) connected to the stem and dig down towards its meaning.

Each lesson comes with an assignment. Be sure to work through it in ways that make most sense for you. One part of the assignment suggests that you look up the word in a dictionary to gain additional insights into the etymology and optional meanings of the word. In this age of technology, you may prefer to "Google it" or check it out on Ask.com or Bing or Metacrawler or one of the many search engines available to you. If you are using Microsoft Office and are on-line, you can **Alt + Click** on a word or phrase and use the Research tool built in to the software to gain additional information. Some on-line dictionaries also offer you the pronunciation of the word. However you choose to do it, the idea is for you to get a deeper understanding of the words. Truthfully, my hope is that you can fall in love with words.

BTW (By The Way), I have included many additional words in the context of the definitions and explanatory sentences that might be new to you. Check them out and see if you wish to include them in <u>your</u> active vocabulary.

Pronunciation – I have never been a big fan of the dictionary style pronunciation guides, so I have taken the liberty of inserting my own version after some of the key words in each lesson. I hope it works for you. If it doesn't work for you, feel free to use the key provided in dictionaries or the pronunciation audio in the on-line dictionaries.

It's rarely possible to learn a word with just one exposure to it, so the more ways you can use a new word, the better chance you have of integrating it into your active vocabulary. Part of the assignment invites you to create a word processing document and **write** a sentence for each new word. If you prefer to keep a notebook or journal, go for it. You can also hand-write a sentence if that works best for you.

If you follow Twitter, consider tweeting your sentence as one option. Start your sentence with **WordsOfWisdom** and tweet away. When you follow it on Twitter or if you are on Facebook, follow the **WordsOfWisdom** face and see what other users have come up with.

If you are a graphical learner and happen to have graphic organization software, such as Inspiration or Kidspiration or even SmartArt in Office 2007, use that to organize the relationships among the various word families. I incorporate some SmartArt graphics to show interconnections.

I am a big fan of summarizing. You can easily incorporate that into your journal or word processing document. Challenge yourself to write a concise definition of the word in your own words. After all, when you are finished with this book, that's what you will do anyway, so start practicing now.

LISTEN and **WATCH** for these words to see how others use them.

The assignment also asks you to be Metacognitive (5-37) in your learning. **Reflect** on what you have learned from the lesson and include a sentence or two containing your insights into those words.

Periodically, look back over the Review at the end of each unit to make sure you can still explain the terms in your own words.

Use a strategy for learning that works for you. This is your vocabulary.

Make these *Words of Wisdom* yours – own them – love them!

Enjoy and learn bunches!

Stan

www.MorePowerfulWords.com

Words of Wisdom

Four minutes a day to a richer and more powerful vocabulary

Table of Contents

Unit Five   **What's going on inside that head of yours?**

Unit Six   **What do you mean "the Romans conjugated"?**

Unit Seven   **I must DECLINE that noun, but thanks for the kind offer**

WORDS of WISDOM

Four Minutes a Day to
A Richer and More Powerful
Vocabulary

by

Stan Dunlap

www.MorePowerfulWords.com
Published by
Fresh Perspectives

Words of Wisdom

Four minutes a day to a richer and more powerful vocabulary
Unit One
Lesson 1

Let's start by looking at some simple words, words that are undoubtedly already part of your active vocabulary, such as **PREFIX**

Where did it come from? The two components of this word came from two Latin words used by the Romans two millennia ago.

Pre – comes from the Latin preposition "*prae-*" or "*pre-*", meaning "in front of" or "before"

fix – comes from the Latin verb "*figere*" {fuh GARE ray}, meaning "to fasten" or "to attach"

As with many other words in American English, this word can be used in several different ways:

> Prefix – (noun or n.) an affix attached to the beginning of a word
> Prefix – (verb or v.) to place in front

One of the ways to assess if this word or phrase is part of your active vocabulary is to see if you can use it in a sentence to effectively demonstrate appropriate understanding and correct usage.

> "He identified the prefix 'pre' attached to the beginning of the word prefix."
> "She planned to prefix the word verse with 're'."

The other component is the root – the simple element that is the basis from which a word is derived. In this case, *fix* comes from the Latin verb

> *figo* (literally *I fix*, first person singular present active indicative tense),
> *figere* (*to fix*, from the infinitive),
> *fixi* (*I have fixed,* first person singular, perfect tense) and
> *fixum* (*to be fixed* or *having been fixed,* past participle or participial).

The stem generally comes from one or more of those Principal Parts by removing the standard verbal endings. In this case, the stem could be "*fig-*" or "*fix-*".

Let's move on to a word that most car drivers use every day – **reverse**. Like many words, this can be used as several different parts of speech.

> **re<u>verse</u>** – {re VURS} (verb or v.) "to turn completely about in position or direction"
> **re<u>verse</u>** – (noun or n.) "a gear that reverses direction, e.g. in a car"

It's time to break it apart and see where it came from.

> **re** – {ree} from Latin preposition "re" {ray}, meaning "back" or "backward";
> in other contexts, re can also mean "again" or "about" or "over"

vers- from Latin verb "vertere", meaning "to turn" (more in lesson 2)
This can also be modified multiple ways and each can have multiple, precise meanings.

> *re**vers**ed* – v. past tense
>
> *re**vers**ing* – present participle
>
> *re**vers**al* – n. the act or process of reversing
>
> *re**vers**ion* – {re VUR zhun} n. the act of turning the opposite way;
>> future interest in property left in control of a grantor
>
> *re**vers**ionary* –adjective (adj.) relating to or involving a legal reversion
>
> *re**vers**ible* – adj. able to be reversed

Observe that the stem in these words is **vers-**.

Now, use each of these words in a sentence that will support clear understanding.

"She reversed her decision."

"He is reversing the direction of his car."

"The Supreme Court ordered a reversal of the lower court's ruling."

"He was sad that the reversion of his father's estate left him penniless."

"She felt the reversionary tactics of the lawyers were disgraceful."

"Since his jacket was reversible, he chose to wear the plaid side out."

Remember that there was another stem available: **vert**. There are several words that flow from that stem.

> *re**vert*** – {re VURT} v. "to return or come back to a former condition"

"Without someone to closely supervise him, he will revert to his old ways."

Beyond that basic word, there are several variants: reverted, reverter, revertible, revertant.

Review:

Prefix	Reversing	Reversion	Revert
Reverse	Reversible	Reversionary	Reverted
Reversed	Reversal	Reverter	Revertant

Assignment:

- Carefully **observe** each of the above words from this lesson. Be sure you can identify the root word and prefix.
- **Create** a word processing document that you can use for this book or **write** in a journal or diary.
- **Explain** each word in your own words (because after you are finished with this book, that's what you will do anyway). You may do this orally, but the impact would stay with you longer if you write it down or type it.
- If you need help or want to find some additional insights into a word, be sure to **refer to a dictionary**. Check the etymology of the word to trace its roots. Check any specific usages and optional meanings.
- **Write a sentence** for each word in which the meaning of the word is clearly discernible to a reader.
- See if these words will "fit" into your vocabulary, especially those words with which you were not previously familiar. **Work them into your conversation**.
- Write a sentence or paragraph in which you **reflect** on what you have learned from this lesson, on any insights or AHA moments

Unit One
Lesson 2

In Lesson 1, we looked at "reverse" and found that the root was the Latin verb "*vertere*". Let's explore that in more detail. The traditional method of presenting verbs to be studied in Latin was to observe the Principal Parts, as you saw with "*figere*" in Lesson 1.

The Principal Parts of "*vertere*" are: *verso, vertere, vertavi, versus*

> *verso* – 1st person singular, present tense – "I turn"
> *vertere* – present infinitive – "to turn"
> *vertavi* – 1st person singular, perfect– "I turned"
> *versus* – past participle – "have turned"

Looking closely at the principal parts, the stems present themselves:

Stems: present - , perfect - , participial -

> **vers**o   – present – vers
> **vert**avi   – perfect tense – vert
> **vers**us   – past participle or participial – vers

So the stems for "vertere" are: **vers**-... or **vert**-...

Sometimes, the stem itself exposes the words in American English (stem underlined).

> **vers**e –n. "a line of metrical writing"
> **vers**ion – n. "a translation, esp. one from another language; an account from a particular viewpoint"
> **vers**us – adv. "against, in contrast to"
> **vers**o –n. "the page being turned, as for a pianist"

These can be demonstrated in sentences such as the following.

"The last verse of her poem moved me to tears."
"His version of the translation of Cicero seemed very fluid and easy to read."
"The main event was Godzilla versus Gigan."
"The assistant lightly grabbed the verso before turning to the next page."

Likewise, the other stem—vert – is also visible in our language.

> **vert**ex (pl. **vert**ices) – n. "██████; point of an angle where two sides meet"
> **vert**igo – n. "a disordered state in which the person's surroundings seem to whirl about dizzily"

"Point A was the vertex of the equilateral triangle."
"He experienced intense vertigo when he looked over the balcony of the penthouse."

Just as we have added prefixes to words in our language today, the Romans also added prefixes to many of their verbs, such as   *reversare* {ray ver SAHR ray}

Principal Parts: reverso, reversere, revertavi, reversus

Consequently, the **stems** are _revers-_ and _revert-_.

4

Understand that words in American English may have evolved either from the basic root or the Latin root with the prefix attached. Either way, the words are ours to use. Let's work with another prefix and the root word "*vertere*".

> *in* – "in" or "inside" or "not"

As mentioned earlier, the Romans also added prefixes to many of their words which changed the meaning.

invertere *inversus*   "to turn inside out or upside down; turned upside down"

> Principal Parts: *inverso, invertere, invertavi, inversus*
> Stems: ***invers***... and ***invert***...

Here are some words that flow from the stem ***invers***.

> ***inverse*** – {in VURCE} adj. "opposite in order or effect"
> ***inversion*** – n. "state of being inverted; a reversal of position"
> "Subtraction is the inverse operation of addition."
> "The inversion layer over the city left a brown layer for people to breathe."

Likewise, several words come directly from the stem ***invert***-.

> ***invert*** – v. "to turn upside down"
> ***inverted*** – v. past tense
> ***inverter*** – n. "one who inverts; a device that changes DC to AC"
> ***invertible*** – adj. "able to be inverted"
> "When the fraction was inverted, the result was a reciprocal of the original number."
> "A fraction, such as 2/3, is invertible and can be inverted to 3/2."
> "He used an inverter to change the direct current to alternating current."

Review:	Verse	Verso	Inverse	Invert
	Version	Vertex	Inversion	Inverted
	Versus	Vertices		Inverter
	Verso	Vertigo		Invertible

Assignment:

- Carefully **observe** each of the above words from this lesson. Be sure you can identify the root word and prefix.
- In your word processing document, **explain** each word in your own words.
- **Refer to a dictionary** or other resource for etymology and specific usages and optional meanings.
- **Write a sentence** for each word in which the meaning of the word is clearly discernible to a reader.
- Try to **work these words into your conversation**.
- Write a sentence or paragraph in which you **reflect** on what you have learned from this lesson

Unit One
Lesson 3

In Lessons 1 and 2, we looked at variations of the Latin verb *vertere*. Let's add several more prefixes and see how that impacts the root.

    sub- "under" or "beneath" or "below"

The Romans also added prefixes such as this to many of their words

    subvertere   To turn from beneath
    Principal Parts: *subverso, subvertere, subvertavi, subversus*
    Stems: *subvers-*, *subvert-*

Several words have come to English from the stem *subvers-*.

    subversion – n. "act of overthrowing, usually a government"
    subversive – adj. "describing activity designed to overthrow or overturn"

Use of these words in a sentence will help insure their inclusion in your vocabulary.

    "Their subversive activities were easily detected by the FBI."
    "Attempted subversion of the government is considered treason."

Likewise, the *subvert-* stem sends words directly into English.

    subvert – v. "to overturn or overthrow"
    subverter – n. "a person who intends to overthrow or undermine morals, faith or allegiance"

    "Socrates was accused of being a subverter of the morals of the young."
    "The underground planned to subvert the corrupt government."

See also: *subversiveness, subversively*

Another prefix that the Romans added to *vertere* was "*intro-*" or sometimes "*intra-*".

    intro- or *intra-* "inside" or "within"
    Principal Parts: *introverso, introvertere, introvertavi, introversus*

introvertere	*introversus*
Infinitive	Participial
Literally, *"to turn inside"*	*"turned within"*

    Stems: *introvers-*, *introvert-*

In English, we find these words from that "*intro-*" stem.

    introvert – n. "a reserved or shy person"; v. "to turn inward"
    introversion – n. "state of being introverted or predominantly interested in one's own mental life"
    introversive or *introverted* – adj. "used to describe a personality characterized by introversion"

    "He is such an introvert that he rarely looks anyone else in the face."
    "When I was in high school, my speech teacher helped me escape my introversion."
    "Her introversive personality kept her from asking anyone to dance."

See also: *introversively*

The Romans balanced the inward movement with a preposition pointing outward.

Extro- or *extra-* "outside" or "without"	
extrovertere	*extroversus*
Infinitive	Participial

Literally, *"to turn outside"*   *"turned without"*

Stems: _extrovert-_, _extrovers-_

These words flow directly ...

extrovert (or extravert) – n. "a gregarious and unreserved person"

extroverted – adj. "characterized by an outgoing or gregarious personality"

extroversion (or extraversion) – n. "state of being predominantly interested in obtaining gratification from what is outside the self"

"He is truly an extrovert; he has never met a person who wasn't his friend."

"Her extraverted personality makes her a pleasure at any party."

"His extroversion has allowed him to meet many interesting people."

Review:

Subversion	Introvert	Extrovert (or extravert)
Subversive	Introverted	Extroverted (or extraverted)
Subvert	Introversive	Extroversion (or extraversion)
Subverter	Introversion	Introversively
Subversiveness		

CHOOSE: Select the word that best fits the sentence –

subvert   introvert   invert   vertigo

Socrates was accused of trying to _____ the morals of the youth of Athens.

extroverted   inverted   subverted   introverted

Once the fraction was _____, the result was the reciprocal of the original.

Assignment:

- When you **observe** each of the above words from this lesson, be sure you can identify the root word and prefix.
- In your word processing document or journal, **explain** each word in your own words.
- **Refer to a dictionary** for etymology and specific usages and optional meanings.
- **Write a sentence** for each word in which the meaning of the word is clearly discernible to a reader.
- Try to **work these words into your conversation**.
- Write a sentence or paragraph in which you **reflect** on what you have learned from this lesson. Capture the insights you had along the way.

Unit One
Lesson 4

In Lessons 1 through 3, we looked at variations of the Latin verb vertere. Let's add several more prefixes.

The Romans had a preposition *"cum"* [koom] which meant "with" or "together" or "jointly". As this was prefixed to a variety of verbs, depending on the following consonant it was adapted to also be *"com-"* or *"con-"* or *"col-"* or *"cor-"*. With *"vertere"*, it typically has taken the *"con-"* form. When affixed to the vertere stems (**vert-** and **vers-**), it shows up in the following words:

> **con**vert – {kun VURT} v. "to turn with, to turn around, to transform"
> **con**vert –{CON vurs} n. "one who is converted"
> **con**vert**ible** – adj. "something that can be changed or converted";
> n. "a car with a flexibly operating roof"
> **con**vert**er** –{kun VURT er} n. "a device to change one form to another"

"He hoped to convert his friend to his religious views."
"He became a convert to Christianity."
"His red convertible drew much attention on campus."
"There are many types of converters – catalytic on a car, a cable converter,
a torque converter, a currency converter."

> **con**vers**e** – {kun VURS} v. "to carry on a conversation"
> **con**vers**e** – {CON vurs} adj. or n. "opposite in order or effect, e.g. a math theorem"
> **con**vers**ion** – n. "process of being converted"; "reduction in math"
> **con**vers**ation** – n. "oral exchange of ideas, opinions, sentiments"

"She agreed to converse with him by phone or in person. "
"His approach to solving the problem was the converse of the teacher."
"Her conversion from Judaism to Buddhism surprised her friends."
"It's difficult to carry on a private conversation in a crowded room."
"A single conversation across a table with a wise man is worth a month's study of books." *Chinese proverb*
See also: **conversationalist, conversance, conversant, conversable, convertibly**

The Romans also had the preposition *"dis-"* which meant "apart". As it evolved into American English, it was shortened to *"di"* and can mean "aside" or "apart". Here are some of the words that come from the Latin word *"divertere"*, with stems of *divert-* and *divers-*.

> **di**vert – {duh VURT} v." to turn from one course to another"

"The baby-sitter tried to divert the baby's attention from the electrical outlet."

   diver**se** {duh VURS} – adj. "differing from one another"

   diver**sion** – n. "the act of diverting from a course, activity or use; amusement"

   diver**sionary** – adj. "tending to draw attention away from the primary concern"

"He has many and diverse interests."

"She practiced yoga as a diversion from the stress of her work."

"The diversionary tactics use by the army distracted the enemy forces."

   diver**sity** – n. "the condition or instance of being diverse"

   diver**sify** – v. "to give variety to; to engage in varied operations"

"Our planet contains an incredible diversity of living creatures."

"His broker suggested that he needed to diversify his stock portfolio."

See also: **diversification, diversifier**

Review:	Convert (v.or n.)	Conversation	Divert	Diversification
	Converter	Conversationalist	Diverse	Diversifier
	Convertible	Conversance	Diversion	
	Converse (v.or adj.)	Conversant	Diversity	
	Conversion	Conversable	Diversionary	
		Convertibly	Diversify	

CHOOSE: Select the word(s) that best fits the sentence –

   converse   diverse   inverse   reverse

His _____ interests allowed him to _____ easily with total strangers.

   diversion   inversion   subversion   introversion

For him, juggling chainsaws was a _____ from his log-cutting duties.

Assignment:
- Carefully **observe** each of the above words from this lesson. Be sure you can identify the root word and prefix.
- In your word processing document, **explain** each word in your own words.
- **Refer to a dictionary** for etymology and specific usages and optional meanings.
- **Write a sentence** for each word in which the meaning of the word is clearly discernible to a reader.
- Try to **work these words into your conversation**.
- Write a sentence or paragraph in which you **reflect** on what you have learned from this lesson

Are you getting comfortable with the process of getting your thoughts down about these new words? Future assignments will be simpler, but the key is for you to find the best way for YOU to absorb these words into your active vocabulary.

Unit One
Lesson 5

In previous lessons, we looked at variations of the Latin verb *vertere*. Let's add several more prefixes.

The Latin preposition *"trans-"* meant "across". When it was attached as a prefix to *"vertere"*, it became *"transvertere"* and left this one stem from the participial: *"transvers-"*.

From this stem, these are some of the words that have evolved:

trans<u>vers</u>e – {trans VURS} adj. "set crosswise"
trans<u>vers</u>e – n. "something that is transverse"
trans<u>vers</u>al – n. "a line that intersects a series of lines"

"The transverse colon extends across the abdominal cavity."
"The hiker encountered a log that was transverse to the trail."
"After drawing two parallel lines, I also drew a transversal that cut across both of them."
See also: **transversely**
In an interesting evolutionary trail, the "ns" was dropped for some terms.

tra<u>vers</u>e – {truh VURS} v. "to go or travel across; to ski across a hill rather than down"
tra<u>vers</u>e – n. "something that crosses or lies across; an obstacle; adversity; a zigzag course for a ship with contrary winds"
tra<u>vers</u>al – n. "the act or an instance of traversing"

"It was fun to watch her traverse the ski slope, zigzagging her way back and forth to the bottom."
"Without sustained winds, the sailboat had to execute a careful traverse."
"The cross country skier's traversal of the avalanche zone loosened the unstable snowpack."
Also:

tra<u>vers</u>ed – (v.) past tense , "I traversed the mountain."
tra<u>vers</u>ing - (v.) present progressive, "I am traversing the mountain."
tra<u>vers</u>er - (n.) one who traverses, "All eyes were on the traverser."
tra<u>vers</u>able - (adj.) can be traversed,
"Though it was a challenge, the steep hillside was traversable."

Sometimes, the Romans wanted to indicate direction. They accomplished this with the preposition "ad" or the shortened form "a" meaning "to" or "toward". This cluster uses the *"advert-"* stem.

*ad***vert** {ad VURT} - v. "to turn the mind or attention"
*ad***vertent** – adj. "paying attention; heedful"
*ad***vertence** – n. "the process of adverting; paying attention"
*ad***vertency** – n. "quality of being advertent; heedfulness"

"The student adverted his attention to his teacher's lecture."
"She was advertent to her parents' warning."
"Advertence to teacher instructions is a great quality for a student."
"Advertency to details was only one of her attributes as a learner."
See also: **Advertently**

In Lesson 6, we will explore many more variations of "*ad-*" and "*a-*" plus "*vertere*".

Review:		
Transverse (v. or n.)	**Traversing**	**Advert**
Transversal	**Traverser**	**Advertent**
Traverse (v. or n.)	**Traversable**	**Advertence**
Traversal		**Advertency**
Traversed		**Advertently**

CHOOSE: Select the word(s) that best fits the sentence –

converse   traverse   inverse   transverse
She plans to _____ the mountain just below the glacier.

diversal   inversion   transversal   transversion
After drawing the two parallel lines, it was easy to draw the _____ to cut across them.

revert   advert   invert   extrovert
A wise student will _____ to teacher instructions.

Assignment:
- **Observe**   Be sure you can identify the root word and prefix.
- **Explain**   In your own words, what dos each word mean?
- **Use a dictionary**   Where did this word come from? What else can it mean?
- **Write a sentence** for each word
- Work these words into your conversation.
- **Reflect**   What have you learned from this lesson?

Unit One
Lesson 6

In Lesson 5, we explored some of the words available in English from "*ad-*" plus "*vertere*." Let's explore a few more.

Flowing from "***advers-***" stem are the following:

*ad**vers**ity* – adj. "acting or turned against or in a contrary direction; hostile"
*ad**vers**ity* – n. "condition contrary to one of well-being"

"The unexpected adverse weather conditions stranded many motorists."
"The adversity of the earthquake victims was painful for the aid workers."

Following the same path, but "turning" a slightly different direction, observe the following terms:

*ad**vers**ary* – n. "one who contends with, opposes or resists; opponent"
*ad**vers**arial* –adj. "characteristic of an adversary"

"The detective once again pursued his old adversary."
"Even though they were once friends, their relationship now was adversarial to say the least."
See also: **Adversariness, Adversative, Adversatively, Adverseness**

Previously, we used the preposition "in-" directly with "*vert*". Remember that one of the meanings of "in" can be negative—"no" or "not". When this is placed before these "advert" terms, the impact is noticeable.

in*advert*ent** – adj. "inattentive, unintentional"
in*advert*ence** – n. "the result of inattention; oversight"
in*advert*ently** – adv. "inattentively, unintentionally"

"His inadvertent remark left a scar."
"His inadvertence cost him a job opportunity."
"She inadvertently omitted the key ingredient in the recipe."

"***Advert***" can be expanded slightly to provide us with terms we hear nearly every day.

*ad**vert**ise* – v. "to make something known; to turn someone's attention to"
*ad**vert**isement* – n. "notice published in the paper or over the air"
*ad**vert**iser* – n. "one who places and pays for an ad"
"The company proposed a large budget to advertise its new product."
"As incredible as it seems, a thirty second advertisement during the Super Bowl cost almost $3 million."
"In tough economic times, it's harder for newspapers to find advertisers."

Finally, remember that the alternative for "*ad-*" is "*a-*". The impact is visible in the nuance.

> *a*<u>vert</u> – {uh VURT} v. "to turn aside or away (as in the eyes) in avoidance"
>
> *a*<u>verse</u> – adj. "having an active feeling of repugnance or distaste"
> *a*<u>vers</u>ion – n. "a feeling of repugnance with something, with a desire to avoid or turn from it"
> *a*<u>vers</u>ive – adj. "tending to avoid a noxious or punishing stimulus"

"The passersby averted their eyes from the horrific accident."
"His averse reaction to the stench was obvious in his facial expression."
"The teenager was accused of having a severe aversion to work."
"His aversive behavior was clearly evident by the circuitous route he took to get home."

Review:	**Adverse**	**Advertise**	**Inadvertent**	**Avert**
	Adversity	**Advertisement**	**Inadvertence**	**Averse**
	Adversary	**Advertiser**	**Inadvertently**	**Aversion**
	Adversarial	**Adversative**		**Aversive**
	Adversariness	**Adversatively**		

CHOOSE: Select the word(s) that best fits the sentence –

adverse   averse   inverse   reverse

The _____ weather conditions caught the meteorologist by surprise.

diversion   inversion   subversion   aversion

She had an intense _____ to snakes and wriggly things.

Assignment:
- **Observe** Identify each root word and prefix.
- **Explain** each word in your own words and write it down.
- **Use a dictionary** for deeper understanding
- **Write a sentence** for each word
- **Use these words into your conversation**.
- Write a sentence or paragraph that describes what you have learned from this lesson

Unit One
Lesson 7 – Review "vertere" *to turn*

In Unit One, we have explored the Latin root word "***vertere***", meaning "to turn". We have also examined the impact of adding a Latin preposition in front of "***vertere***" to see how that can significantly change the meaning of the root word. Now it's time to take a look back and see how things are fitting into your active vocabulary. Answers can be found on pages 18-19.

Prepositions: We worked with 10 different prepositions that can be "prefixed" to root words, both in Latin and in American English. Explain the basic meaning(s) of each word.

> *Ad- or a-*
> *Con-*
> *Di-*
> *Extro- or extra-*
> *In-*
> *Intro- or intra-*
> *Pre-*
> *Re-*
> *Sub-*
> *Trans-*

In the upcoming sections, identify the word that best completes the sentence or matches the definition. If you don't get it correct, just go back and look at the original lesson.

Words directly from the root word "*vertere*"

> The last _____ of her poem moved me to tears.
> In a triangle, the point at which two sides meet is called the _____.
> He experienced an intense feeling of _____ when he looked over the railing of the penthouse.
>
> Noun- the page to be turned by a pianist's assistant: _____
> Noun - an account from a particular viewpoint; a translation: _____
> Adverb - against; in contrast to: _____

Words from the root word "vertere" and the prefix "sub"

_____ is considered treason and can result in a sentence of death.
Socrates was accused of being a _____ of the morals of young people.
Adjective describing activity designed to overthrow or overturn: _____
Verb meaning to overthrow or overturn: _____

Words from the root word "vertere" and the prefix "re"

Since his coat was _____, he chose to wear the green side out for the game.
When the stock market dropped, he experienced a serious _____ of
fortune.

Verb – to change direction and go backwards: _____
Verb – to return to a former condition or pattern of behavior: _____

Words from the root word "vertere" and the prefix "trans"

Verb – to go or travel across; to ski across a hill rather than down: _____
Noun –an act or instance of traversing: _____

The _____ colon extends across the abdominal cavity.
After drawing two parallel lines, I also drew a _____ that cut across
        both of them.

Words from the root word "vertere" and the prefix "di-"

Verb – to turn from one course to another: _____
Adj. – tending to draw attention away from the primary purpose
Verb – to give variety to

Charles Darwin observed the incredible _____ of life on our planet.
There were many _____ opinions about the candidates.
The rebels created a _____ to distract the soldiers.

Words from the root word "vertere" and the prefix "intro-" & "extro-"

His _____ kept him from making friends.
He was such an _____ that a stranger was just a friend he hadn't met yet.

Noun – a person who is shy or reserved: _____
Noun –state of being predominantly interested in obtaining gratification
from what is outside the self: _____

Words from the root word "vertere" and the prefix "con"

Verb – to turn with, to turn around, to transform; to bring about a
religious conversion in: _____
Verb – to carry on a conversation: _____
Adjective – something that can be changed or converted;
n. a car with a flexibly operating roof: _____
Adjective or noun – opposite in order or effect, e.g. a math theorem: _____
He became a _____ to Christianity.
Her _____ from Judaism to Buddhism surprised her friends.
The catalytic _____ on his car failed to control emissions.
"A single _____ across a table with a wise man is worth
a month's study of books." *Chinese proverb*

Words from the root word "vertere" and the prefix "ad-"

Verb – to turn the mind or attention: _____
Noun –the process of adverting; paying attention: _____

She was wise to be _____ to her parents' warning.
_____ to details was only one of her attributes as a learner.

Words from the root word "vertere" and the prefixes "in-" and "ad-"

Noun – the result of inattention; oversight: _____
His _____ remark left a scar.
She _____ omitted the key ingredient in the recipe.

Words from the stem "vers" and the prefixes "ad-"

Noun – condition contrary to one of well-being: _____
Noun – one who contends with, opposes or resists; opponent

The unexpected _____ weather conditions stranded many motorists.
Even though they were once friends, their relationship now was _____
to say the least.

Words from the stem "vert" and the prefixes "ad-"

Verb – to make something known; to turn someone's attention to: _____
Noun – one who places and pays for an ad: _____

As incredible as it seems, a thirty second _____ during the Super Bowl costs
about $3 million.

Words from the root word "vertere" and the prefix "a-"

Adjective – having an active feeling of repugnance or distaste
Adjective— tending to avoid a noxious or punishing stimulus
The passersby _____ their eyes from the horrific accident.
The teenager was accused of having a severe _____ to work.

Words from the root word "vertere" and the prefix "in-"

Adjective – opposite in order or effect: _____
Noun – state of being inverted; a reversal of position: _____
Verb – to turn upside down: _____
Noun – one who inverts; a device that changes DC to AC: _____
When the fraction was _____, the result was a reciprocal of the original number.
A fraction, such as 2/3, is _____ and can be inverted to 3/2.
Subtraction is the _____ operation of addition.
The _____ layer over the city left a brown layer for people to breathe.

Unit 1 REVIEW Answers:

Prepositions

Ad- or a-	to or toward
Con-	with or together or jointly
	(or cum or com or col or cor or cof)
Di-	aside or apart (from the Latin "dis" apart)
Extro- or extra-	outside or without
In-	in or inside or not
Intro- or intra-	inside or within
Pre-	before
Re-	back or backward; again; about
Sub-	under or beneath or below
Trans-	across

Words from the root word "vertere"

verse   vertex   vertigo   verso   version   versus

Words from the root word "vertere" and the prefix "sub-"

subversion   subverter   subversive   subvert

Words from the root word "vertere" and the prefix "re-"

reversal   reversible   reverse   revert

Words from the root word "vertere" and the prefix "trans-"

traverse   traversal   transverse   transversal

Words from the root word "vertere" and the prefix "di-"

divert   diversionary   diversify   diversity diverse   diversion

Words from the root word "vertere" and the prefix "intro-" & "extro"

introversion   extrovert   introvert   extroversion

Words from the root word "vertere" and the prefix "con-"

convert   converse   convertible   converse
convert   conversion   converter   conversation

Words from the root word "vertere" and the prefix "ad-"

advert   advertence   advertent   advertency

Words from the stem "vers" and the prefixes "ad-"

adversity   adversary   adverse   adversarial

Words from the root word "vertere" and the prefix "ad-" and "in-"

inadvertence   inadvertent   inadvertently

Words from the stem "vert" and the prefixes "ad-"

advertise   advertiser   advertisement

Words from the root word "vertere" and the prefix "a-"

averse   aversive   averted   aversion

Words from the root word "vertere" and the prefix "in-"

inverse   inversion   inverse   inversion

invert   inverter   inverted   invertible

CONGRATULATIONS!

You have just cemented 10 prefixes and 97 words into your active vocabulary.

Words of Wisdom

Four minutes a day to a richer and more powerful vocabulary
Unit Two

In Unit Two, we will use the same approach as we used in Unit One. Your challenge is to train yourself to look carefully at words and begin to see the components – stems and affixes (prefixes and suffixes). Be sure to cement your learning by writing down the meaning of the words in words that make sense to you. Also, be sure that you can use each word in a sentence that will communicate its meaning to your readers.

ENJOY!

Unit Two
Lesson 8

Time to add a new Latin verb for your consideration: *mittere* {MIH tuh ray} "to send"
As we did with *vertere*, let's start by taking a quick look at the principal parts and their meanings.

> **Principal Parts**: *mitto, mittere, missi, missum*
> *mitto* – 1st person singular, present tense – "I send"
> *mittere* – present infinitive – "to send"
> *missi* – 1st person singular, perfect– "I sent"
> *misssum* – past participle – "have sent"

As you learned to observe carefully in Unit One, feast your eyes on the stems hidden in these parts.

> <u>mitt</u>o – present –   *mit-* or *mitt-*
> <u>miss</u>i – perfect tense –   *mis-* or *miss-*
> <u>miss</u>um – past participle – participial   *mis-* or *miss-*

Observe that these double consonants allow "*mittere*" to have stems with either one or two of the final consonants depending on the following consonant.

> **Stems**: *mis-… miss-… or mit-… mitt-…*

The following words have evolved from these stems into contemporary English:

> **mission**– n. "a ministry by a religious organization to propagate its faith; a vocation; a local church dependent on a larger church for support"
> **missionary** – n. "a person undertaking a mission, esp. a religious mission; in the fashion of a missionary"
> **missionize** – v. "to carry on missionary work"
> **mittimus** –n. "a warrant of commitment to prison" (lit. "we send" or "we are sending" –first person plural, present tense – *more on this in Unit 6*)

See also: **Missiology, Missioned, Missioning, Missionaries, Missionizer**

Like all words, these find their meaningful place in the context of a sentence.

"The church planned to establish a mission in Central America."
"The missionary labored with great zeal to help the indigenous peoples."
"Their plan was to missionize throughout the region."
"The deputy carried to mittimus for his convict to the new prison."

One of the ways "to send" something is "to throw" or "to hurl" it. Just ask any little boy.

> **missile** – n. "an object thrown or projected so as to strike something"
> **missile** – adj. "capable of being thrown; adapted for throwing missiles"
> **missive** – n. "a written communication; a letter"

"They launched an intercontinental ballistic missile."
"The missile launcher moved into position near the border."
"She sent him a scented missive to get his attention."

See also: **Missileer, Missileman, Missilery**

As we saw with "*vertere*", the Romans also added the "re" prefix to "*mittere*".

> *re* – "back" or "before"   **re<u>mitt</u>ere** – "to send back"

Stems: *remis-*… *remiss-*… or *remit-*… *remitt-*…

The words in our current language just flow right out of the stems.

> *remit* – v. "to send back"; "to give relief from suffering"; "to refer for consideration or action"
>
> *remiss* – adj. "negligent in the performance of work; careless"
>
> *remission*– n. "act or process of sending back or remitting"; "the period of relief from suffering"
>
> *remittance* – n."a sum of money remitted; transmittal of money"

"Please remit your payment promptly."

"I would be remiss in my duties if I didn't warn you about the hazards of smoking."

"Her leukemia is in remission and she is temporarily spared that agony."

"Please return your payment in the enclosed remittance envelope."

There are several other less-frequently used terms that may be just what you need.

> *remittent* – adj. "marked by alternating periods of abatement and increase of symptoms"
>
> *remise* [ree MIZE] – v. "to give, grant or release a claim"
>
> *remissible* – adj. "capable of being forgiven or released"

"The remittent nature of his illness was puzzling to his doctors."

"The prospector planned to remise the claim to a local charity."

"His minor sins were easily remissible."

> See also: **Remittal, Remitter, Remittable**

There is also an English derivative from *supermittere*

> *Surmise* – v. "to imagine or infer on slight grounds"; n. "a thought or idea based on scanty evidence, conjecture"

"Based on its design and power source, I surmised that the craft was from outer space."

Review:			
Mission	Missile (n. or adj.)	Remit	Remittent
Missionary	Missileer	Remiss	Remissible
Missionize	Missileman	Remission	Remise
Mittimus	Missilery	Remittance	Remitter
Missiology	Missive	Remittal	Remittable
Missioned	Missionaries	Missionizer	Surmise

CHOOSE: Select the word(s) that best fits the sentence –

mission   remission   mittimus   missionary

The _____ established the _____ in the lush jungle.

missile   missive   remittance

The_____ envelope required a stamp.

Assignment:

• In your word processing document, **explain** each word and use it in a sentence.

• **Use these words into your conversation**.

• **Reflect** on what you have learned.

Unit Two
Lesson 9

Previously, you have worked with variants of the Latin preposition *"cum"* meaning "with" or "together" or "jointly". The Latin verb that incorporated *mittere* was *committere* – "to entrust". The words here all begin with *"com"*, which typically doubles the "m" in English to help create the soft "o" sound.

> ***commit*** – v. "to connect, to entrust; to perpetrate (e.g. crime); to pledge oneself"
>
> ***committee*** – n. "a group of persons assigned to consider & report on some matter"
>
> ***commission*** – n. "a group of persons directed to perform some duty"; "certificate conferring military rank"; "a fee paid to an agent"
>
> ***commitment*** – n. "act of committing to a charge or trust"; "assignment to a penal or mental institution"

Work these into a sentence, such as these.

"His fear of commitment kept him from getting married."
"He planned to commit his entire wealth and energy to fighting disease."
"The committee met on Monday to begin its series of meetings."
"The Election Commission made the final decision on voter eligibility."

"Comm-" lends itself to the development of related nouns.

> ***commissioner*** – n. "a person with a commission or a member of a commission"; "officer in charge of a commission"; " administrative head of a professional sport"
>
> ***commissary*** – n. "one delegated to execute a duty or office"; "a store for equipment and provisions; food supplies"

"The NBA commissioner suspended the player for violation of league rules."
"Generally, a commissary on a military base offers service people excellent quality and prices."

> ***commissure*** – n. "a juncture of two anatomical parts, such as adjacent heart valves"
>
> ***committal*** – n. "commitment or consignment; something pledged or committed"

"The cardiologist explained the faulty commissure that was causing his patient's pain."

"The second-hand shop accepted her committal of children's clothing."

See also: *Com**miss**ioned, Com**miss**ioning, Com**miss**ionaire, Com**miss**ionership, Com**mit**ted, Com**mit**ting, Com**mit**table*

As we saw earlier, there are some words to which the additional prefix "in" meaning "not" can be added.

> *non**commit**tal* – adj. "giving no clear indication of attitude or feeling"

"His noncommittal attitude did not endear him to his supervisor."

Review:

Commit	Commission	Commissioner
Commissure	Noncommittal	Commissioning
Commissionership	Committing	Commissary
Committee	Commitment	Commissionaire
Committal	Commissioned	
Committed	Committable	

CHOOSE: Select the word(s) that best fits the sentence –

commissioner   committal   committee
The _____ demanded that the contractor submit his _____ to the _____.
Sorry – I was just having fun.

Assignment: In your word processing document, **explain** each word in your own words, **write a sentence** using the word, and **work these words into your conversation**. Well, what did you learn about words from this lesson?

Unit Two
Lesson 10

The Romans also had a preposition (occasionally used as a prefix) to indicate the direction "through" – *per-*. When it was prefixed to *mittere*, it became *permittere* – {pear MIT tuh ray} "to let through" or "to let go" or "to permit".

This time, observe and identify the words from this root in the following sentences.
"As Principal, I cannot permit you to let your students run wild around the building."
"The old adage suggests that it is better to ask forgiveness rather than permission."
"Some people are concerned that our society is becoming too permissive."
"Parking is permissible only in designated areas."

Congratulations! Here they are. As you read through them, notice the subtle—and sometimes not-so-subtle variations – that occur within the definitions. This is where you begin to access the power you are developing in your vocabulary.

> *per**mit*** – v. "to let go; to allow"; n. "written license granted by one in authority"
> *per**miss**ion* – n. "act of permitting"; "formal consent; authorization"
> *per**miss**ive* – adj." tolerant; indulgent"; "allowing discretion; granting permission"
> *per**miss**ible* – adj. "allowable"; "something that can be permitted"

See also: **Per*mit*ted, Per*mit*ting, Per*mit*ter, Per*mit*tee, Per*miss*ibility, Per*miss*ibly, Per*miss*ively, Per*miss*iveness**

Add yet another preposition to our repertoire – *inter-* "between".
When added as a prefix, it became *intermittere* – "to be intermittent" – "to cease for a while at intervals"
"Idleness of body is nothing but a kind of benumbing laziness, intermitting exercise, which makes them unapt to do anything whatever."
Robert Burton, *The Anatomy of Melancholy*
"The intermittent power outages were caused by ice on the lines."
"During the intermission, the theatre-goers enjoyed a glass of Merlot."

As you observed, here are the words that flowed from "*intermittere*".

> *inter**mit*** – v. "to cause to cease for a time at intervals"; "to discontinue"; "to be intermittent"
> *inter**mit**ting* – adj. "characterized by stopping and starting"
> *inter**mit**tent* – adj. "coming and going at intervals; not continuous; occasional"
> *inter**miss**ion* – n. "act or state of being intermitted"; "an interval between the parts of an entertainment, such as a play"

See also: *Inter**mit**tence, Inter**mit**tently, Inter**mit**ter*

Time for a "**By The Way" (BTW).**
The newly added preposition "per" can also be prefixed to "vertere" – "*pervertere*" =
"to upset, to corrupt, to ruin, to destroy".
Take a look at these terms.

> **Per*vers*e** [pur VURS] —adj. "turned away from what is right or good;
> improper, incorrect; obstinate in opposing what is right or good"
> **Per*vers*ion** – n. "action or condition of being perverted"
> **Per*vers*ive** – adj. "arising from or indicative of perversion"
> **Per*vert*** – n.[PURR vurt] "a person given to some form of perversion"
> **Per*vert*** – v. [purr VURT] "to cause to turn away from what is right or good";
> "to corrupt, to misdirect; to misuse"

When these work their way into sentences, the depth of the perversion becomes
obvious.
   "He remained perverse in his attitude toward civilized society."
   "His perversion led him into many difficult situations."
   "His perversive behavior left him bereft of close friends."
   "She knew from his actions that he was a pervert."
   "He always seemed eager to pervert the innocent."

Review:	Permit	Permitter	Intermit
	Permission	Permittee	Intermitting
	Permissive	Permissibility	Intermittent
	Permissible	Permissibly	Intermission
	Permitted	Permissively	Intermittence
	Permitting,	Permissiveness	Intermittently
			Intermitter

Assignment: In your word processing document, **explain** each word in your own
words, **write a sentence** using the word, and **work these words into your
conversation.**
Reflect on what you have learned in this lesson.

Unit Two
Lesson 11

Previously we saw the preposition "*ad-*" meaning "to" or "toward". When it was prefixed to *mittere*, it became *admittere* – "to send" or "to let in" or "to allow".

Since you did so well last time, observe and identify the words from this root in the following sentences.

"Starting the fight was an admitted error."
"Admittedly, the department was under-staffed to deal with the volume of work."
"His admission of guilt made him eligible for prison, but saved him from the death penalty."
"The judge ruled that the evidence was indeed admissible."
"She was granted admittance to the concert only after she paid her admission fee."

Congratulations! Here they are. This is where you can really begin to access the power and flexibility you are developing in your vocabulary.

> **ad**mit – v. "to allow, to permit; to concede as true"
> **ad**mitted – adj. "accepted as true"; v. past tense
> **ad**mittedly – adv. "has been or must be admitted"
> **ad**mission – n. "act of admitting"; "acknowledgement that a statement is true"; "the fee paid for admission"
> **ad**missible – adj. "permissible; capable of being allowed or conceded or considered"
> **ad**mittance – n. "permission to enter"

See also: **Admitting, Admissibility, Admissive**

Remember yet another preposition from your repertoire: *ex- or e-* "from" or "out of". When added as a prefix, it became "*emittere*" [ee MIT tuh ray] – "to send out" or "to send forth" or "to let fly" or "to publish". With this many meanings from the Latin, think of what it offers us in our American English.

> **e**mit – v. to send out; to give off or to give voice to; to eject; to publish; to issue with authority; to give utterance or voice to
> **e**mitted – v. past tense
> **e**mitted – adj. that which has been given off
> **e**mission– n. act of sending out; something sent forth by emitting; substances discharged into the air; publication
> **e**missary [EH mis sair ee] – n. one designated as the agent of another; one sent forth; a secret agent

emittance – n. [ee MITT unce] "the energy radiated by the surface of an area per second per unit area"

emissivity – n. "the relative power of a surface to emit heat by radiation"

See also: *Emissive, Emitting, Emitter,*

Appropriate use of these terms adds a definite level of specificity to your writing.

"The ghost emitted an eerie groan."

"Carbon emissions have skyrocketed in the last two decades."

"The Romans sent an emissary to talk with the Angles."

"The scientists carefully studied the radioactive emittance from the old smelter."

"The technicians considered the emissivity of the old factory to be dangerously high."

OOPS, sorry but I just about omitted **OMIT**, "to leave out".

"OOPS, sorry but I just about omitted OMIT."

See also: *Omitted Omitting Omission Omissible*

CHOOSE: Select the word(s) that best fits the sentence –

Admittedly emissary's admission commission emissions emissivity

_____, the _____'s _____ to the _____that the _____ were too high led to concerns about the potential levels of _____.

(OK, forgive me. I was just having some more fun, trying to use multiple words in one sentence.)

Review:			
Admit	Admitting	Emit	Omit
Admitted	Admissibility	Emitted	Omitted
Admittedly	Admissive	Emission	Omitting
Admission	Emissary	Emissive	Omission
Admissible	Emittance	Emitting	Omissible
Admittance	Emissivity	Emitter	

Assignment: In your word processing document, **explain** each word in your own words, **write a sentence** using the word, and **work these words into your conversation**.

Unit Two
Lesson 12

Let's add several more prefixes.

Start with *trans-* = "across" ***transmittere*** = "to send across"

    Stems: *transmit-* and *transmis-*

       transmit – v. "to send or convey from one person to another"

       transmitter – n. "an apparatus for transmitting radio or television signals"

       transmission – n. "act or process of transmitting, e.g. a radio wave"; "device for passing power from an engine to the wheels"

       transmissible or ***transmittable*** – adj. "capable of being transmitted, e.g. diseases"

As before, these words are best understood when used in a sentence.

    "Radio Free Europe was built to transmit information to people living behind the 'Iron Curtain'."

    "The loss of power to the radio station's transmitter knocked it 'off the air'."

    "The transmission on my car needed serious mechanical assistance."

    "The Center for Disease Control monitors transmissible diseases."

See also: **Transmissibility, Transmissive, Transmitted, Transmitting, Transmittal, Transmittance**

Now apply the prefix "sub" = under or below   *submittere* = to lower, to submit

Stems: *submit-* and *submis-*

       submit – v. "to lower"; "to yield to governance or authority"; "to surrender"

       submission – n. "act of submitting something for consideration"; "the product that is being submitted"; "acknowledging defeat"

       submissive – adj. "yielding or submitting to others"

       submittal – n. "in construction management shop drawing, material data, and sample"

    "His submission of the research paper was after the deadline."

    "The rebels agreed to submit to the authority of the new regime."

    "The prisoner demonstrated submissive behavior toward his captors."

    "The contractor forwarded his submittals to the county officials."

    See also: **Submitted, Submitting, Submissively, Submissiveness**

Review:

Transmit	Submit
Transmitter	Submission
Transmission	Submissive
Transmissible or transmittable	Submittal
Transmissibility	Submitted
Transmissive	Submitting
Transmitted	Submissively
Transmitting	Submissiveness
Transmittal	
Transmittance	

CHOOSE: Select the word(s) that best fits the sentence –

remit   transmit   submit

You must _____ your thesis to the instructor by the deadline.

remittance   submission   remission   transmission

Fortunately, her illness was in _____ .

Assignment:

In your word processing document, **explain** each word in your own words, **write a sentence** using the term, and **work these words into your conversation**.

Unit Two
Lesson 13 – **Review** *"mittere"*

In Unit Two, we have explored the Latin root word *"mittere"*, meaning "to send". We have also examined the impact of adding a Latin preposition in front of *"mittere"* to see how that can significantly change the meaning of the root word. Now it's time to take a look back and see how things are fitting into your active vocabulary. Answers can be found on pages 33-34.

Prepositions: We worked with 2 new prepositions that can be "prefixed" to root words, both in Latin and in American English. Explain the basic meaning(s) of each word.

> *Per-*
> *Inter-*

In the upcoming sections, identify the word that best completes the sentence or matches the definition. If you don't get it correct, just go back and look at the lesson.

Words from the root word *"mittere"*

> Noun – a ministry commissioned by a religious organization to propagate its faith; a calling or vocation; a local church dependent on a larger church for support: _____
> Verb – to carry on missionary work: _____
> The _____ labored with great zeal to help the indigenous peoples.
> The deputy carried the _____ for his convict to the new prison.
> Adjective – capable of being thrown; adapted for throwing or hurling missiles: _____
> They launched an intercontinental ballistic _____.
> She sent him a scented _____ to get his attention.

Words from the root word "mittere" and the prefix "re-"

> Verb – to send back; to give relief from suffering; to refer for consideration or action: _____
> Noun – act or process of sending back or remitting; the period of relief from suffering: _____
> I would be _____ in my duties if I failed to warn you about the hazards of smoking.
> Please return your payment in the enclosed _____ envelope.
> Adjective – marked by alternating periods of abatement and increase of symptoms: _____
> Adjective – capable of being forgiven: _____
> The prospector planned to _____ the claim to a local charity.

Words from the root word "mittere" and the prefix "trans-"

Noun – an apparatus for transmitting radio or television signals: _____

Adjective – capable of being transmitted, e.g. diseases: _____

Radio Free Europe was built to_____ information to people living behind the 'Iron Curtain'.

The _____ on my car needed serious mechanical assistance.

Words from the root word "mittere" and the prefix "sub-"

Adjective – yielding or submitting to others: _____

Noun – in construction management shop drawing, material data, and sample: _____

His _____ of the research paper was late.

The rebels agreed to _____ to the authority of the new regime.

Words from the root word "mittere" and the prefix "per-"

The old adage suggests that it is better to ask forgiveness rather than _____.

Parking is _____ only in designated areas.

Verb – to let go; to allow;   Noun— written license granted by one in authority: _____

Adjective – tolerant; indulgent; allowing discretion; granting permission:_____

Words from the root word "mittere" and the prefix "inter-"

The _____ power outages were caused by accumulations of ice on the lines.

During the _____, the theatre-goers enjoyed a glass of Merlot.

Verb – to cause to cease for a time at intervals; to discontinue; to be intermittent: _____

Adjective – characterized by stopping and starting: _____

intermittent – adj. coming and going at intervals; not continuous; occasional

intermission – n. act or state of being intermitted; an interval between the parts of an entertainment, such as a play

Words from the root word "mittere" and the prefix "ad-"

He finally _____ that hitting his friend was a serious error.

HIs _____ of guilt made him eligible for prison.

The judge ruled that the evidence was indeed _____.

Verb – to allow, to permit; to concede as true: _____

Adverb– has been or must be admitted: _____

Noun – permission to enter: _____

Words from the root word "mittere" and the prefix "ex-" or "e-"

Verb – to send out; to give off or to give voice to; to eject; to publish; to issue with authority; to give utterance or voice to: _____

Noun – the energy radiated by the surface of an area per second per unit area: _____

Noun – the relative power of a surface to emit heat by radiation: _____

The ghost _____ an eerie groan.

Carbon _____ have skyrocketed in the last two decades.

The Romans sent an _____ to talk with the Angles.

Words from the root word "vertere" and the prefix "per-"

Adjective — turned away from what is right or good; improper, incorrect; obstinate in opposing what is right or good: _____

Verb – to cause to turn away from what is right or good; to corrupt, to misdirect; to misuse: _____

His _____ led him into many difficult situations.

His _____ behavior left him bereft of close friends.

She knew from his actions that he was a _____.

CHOOSE: Select the word(s) that best fits the sentence –

converse   diverse   inverse   reverse

His _____ interests allowed him to _____ easily with total strangers.

diversion   inversion   introversion   subversion

Juggling chainsaws was a _____ for him from his log-cutting duties.

converse   inverse   transverse   traverse

She plans to _____ the mountain just below the glacier.

diversion   inversion   transversal   transversion

After drawing the two parallel lines, I drew the _____ to cut across them.

advert   extrovert   invert   revert

A wise student will _____ to teacher instructions.

commissioner   committal   committee

The _____ demanded that the contractor submit his _____ to the _____.

Answers:

Prepositions

Per-	through
Inter-	between

Words from the root word "mittere"

mission	missionize	missionary	mittimus
missile	missile	missive	

Words from the root word "mittere" and the prefix "re-"

remit	remission	remiss	remittance
remittent	remissible	remise	

Words from the root word "mittere" and the prefix "trans-"

transmitter	transmissible or transmittable
transmit	transmission

Words from the root word "mittere" and the prefix "sub-"

submissive	submittal	submission	submit

Words from the root word "mittere" and the prefix "per-"

permission	permissible	permit	permissive

Words from the root word "mittere" and the prefix "inter-"

intermittent	intermission	intermit	intermitting

Words from the root word "mittere" and the prefix "ad-"

admitted	admission	admissible
admit	admittedly	admittance

Words from the root word "mittere" and the prefix "e-"

emit	emittance	emissivity
emitted	emissions	emissary

Words from the root word "vertere" and the prefix "per-"

perverse	pervert	
perversion	perversive	pervert

His <u>diverse</u> interests allowed him to <u>converse</u> easily with total strangers.

Juggling chainsaws was a <u>diversion</u> for him from his log-cutting duties.

She plans to <u>traverse</u> the mountain just below the glacier.

After drawing the two parallel lines, I drew the <u>transversal</u> to cut across them.

A wise student will <u>advert</u> to teacher instructions.

The <u>commissioner</u> demanded that the contractor submit his <u>committal</u> to the <u>committee</u>.

Congratulations! You have been presented with 2 new prepositions and 97 words from this Unit. What do you need to do to incorporate some or all of these into your active vocabulary?

Words of Wisdom

Four minutes a day to a richer and more powerful vocabulary
Unit Three

In Unit Three, we will use the same approach as we used in the previous units. Your challenge remains: **train yourself to look carefully at words and see the components** – stems and affixes (prefixes and suffixes). Be sure to cement your learning by writing down the meaning of the words in words that make sense to you. Also, be sure that you can use each word in a sentence that will communicate its meaning to your readers.

ENJOY!

Unit Three
Lesson 14

OBSERVE the word   **suffix**

suf – variation from **sub** "under"   as the prefix &
-fix from *figere* – "to fix" or "to attach" as the root or stem

OBSERVE these words
- Admissible
- Convertible
- Permissible
- Remissible
- Reversible
- Transmittable

Add and OBSERVE their meanings
- Admissible   ABLE to be admitted
- Convertible   Able to be converted
- Permissible   Can be permitted
- Remissible   Can be remitted
- Reversible   Can be reversed
- Transmittable   Able to be transmitted

Next focus on the suffix of these words
- Admiss<u>ible</u>
- Convert<u>ible</u>
- Permiss<u>ible</u>
- Remiss<u>ible</u>
- Revers<u>ible</u>
- Transmitt<u>able</u>

When you **observe** this suffix   *-ible* or *-able*
understand that it usually is an adjective that means
- capable of, fit for, worthy of
- tending, given, or liable to

Now **observe** these words and their meanings

- Permissive   TENDING to grant permission
- Submissive   Tending to submit to others
- Aversive   Tending to avoid a noxious substance
- Subversive   Tending to subvert or undermine

Observe the suffix

- Permiss<u>ive</u>
- Submiss<u>ive</u>
- Avers<u>ive</u>
- Subvers<u>ive</u>

When you **observe** this suffix   *-ive*
understand that it usually indicates an adjective and means
                - tending, given, or liable to
                  -that performs or tends toward an indicated action

Remember these words and their meanings. **Observe** the suffix

- Admiss<u>ion</u>   Act of admitting
- Commiss<u>ion</u>   Act of committing
- Emiss<u>ion</u>   Act of emitting
- Avers<u>ion</u>   Act of averting
- Convers<u>ion</u>   State or act of converting
- Extrovers<u>ion</u>   Act, state or habit of ...
- Introvers<u>ion</u>   Act, state or habit of ...
- Revers<u>ion</u>   etc.
- Subvers<u>ion</u>
- Intermiss<u>ion</u>
- Permiss<u>ion</u>
- Remiss<u>ion</u>
- Submiss<u>ion</u>
- Transmiss<u>ion</u>

I'm sure you get the picture. Typically, when a word in English comes from a Latin verb and is converted into a noun in English, the suffix is frequently *-ion* meaning
         - act or process
         - result of an act or process
         - state or condition
As you encounter unfamiliar words, train yourself to look for prefixes and suffixes. Together, these are called affixes, from "ad" or "a" plus "fix from "figere".

Summary

-ible or -able   usually an adjective that means
- capable of, fit for, worthy of
- tending, given, or liable to

-ive adjective meaning
- tending, given, or liable to
-that performs or tends toward an indicated action

-ion   noun meaning
- act or process
- result of an act or process
- state or condition

Assignment: In your word processing document, **explain** each suffix in your own words, **write a sentence** using each suffix, and **work these words into your conversation**.
Be alert to seeing suffixes when you read and listen for them in oral conversation.
Reflect on what you have learned from this lesson.

Pop quiz:
Based on what you have learned, explain the term "**resubmission**".

Unit Three
Lesson 15

Time to add a new Latin verb for your consideration:
> *ducere*   {due SAIR ray} "to lead" "to bring"

Principal Parts: *duco, ducere, duxi, ductum*
> *duco* – 1st person singular, present tense – "I lead"
> *ducere* – present infinitive – "to lead"
> *duxi* – 1st person singular, perfect– "I led"
> *ductum* – past participle – "have led"
> **Stems**:   **duc-** and **duct-**

Observe and find the words that evolved from *ducere*

"She had something in her tear duct."
"The ductile iron was fashioned into a sword."
"The ductule was blocked."
"The duke waved to the crowd in his duchy."
"Benito Mussolini was known in Italy as 'il Duce' for his leadership of the National Fascist Party from 1922 to 1943."

Well, here are the words in English ... and even one in Italian
> **duct** – n. "a tube or vessel that carries a substance"
> **ductile** – adj. "capable of being drawn out or hammered thin"
> **ductule** – n. "a small duct"
> **duke** – n. "a sovereign male ruler of a European duchy"
> il **Duce** – n. "'the leader'- term used for Mussolini in WWII Italy"
See also: **Ductal, Ductless, Ducting, Ductility, Ducal, Ducat, Duchy, Duchess**

Here is a prefix that you have used previously to work with *ducere*
> *re-*   "back" or "before"
> *reducere* – "to lead back" or
>   "to withdraw" or
>   "to recollect" or
>   "to reduce"
> **Stems**:   **reduc-** and **reduct-** and sometimes just **red-**

Again, some of the words just seem to flow right out of the stems.
> **reduce** – v. "to lead back; to consolidate"; "to diminish in size, amount, extent or number"
> **reduction** – n. "act or process of reducing"; "something made by reducing"
> **reductive** – adj. "of, relating to, causing or involving reduction"
> **reducible** – adj. "able to be reduced

Some have evolved from the stem, but are a bit removed.

> **re**doubt – n. "a small, enclosed defensive position; a defended position"; "a stronghold"

"The chemical reaction was reductive in nature."
"A reduction in force is usually very hard on the morale of the organization."
"The economy has caused many schools to reduce faculty size."
"When I saw the fraction 8/10, I knew right away it was reducible."
"When I visited the old fort overlooking the harbor, I was fascinated by the narrow rifle slits in the walls of the redoubt."

> See also: **Reduced, Reducing, Reducer, Reducibly, Reductant, Reductionism, Reductionist, Reductionistic**

Review:

Duct	**Ductal**	**Reduce**	**Reduced**
Ductile	**Ductless**	**Reduction**	**Reducing**
Ductule	**Ducting**	**Reductive**	**Reducer**
Duke	**Ductility**	**Redoubt**	**Reducibly**
il Duce	**Ducal**		**Reductant**
	Ducat		**Reductionism**
	Duchy		**Reductionist**
	Duchess		**Reductionistic**

Think about the various suffixes in the additional words. We will explore these in details in future lessons. For now, ask yourself how these might impact meaning?

CHOOSE: Select the words that best fits this sentence –

    duke   submittal   redoubt   transmitted
The _____ had no doubt the _____ for the new _____ he electronically _____ to the

committee   reduce   commission
_____ would _____ his _____.

(OK, sorry – I was just having a little fun.)

Assignment: In your word processing document, **explain each word** in your own words, **write a sentence** using the word, and **work these words into your conversation**.
Observe your reading carefully to see if any of these words appear. How are they used?

Unit Three
Lesson 16

Here is another prefix you have used before that works with the root word - *ducere*

ex- or e-   "out" or "out of"

Principal parts: *educo, educere, eduxi, eductum*

educere – "to lead out" or {a DUE sair ray}

"to extract" or

"to rear" or

"to nurture" or

"to rescue"

Stems: *educ-* or ***educt-***

educe [ee DOOS] – v. "to bring out; to consolidate"; Syn: "evoke, elicit, extract"

educate – v. "to provide schooling for"; "to develop mentally, morally or aesthetically"; "to inform; to train by formal instruction & practice"

education – n. "process of educating or being educated; the knowledge and development resulting from the educational process"

educator – n. "one skilled in teaching"; "a student of the theory & practice of education"

Work these into sentences, such as:

"It is a beautiful feeling to know that you have helped educate a young person."

"I hope that every student has at least one dedicated, concerned, supportive educator during his or her educational process."

"It's impossible to place a dollar value on a great education."

"She has an uncanny ability to educe latent evidence to support her case."

You may recognize these variations on the theme:

Educated, Educationese, Educationist, Eductor

Now, based on the discussion of suffixes in the previous lesson, see if you can deduce the meanings of these terms:

educable or **educible** (what would make the difference?)

educative

Here is another prefix that works with the root word - *ducere*

ab – "from" or "away" or "off"

abducere – "to lead away"

Stems: ***abduc-*** and ***abduct-***

Again, the words seem to flow directly from the stems:

> **ab**<u>duct</u> – v. "to lead away; to carry off by force"
> **ab**<u>duct</u>ion – n. "act or process of abducting"; "the unlawful carrying away of a woman for marriage"
> **ab**<u>duct</u>or – n. "person who carries someone off by force"

"In some parts of the world, it was customary to abduct a woman to become a bride."

"The abduction of the soldier was blamed on the Taliban."

"The police promptly captured the abductor."

Review:

Educe	Educible	Eductor
Educate	Educable	Abduct
Education	Educated	Abduction
Educator	Educationist	Abductor
Educable	Educative	
Educated	Educationese	

CHOOSE: Select the words that best fits this sentence –

education	abduction	reduction	duction

The value of a great _____ is truly priceless.

Assignment: In your word processing document, **explain** each word in your own words, **write a sentence** using the word, and **work these words into your conversation.** In reflecting on the lesson, what did you learn?

Unit Three
Lesson 17

Here are two additional prefixes that work with the root word - *ducere*

   de- "from" or "down" or "away"

      deducere –

            "to lead away" or

            "to bring down" or

            "to deduce"

  in- "in" or "into" or "toward"

      inducere –

            "to lead into" or

            "to bring in" or

            "to induce"

deducere –	*inducere* –
deduce	induce
deduction	induction
deductive	inductive

Sounds reasonable to me, but I never can remember which is which???

So let's explore…

Here are some words that come directly from the root words

      Deduce – v. "to determine by deduction"

            "to trace the course of" (syn. Infer)

            "to infer from a general principle"

      Deduction – n. "the deriving of a conclusion by reasoning or inferring from a universal premise"

      Deductive – adj. "provable by deduction"; "employing logical deduction" (~reasoning)

These sentences hopefully will help elucidate the meaning.

  "Now that I understand Newton's second law, I can deduce that I should not sit under this particular apple tree."

  "A deduction from the law of momentum explains why this car slows down so slowly."

  "There is a fine line between accurate deductive reasoning and fallacious thinking."

Induce is the antonym of deduce … but what does that mean?

        Induce – v. "to move by persuasion or influence"

            "to cause the formation of"

            "to infer from particulars"

      Induction – n. "the inference of a generalized conclusion from particular instances"

      Inductive – adj. "leading on; employing mathematical or logical induction" (~reasoning)

"After seeing all the apples on the ground under this tree, I can begin to understand how Newton induced the second law of gravity."

"Induction builds a general principle from analysis of multiple specific examples."

"After examining a few instances, some people succumb to fallacious thinking and induce an inaccurate conclusion."

Visualize this triangle and see if it helps.

The General Principle is unique and at the top.

The specific examples are many and are at the bottom.

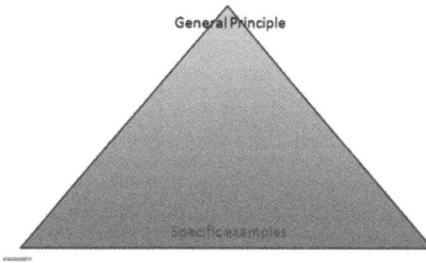

Deductive reasoning starts at the top and goes **down** to the specifics.

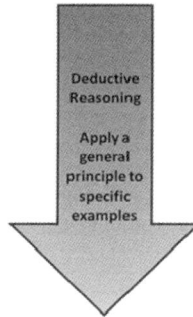

Deductive Reasoning

Apply a general principle to specific examples

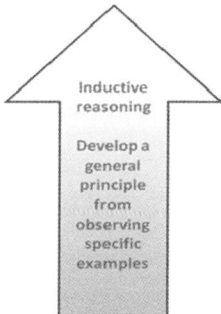

Inductive reasoning

Develop a general principle from observing specific examples

Inductive reasoning starts with specifics and builds **up** to a general principle.

Put them all together and you get this visual:

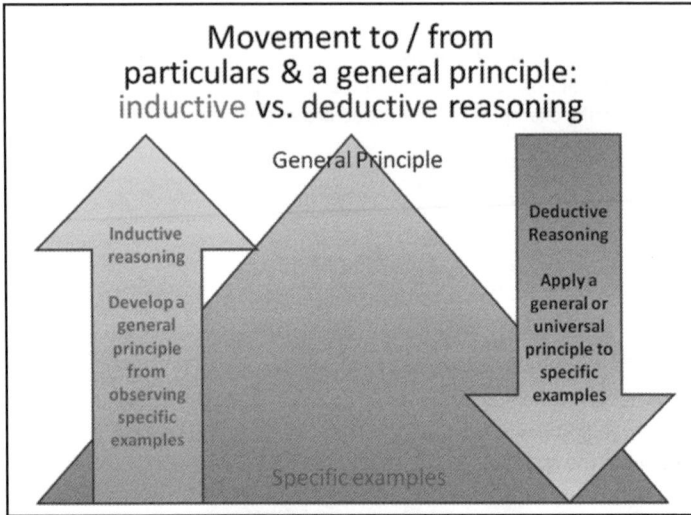

Movement to / from
particulars & a general principle:
inductive vs. deductive reasoning

General Principle

Inductive reasoning

Develop a general principle from observing specific examples

Deductive Reasoning

Apply a general or universal principle to specific examples

Specific examples

More in Lesson 18

Assignment: Be sure you can explain in your own words the difference between **Deductive** and **Inductive** reasoning.

Unit Three
Lesson 18

Here are some other words & meanings that come directly from the root words –
deducere and *inducere*

> **Deduct** – v. "to take away an amount from a total"; "to subtract"
> **Deductible** – n. "clause in an insurance policy that relieves the insurer of responsibility for specific conditions"; "something allowable as a deduction (~tax)"
> **Deduction** – n. "act of taking away (~ of legitimate business expenses from taxes)"

"His employer had to deduct one hour's pay for his tardiness."
"Legitimate use of your vehicle for business purposes is deductible."
"He claimed every possible deduction on his income taxes."

> **Induct** – v. "to put in a formal possession"; "to install"; "to admit as a member"; "to initiate"
> **Induce** – v. "to call forth or bring about by influence or stimulation"
> **Inducement** – n. "motive or consideration that leads one to action;" syn. motive
> **Inducible** – adj. "capable of being induced (cf. biology of cells)"

"The Rotarians met to induct the new members."
"The obstetrician decided it was time to induce labor."
"He fell for the 'bonus gift' as an inducement to buy a large quantity that he didn't really need."
"The biologist determined that the cell development made them inducible due to their response to the enzymes."

> **Induction** – n. "act or process of inducting, as into an office"; "initiation"; "formality by which a civilian is inducted into the military"
> **Inductor** – n. "one who inducts; reactor; organizer"; "part of an electrical apparatus"
> **Inductance** – n. "a property of an electric circuit by which an electromotive force is induced in it"
> **Inductee** – n. "one who is inducted"

"As president, she was the primary inductor of new members."
"Once he installed the new coil inductor, the machinery worked fine."
"The mechanic determined that it was an inductance problem."
"He is a worthy inductee into the hall of fame."

See also: **Deduced, Deducing, Deductively, Deductibility, Induced, Inducing, Inducer, Inducibility, Inductively**

REVIEW:

deducere		*inducere*	
Deduce	**Deduced**	**Induce**	**Induced**
Deduction	**Deducing**	**Induction**	**Inducing**
Deductive	**Deductively**	**Inductive**	**Inducer**
Deduct	**Deductibility**	**Inductor**	**Inductively**
Deductible		**Inductance**	**Inducibility**
		Inductee	
		Inducible	
		Inducement	

Word choice: **induced**   or   **Deduced**

After examining all the evidence, the jury _____ that his guilt.

Drawing on his extensive knowledge of plant classification, the biologist _____ that this plant was indeed a geranium.

Assignment: Write several sentences using various forms of induce and deduce to make sure you are comfortable with correct usage.

Unit Three
Lesson 19

Now look at some words from the root word *ducere* and the prefix *"con..."* *"with"*

   conducere to conduce or to conduct; stems: **conduc-** or **conduct-**

conduce [kuhn DOOS] – v. "to lead or tend to a particular and usually desirable result; contribute"

conducive [kuhn DOO sive] – adj. tending to promote or assist

 "Your positive insights are appreciated and will undoubtedly conduce a successful outcome."

 "Congratulations! You have created an atmosphere is your classroom that is conducive to learning."

conduct– v. [kuhn DUCT] "to bring by as if by leading; to lead from a position of command; to cause to act or behave in a particular way; to manage, to control"

conduct – n. [KOHN duct] act of leading; the act, manner or process of carrying on; a mode or standard of personal behavior

 "Please conduct yourself appropriately for your visit to the museum."

 "We have a high standard of conduct here in our school."

conduction – n. "act of conducting or conveying; transmission through a conductor; transfer of heat through matter by communication of kinetic energy from particle to particle"

conductor – n. "the leader of a musical ensemble or public conveyance"; " material that permits the easy flow of electric current"

 conductance – n. "conducting power or the power to conduct electricity"

 "The students watched in awe at the physicist's conduction demonstration."

 "The train's conductor would not allow the salesman to transport his electrical conductor."

 "The electrical engineer measured the conductance of the new material."

conductible – adj. "able to conduct; conductibility" – n. "the ability to conduct"

conductive – adj. "having conductivity; relating to conduction (as of electricity)"

conductivity – n. "the power or quality of conducting or transmitting; the reciprocal of electrical resistivity"

 "The copper wire had a higher quality of conductibility than the aluminum."

 "The copper wire had a strong conductive quality."

 "Copper wire is recommended for its conductivity."

Review:

		Other words	
Conduce	Conductor	Conducted	Conductometric
Conducive	Conductance	Conducting	Conductorial
Conduct v.	Conductible	Conductress	Conducing
Conduct n.	Conductive	Conduced	Conduciveness
Conduction	Conductivity		

47

Unit Three
Lesson 20

Now look at some words from the root word *ducere* and
  the prefix "*intro-*" which means "inside" or "inward".
The Latin verb became "**introducere**" (= to introduce, to insert, to establish) and the
stems became **introduc-** and **introduct-**.

> **Intro*duc*e** – v. "to lead or bring in, esp. for the first time; to bring into play
> or practice or use"
> **Intro*duct*ion** – n. "to lead or bring in, esp. for the first time; to bring into
> play or practice or use"
> **Intro*duct*ory** – adj. "relating to or being a first step that sets something
> going or in proper perspective"

These words flow easily into sentence form, even in the past tense of the verb.

> "The consultant introduced a new teaching method to help students learn math."
> "The introduction to the book was actually more interesting than the book itself."
> "The emcee's introductory remarks made everyone feel at home."
> See also: **Introduced, Introducing, Introducer, Introductorily**

Now look at some words from the root word *ducere* and
  the prefix "*pro-*" which means "forward" or "before" or "forth"
The Latin verb became "**producere**" (= to bring forward, to bring out, to make to
appear) and the stems became **produc-** and **product-**.

Find the words in these sentences.
> "The grocer expected the farmer to produce the produce … promptly."
> "The third grader finally understood how to arrive at the product of the
> multiplication problem."
> "The high school's production of 'High School Musical' was outstanding."

> **Pro*duc*e** – [pro DOOS] v. "to lead forward; to offer to view or notice"; "to
> bring about"; "to present to the public"; "to cause to happen"
> **Pro*duc*e** [PRO doos] n. "something produced"; "the yield"; "agricultural
> products"
> **Pro*duct*** – n. "something produced"; "the number result of a multiplication
> of numbers"; "the amount or quantity produced"
> **Pro*duct*ion** – n. "something produced"; "the making of goods available for
> use"; "a literary or artistic work"

Now look at more words from the root word *ducere* and the prefix "*pro-*" "forward".

Pro*ductive* – adj. "having the quality or state of producing, esp. in abundance"; "effective in bringing about results, benefits or profits"

Pro*ductivity* – n. "the quality or state of being productive; the rate of production"

Pro*ducer* – n. "one who produces especially agricultural products or manufactures raw materials into useful products"; "the person who supervises or finances the production of a stage or screen event"

"She was one of the most productive young writers I have known."

"The managers were concerned about the lack of productivity in the plant."

"Generally the producer of a film is not as well known as the director."

See also: **Produced, Producing, Producible, Productional, Productively, Productiveness**

Now look at more words from the root word *ducere* and the prefixes *"re-"* and *"pro-"*.

Repro*duce* – v. "to produce again"; "to produce new individuals of the same kind"

Repro*ductive* – adj. "of or related to reproduction"

Repro*duction* – n. "act or process of reproducing"; "something reproduced"; "a duplicate or copy of an original, facsimile, replica"

"He struggled to reproduce the original piece of art."

"The gynecologist said her reproductive organs were fine."

"The art critic was convinced the piece was only a reproduction."

See also: **Reproducible, Reproducibility, Reproducer**

Review:

Introduce	**Introduced**	**Produce (n.)**	**Produced**
Introduction	**Introducing**	**Produce (v.)**	**Producing**
Introductory	**Introducer**	**Product**	**Producible**
Introductorily		**Production**	**Productional**
Reproduce	**Reproduced**	**Productivity**	**Productively**
Reproductive	**Reproducing**	**Producer**	**Productiveness**
Reproduction	**Reproducible**		
Reproducibility	**Reproducer**		

Assignment: In your word processing document, **explain** each word in your own words, **write a sentence** using the word, and **work these words into your conversation**. What "big picture" ideas did you come up with about this lesson?

Unit Three
Lesson 21

Now look at some words from the root word *ducere* and
the prefix "*sub-*" which means "under"
The Latin verb became "*subducere*" (= to withdraw, to haul {ships} onto land, to remove secretly) and the stems became *subduc-* and *subduct-* and sometimes *subdu-*.

> **sub*due*** – v. to conquer and bring into subjection; to bring under control or cultivation; to vanquish
> **sub*due*d** – adj. lacking in vitality, intensity or strength
> **sub*duct*ion** – n. the process of the edge of one earth crustal plate descending below the edge of another
> **sub*duct*** – v. to push one tectonic plate under another
> See also: **Subduedly, Subduing, Subduer**

Inclusion in a sentence provides the basis for deeper understanding – contextual understanding.

> "The general's plan was to subdue the insurgents with a massive assault."
> "The mood in the office was quite subdued after the merger was announced."
> "Subduction, which occurs when one tectonic plate slides under the adjacent plate, is often accompanied by earthquakes or other seismic activity."
> "When one plate subducts an adjacent plate, people on the ground frequently experience an earthquake."

Now look at some words from the root word *ducere* and the prefix "*se*..." "apart"
The Latin verb became "*seducere*" "to lead aside" and the stems became **seduc-** and **seduct-**.

> **se*duce*** – v. "to lead astray, usually by false promises"; "to persuade to disobedience or disloyalty; syn. to attract, to lure, to entice"
> **se*duct*ion** – n. "act of seducing to wrong"; "unlawful enticement of someone, frequently a female"; "something that attracts or charms"; "temptation"
> **se*duct*ive** – adj. "having alluring or tempting qualities"
> **se*duct*ress** – n. "a woman who seduces"

See also: **Seduced, Seducing, Seducer, Seducement, Seductively, Seductiveness**
These words tend to create their own tone when used in a sentence.

> "She planned to seduce him with her charm and guile".
> "It's easy to yield to the seduction of a low interest credit card and end up facing financial ruin."
> "She had a seductive personality."
> "Mata Hari was described as being a beautiful seductress before she was executed for being a spy in 1917 near the end of WW I."

Here are some other words & meanings that come directly from the root word - *ducere*

These however are appended to a noun.

> **Aque<u>duct</u>** – n. *(from the Latin "aqua" "water" and "duct" "conduit")* a conduit for carrying a large amount of flowing water.
>
> **Via<u>duct</u>** – n. *(from the Latin "via" "road" or "way" and "duct" "conduit")* a long elevated roadway, usually consisting of a series of short spans supported on arches, piers or columns
>
> "The aqueduct dated from Roman times and was still functional for delivering water to the village."
>
> "The Millau viaduct in southern France is a remarkable piece of engineering and a time-saver for travelers driving south to the Mediterranean."

Review:

Subdue	Subduer	Seduce	Seduced
Subdued	Subduedly	Seduction	Seducing
Subduction	Subduing	Seductive	Seductively
Subduct		Seductress	Seducer
Aqueduct	Viaduct	Seducement	Seductiveness

Word choice: seduction   subduction   reduction

His attempted _____ of the beautiful young woman was met with appropriate resistance.

Assignment: In your word processing document, **explain** each word in your own words, **write a sentence** using the word, and **work these words into your conversation. Reflection**?

Unit Three
Lesson 22

This group of words comes from the root word *ducere* and the prefix *"ad…"* "to" "toward" and became *adducere* "to lead to" or "to draw to".
  The **stems** are ***adduc-*** and ***adduct-***.

> ***ad<u>duce</u>*** – v. "to offer as example, reason or proof in discussion or analysis"
> ***ad<u>duct</u>***– v. "to draw a limb toward or past the median axis of the body";
> n. " a chemical addition product"
> ***ad<u>duct</u>ion*** – n. "the action, act or state of adducing or being adducted"
> ***ad<u>duct</u>or*** – n. "a muscle that draws a part toward the median line of the body"; "a muscle that closes the valves of a bivalve mollusk"

See also: **Adduced, Adducing, Adducer, Adductive**

The sentences may sound a bit strange – but that's only because this is not a frequently utilized family of words.
  "I intend to adduce multiple specific cases of this abuse to convince you of the need for change."
  "He adducted his right arm to his left shoulder."
  "Her successful adduction of many pieces of evidence convinced the jury of her client's innocence."
  "When the mollusk closed his valves using his adductor muscles, it was obvious he was going to clam up."

Now look at some words from the root word *ducere* and the prefix *"trans-"* meaning "across".
  transducere "to lead across" with stems ***transduc-*** and ***transduct-***

Find the suspicious characters based on these stems in this group of sentences.
  "He used the small device to transduce the electrical power into sounds through the loudspeaker."
  "The microbiologist was excited at the success of his transduction experiments."
  "He used a transducer to change the electrical power into audible sounds that could be broadcast over the public address system."
… and their meanings …

> ***trans<u>duce</u>***– v. "to convert into another form (e.g. energy or a message)"; "to bring about the transfer from one microorganism to another"
> ***trans<u>duct</u>ion*** – n. "the transfer of genetic determinants from one microorganism to another by a viral agent"
> ***trans<u>duce</u>r*** – n. "a device actuated by power from one system that supplies power in another form to a second system"

See also: **Transduced, Transducing, Transductant, Transductional**

Review:

Adduce	**Adduced**	**Transduce**	**Transduced**
Adduct	**Adducing**	**Transduction**	**Transducing**
Adduction	**Adducer**	**Transducer**	**Transductional**
Adductor	**Adductive**	**Transductant**	

Word Choice:
   abduction   adduction   seduction   subduction   transduction

The entire region felt the trembling of the earthquake after the _____ of one tectonic plate under the adjacent one.

When the microbiologist observed the similar genetic determinants in the smaller microorganism, he knew that _____ had occurred.

Assignment: In your word processing document, **explain** each word in your own words, **write a sentence** using the word, and **work these words into your conversation**.

BE SURE you can explain the sometimes subtle differences among all the "-*duction*" words. Once you get that straight, the whole family will be yours. Now is the time for a broad reflection on all the words from the *ducere* root.

Unit Three
Lesson 23 – **Review** "ducere"

In Unit Three, we have explored the Latin root word "ducere", meaning "to lead". We have also examined the impact of adding a Latin preposition in front of "ducere" to see how that can significantly change the meaning of the root word. Now it's time to take a look back and see how things are fitting into your active vocabulary. Answers can be found on pages 60-61.

 Prepositions: We worked with 2 new prepositions that can be "prefixed" to root words, both in Latin and in American English. Explain the basic meaning(s) of each word.

   Se-
   Pro-

Suffixes

Which of these correlates with the following descriptions?

   -ible or -able   -ion   -ive

_____Usually an adjective that means - capable of, fit for, worthy of
                 - tending, given, or liable to

_____Usually an adjective that means - tending, given, or liable to
                 -that performs or tends toward an indicated action

_____Usually a noun meaning   - act or process
                - result of an act or process
                - state or condition

In the upcoming sections, identify the word that best completes the sentence or matches the definition. If you don't get it correct, just go back and look at the lesson.

Words from the root word "ducere"

   She had something in her tear _____ .
   When iron is sufficiently _____, it can be fashioned into a sword.
   While the duct was open, the smaller _____ was blocked.
   Since it was his duchy, the _____ waved to the crowd.

Words from the root word "ducere" and the prefix "re-"

A RIF, or_____ in force, is very hard on morale in an organization.
His New Year's resolution was to _____ his weight.

Adjective – of, relating to, or involving reduction: _____
Noun – a small, enclosed defensive position; a stronghold:_____

Words from the root word "ducere" and the prefix "e-"

Noun – process of educating or being educated; the knowledge and
development resulting from the educational process: _____
Verb – to bring out; to consolidate; syn: evoke, elicit, extract: _____

It's a beautiful feeling to know that you have helped to _____ a young
person.
My sincere hope is that all students have at least one dedicated, supportive
_____ during his or her schooling to bring out their best.

Words from the root word "ducere" and the prefix "ab-"

In some parts of the world, it was customary for a man to _____ a
woman to become his bride.
The soldier's _____ was blamed on the Taliban.

Noun – person who carries someone off by force: _____

Words from the root word "ducere" and the prefix "de-"

Verb – to determine by deduction; to trace the course of (infer); to infer
from a general principle: _____
Adjective – provable by deduction; employing logical deduction
(~reasoning): _____

A _____ from the law of momentum explains why this car slows down so
slowly.

Words from the root word "ducere" and the prefix "in-"

Verb – to move by persuasion or influence; to cause the formation of; to
infer from particulars: _____

_____ builds a general principle from analysis of multiple specific
examples.
After examining a few instances, some people succumb to fallacious
thinking and _____ an inaccurate conclusion.

Reasoning:

_____ reasoning develops a general principle from observing specific examples.

_____ reasoning applies a general or universal principle to specific cases.

More from "de-"

Noun – clause in an insurance policy that relieves the insurer of responsibility for specific conditions; adj. something allowable as a deduction (tax): _____

His employer had to _____ one hour's pay for his tardiness.
The IRS agent questioned several _____ on his income taxes.

Words from the root word "ducere" and the prefix "in-"

Verb – to put in a formal possession; to install; to admit as a member; to initiate: _____
Adjective – adj. capable of being induced (cf. biology of cells): _____
Noun – act or process of inducting, as into an office; initiation; formality by which a civilian is inducted into the army: _____
Noun – a property of an electrical circuit by which an electromotive force is induced: _____

The used car salesman offered free gas for a year as an _____ to buy.
The obstetrician decided it was time to _____ labor.
As president, she was the primary _____ of new members.
He is a worthy _____ into the hall of fame.

Words from the root word "ducere" and the prefix "se-"

Verb – to lead astray, usually by false promises; syn: to attract, to lure, to entice: _____
Noun – a woman who seduces: _____

Some young people yield to the _____ of a low interest credit card and end up facing financial ruin.
She displayed a _____ personality.

Words from the root word "ducere" and the prefix "sub-"

Verb – to conquer and bring into subjection; to bring under control or cultivation; to vanquish: _____

Verb – to push one tectonic plate under another: _____

The mood in the classroom was quite _____ after the grades were announced.

_____, which occurs when one tectonic plate slides under the adjacent plate, is often accompanied by earthquakes or other seismic activity.

Words from the root word "ducere" and the prefix "ad-"

Verb – to offer as an example, reason or proof in discussion or analysis: _____

Verb – to draw a limb toward or past the median axis of the body; Noun a chemical addition product: _____

Her successful _____ of many pieces of evidence convinced the jury of her client's innocence.

When the mollusk closed his valves using his _____ muscles, it was obvious he was going to clam up.

Words from the root word "ducere" and the prefix "trans-"

Verb – to convert into another form (e.g. energy or a message); to bring about the transfer from one microorganism to another: _____

Noun – a device actuates by power from one system that supplies power in another form to a second system: _____

The microbiologist was excited at the success of his _____ experiments.

Words from the root word "ducere" and the prefix "intro-"

Noun – act of process of introducing; something that introduces (e.g. a book or short introductory musical passage): _____

The teacher used an interactive applet to _____ the new math concept.

The emcee's _____ remarks made everyone feel at home.

Words from the root word "ducere" and the prefix "pro-"

Verb – to lead forward; to offer to view or notice; to bring about; to present to the public; to cause to happen: _____

Noun – the quality or state of being productive; the rate of production: _____

Noun – one that produces, esp. agricultural products or manufactures raw materials into useful products; the person who supervises or finances the production of a stage or screen event: _____

The third grader finally figured out how to arrive at the _____ of the multiplication problem.

The Broadway _____ of "Les Mis" was outstanding.

Words from the root word "ducere" and the prefixes "re-" and "pro-"

Adj. of or related to reproduction: _____

Adj. able to be reproduced: _____

He struggled to _____ the original piece of art.

The art critic was convinced the piece was only a _____.

Now identify words from the root word "ducere" and the "duct…" _suffix_

The _____ dated from Roman times and was still fulfilling its function of delivering water to the city.

Noun – (from the Latin "aqua" water and "duct" conduit) a long elevated roadway, usually consisting of a series of short spans supported on arches, piers, or columns: _____

Words from the root word "ducere" and the prefix "con-"

Verb – to lead or tend to a particular and usually desirable result; contribute: _____

Verb – to bring by as if by leading; to lead from a position of command; to cause to act or behave in a particular way; to manage, to control, to direct: _____

Noun – act of conducting or conveying; transmission through a conductor; transfer of heat through matter by communication of kinetic energy from particle to particle: _____

Noun – the power or quality of conducting or transmitting; the reciprocal of electrical resistivity: _____

Examine the key words from the various roots. Explain each term in your own words.

If the definition/explanation doesn't come easily, try using the word in a sentence.
Identify which words are nouns, verbs or possibly either one.

Advert	Admit	Aqueduct	Adduce
Avert	Emit	Abduct	Conduce
Convert	Permit	Conduct	Deduce
Divert	Remit	Duct	Educe
Extrovert	Submit	Deduct	Induce
Introvert	Transmit	Induct	Introduce
Invert		Product	Produce
Pervert		Subduct	Reduce
Revert		Viaduct	Seduce
Subvert			Transduce

Recall the suffixes: -able or –ible, -ion, & -ive

Which of these suffixes could be applied to these base words?

What changes would you need to make to some of the base words to affix the suffixes?

<u>Answers:</u>

2 prepositions for prefixes, 142 words and 3 suffixes

Prepositions

Se-	"away"	
Pro-	"before", "in front of", "forth", "for"	

Suffixes

-ible   Usually an adjective that means - capable of, fit for, worthy of
-able   - tending, given, or liable to

-ive   Usually an adjective that means - tending, given, or liable to
                                                            -that performs or tends toward an indicated
                                                            action

-ion   Usually a noun meaning   - act or process
                                                            - result of an act or process
                                                            - state or condition

Words from the root word "ducere"

duct   ductile   ductule   duke

Words from the root word "ducere" and the prefix "re-"

reduction   reduce   reductive   redoubt

Words from the root word "ducere" and the prefix "e-"

education   educe   educate   educator

Words from the root word "ducere" and the prefix "ab-"

abduct   abduction   abductor

Words from the root word "ducere" and the prefix "de-"

deduce   deductive   deduction

Words from the root word "ducere" and the prefix "in-"

induced   induction   induce

Reasoning: inductive   deductive

Words from the root word "ducere" and the prefix "de-" & "in-"

deductible   deduct   deductions

induct   inducible   induction   inductance

inducement   induce   inductor   inductee

Words from the root word "ducere" and the prefix "se-"

seduce   seductress   seduction   seductive

Words from the root word "ducere" and the prefix "sub-"

subdue   subduct   subdued   subduction

Words from the root word "ducere" and the prefix "ad-"

adduce   adduct   adduction   adductor

Words from the root word "ducere" and the prefix "trans-"

transduce   transducer   transduction

Words from the root word "ducere" and the prefix "intro-"

introduction   introduce   introductory

Words from the root word "ducere" and the prefix "pro-"

produce   productivity   producer

product   production

Words from the root word "ducere" and the prefixes "re-" and "pro-"

reproductive reproducible reproduce reproduction.

Words from the root word "ducere" and noun prefixes

aqueduct   viaduct

Words from the root word "ducere" and the prefix "con-"

conduce   conduct   conduction   conductivity

conducive   conduce   conductor / conductor

Congratulations! You have cemented 3 suffixes, 2 new prepositions and 142 words from this Unit into your active vocabulary.

Be sure to take a few minutes and go back to the Review lessons from Units 1 and 2 to make sure you keep those words updated in your vocabulary.

Words of Wisdom

Four minutes a day to a richer and more powerful vocabulary

Lesson 24   Graphical Review of Units One - Three

Before we move on into Unit Four, take a look at these graphics. Some people (graphical learners) find them a helpful tool for organizing their understanding of the relationships among words. Here are just a few of the key words that evolved from the Latin roots.

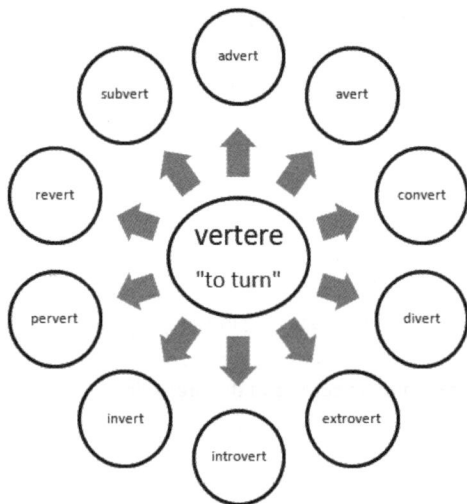

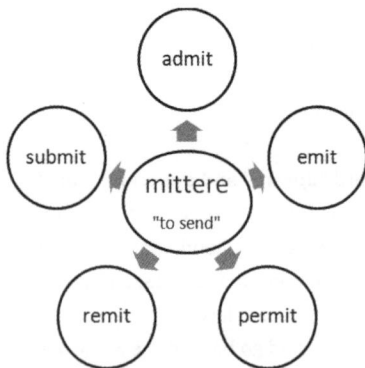

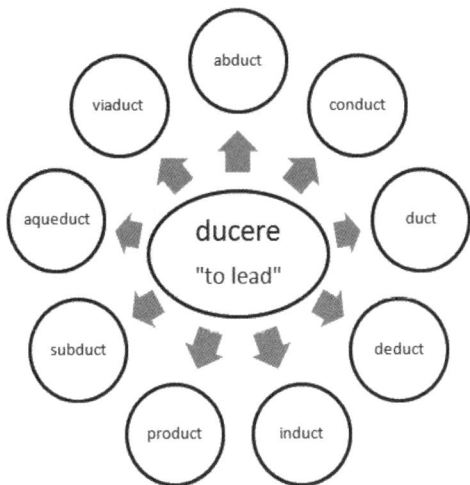

Word web — center: ducere "to lead"

Surrounding words: abduct, conduct, duct, deduct, induct, product, subduct, aqueduct, viaduct

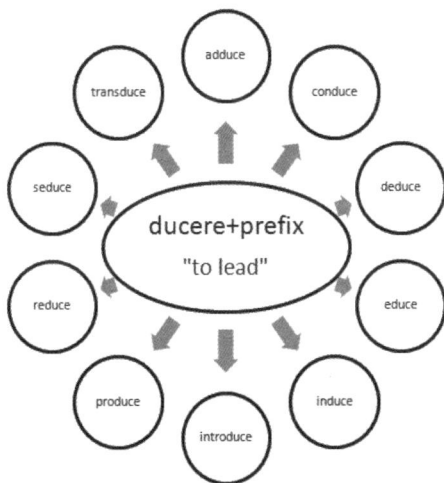

Word web — center: ducere+prefix "to lead"

Surrounding words: adduce, conduce, deduce, educe, induce, introduce, produce, reduce, seduce, transduce

Words of Wisdom

Four minutes a day to a richer and more powerful vocabulary

Unit Four

In Unit Four, the pace picks up. Now that you are developing great observational skills in looking at words and analyzing them, we should be able to build on your skills.

Unit Four
Lesson 25

The words we will be working with in the upcoming lessons fit under the umbrella of communication. Let's start with "audire", the Latin word for "to hear" or "to listen".

Principal Parts: audio, audire, {ow DEER ay} audivi, auditum

The basic **stem** is *audi*- (No, not the German car), but it may also surface as *audit*-.

> *Actually, the Audi company name is based on the surname of the founder August Horch. The name Audi itself is a cognate with the English word* **HARK**, *meaning* **listen**- *which translated to/from Latin becomes* **Audi**.

The word "audio" has come directly into English. However, in English it is used as a noun and an adjective, as opposed to its use in Latin as a first person, singular verb – "I hear".

As a noun, **audio** refers to "sound", usually a radio signal, but frequently as the section of television, motion picture or video equipment that deals with sound.

"The picture was beautiful, but the audio was garbled."

As an adjective, **audio** refers to just about anything that relates to sound.

"The audio channel of the movie was garbled."

The stem itself exposes multiple words in American English.

audible –adj. heard or capable of being heard (note the suffix "ible").

From this word come **"audibility", "audibly", "inaudible", "inaudibly" and "inaudibility"**.

What would an actor be without an **audience**? n. "a group of listeners, or as the act or state of hearing and even a formal hearing or interview"

"She felt fortunate to be granted an audience with the pope."

Obviously, the audience has to sit somewhere.

auditorium – n. "part of a building where an audience sits"

"The new school had a huge auditorium that seated 750 people."

If an actor wished to participate in a play in that auditorium, they would first need to

audition – v. "to test or give a trial performance"; n. "a trial performance to assess an entertainer's merits"

"She looked forward to auditioning for the part."

"He was very nervous before his audition."

audiovisual –adj. "of or relating to both hearing and sight; utilizing both audible and visual components"

"The audiovisual aspect of the presentation was quite absorbing."

auditory –adj. "of or relating to hearing or experienced through hearing"

"The fireworks display was an awesome auditory and visual experience."

audiology –n. "the branch of science dealing with hearing"

audiologist –n. "a person trained in the branch of science dealing with hearing"

audiometer –n. "n instrument used in measuring the acuity of hearing"
    "After earning her degree in audiology and practicing many years with her audiometer, she was widely acknowledged as the best audiologist in the region."

audit –n. "a formal examination of a company's records"; "a methodical examination and review"; v. "to perform an audit or examination of books or records"
    "The financial audit revealed many glaring accounting errors."
Obviously, an audit is conducted by an **auditor** – n. "a person authorized to examine and verify accounts"
    "The auditor discovered outright fraud in the company's accounting procedures."

audiocassette –n. "an audiotape recording mounted in a cassette"
    "The audiocassette tape is almost a relic of the past."

Examine the word **subaudition**. It is a noun that refers to the act of understanding or supplying something that is not expressed, a "reading between the lines". From this comes the adverb **subaudibly**, meaning barely audible.
    "The neophyte actor spoke so softly as to be subaudible."

Well, where did all of this come from? The Latin word **"auris"** {ORR iss} refers to the ear.
This yields the English term **aural**, an adjective meaning of or relating to the ear or the sense of hearing.
    "The gentleman had a serious aural deficiency and required hearing aids."
This is different from the term **auricular,** {or RIK u lar} which is an adjective meaning something told privately.
    "His attempt at making an auricular confession fell apart when he learned the priest was almost deaf."

The Romans even had a term they used to describe a person having large or long ears, **auritus,** which fortunately did not survive the transition into English.
BTW, did you figure out the meaning of the noun "cognate" used earlier in this lesson? Check out the meaning of the adjective "cognate" for clarification.

Review:	Audio	Audiology	Audibility	Audit
	Audible	Audiologist	Audibly	Auditor
	Audience	Audiometer	Inaudible	Auditory
	Auditorium	Subaudible	Inaudibly	Aural
	Audition	Subaudibly	Inaudibility	Auricular
	Audiovisual	Subaudition	Audiocassette	

Assignment: OK, now how are you going to sort these words out and figure out the best way to incorporate them into your active vocabulary?
Reflection: What have you learned from this lesson? How might you use this knowledge to add power and fluency to your writing and speaking?

Unit Four
Lesson 26

Next, let's work with "*videre*", the Latin word for "to see" or "to look at".

Principal Parts: *video, videre*, {vee DAIR ray} *vidi, visum*

The basic **stem** is **vid-**, but it also frequently surfaces as **vis-**.

As we saw in the previous lesson with audio, video has translated itself directly into English. **Video** surfaces as a noun meaning "the visual portion of television, video or film"; it is also referred to as "the finished or broadcast product ready to be viewed through an electronic medium".

"The video of the sports coverage provided great detail for all the armchair quarterbacks."

video – adj. of or relating to images seen through an electronic medium, such as television or computer display

"The video display on her computer tended to distort enlarged images."

Videography and **videographer** refer to the nouns describing the practice or art of recording images with a video camera & the person who does so. Wait a minute –

"With access to video camera technology being so prevalent, just about everyone can consider himself or herself a videographer."

Video morphs into **visible** –adj. capable of being seen (note the "-ible" suffix)

"The colors displayed were all in the visible spectrum."

While it starts as "something that can be seen", **vision** frequently connotes "a lovely or charming sight or even something seen in a dream, a trance or ecstasy".

"She was truly a vision of loveliness in her wedding gown."

Visionary shows up as a noun – "one who see visions, but whose projects may be viewed as unrealistic" or an adjective – "characterized by visions or the power of visions; dreamy, existing only in imagination".

"While he considered himself a visionary, his acquaintances described him as 'some sort of kook'."

"The architect's visionary plans challenged all the contractor's skills."

Without sounding too negative, there is also "**invisible**" (adj.), "**invisibility**" (noun) and "**invisibly**" (adv). This also includes someone who is totally **visionless**.

A related word that is almost disappearing from our electronic vocabulary is **videotape.** It has been used as a noun meaning a recording of visual images and sound on magnetic tape or as a verb to describe the action of making a recording.

"After they finished videotaping the game, they decided to try to sell copies of the videotape at an exorbitant price."

Audiovisual – hey, wait a minute. We already had that in the last lesson.

Visit is the verb coming from *videre* through *visitare* {viz i TAR ray} "meaning to go to see" referring "to go to see as an act of comfort or help". **Visit** as a noun is "a short stay".

Based on this word, a *visitor* is a "person who visits", a **visitation** is "an instance of visiting or temporary custody of a child given to a noncustodial parent", with the adjective **visitable** as "socially eligible to receive visits". *Again, observe the "-able".*

"As a visitor to the state, he was not eligible for visitation rights."
"After her release from intensive care, she was visitable."

Vista [VIZ tuh] refers to "a distant view through or along an opening".

"Visitors from the eastern part of the U.S. are usually amazed at the extensive vistas they encounter while traveling in the American West."

Visor [VI zur] is the front piece of a helmet or the brow of a cap.

"The knight lowered his visor, indicating that he was ready for the joust."

As an adjective, **visual** means "of, relating to, or used in vision", "producing mental images". As a noun, a **visual** refers "something that appeals to sight; something used for illustration, demonstration or promotion:.

"Since he was a visual learner, he really needed to see the content instead of just hearing it."

As a verb, **visualize** means "to make something visible; to see or form a mental image; to envisage". *Observe the suffix "-ize".*

"Athletes are taught to visualize a successful performance before they begin."

Finally, there are two other words from this root that have flowed directly from Latin into English.

Vide – meaning to "**look at**" ... or **See**... (command, imperative) to direct you to additional information. (Note: you will see this throughout the rest of the lessons.)

"**Vide**: visualization."

Videlicet – from a combination of *videre* (to look at) + *licere* (to be permitted) meaning "that is to say" or "Namely"; sometimes abbreviated **viz**.

"The jury will examine the evidence, **viz**. the murder weapon."
"The jury will examine the evidence, **videlicet**, the murder weapon."
"The jury will examine the evidence, **namely**, the murder weapon."

Visual is often used in combination with a variety of other terms, such as "visual literacy", "visual learner", "visual acuity", "visual aid", or "visual field".

The next lesson will continue this, so let's **see** what happens then.

Review:	Video (v. or n.)	Invisible	Visit	Visual
	Videography	Invisibility	Visitor	Visualize
	Videographer	Invisibly	Visitation	Vide:
	Visible	Visionless	Visitable	Videlicet
	Vision	Videotape	Vista	viz.
	Visionary	Audiovisual	Visor	

Unit Four
Lesson 27

Previously, we worked with *videre* ("to see") and explored several dozen words directly from that root. In this lesson, we will look at adding prepositions to the root. Then, we will examine two related Latin roots.

One additional word that flowed from *videre* was the English word "**view**". As a verb, it means "to look at attentively" or "to examine". It can also mean "to survey or examine mentally".

As a noun, among other definitions it can mean "inspection" (*watch for more on this word shortly*) or "an opinion or judgment colored by the individual's bias" or simply the "scene or the sight or the prospect". This can be a very flexible word for your vocabulary.

"He was called in to view the remains of the crash victim."

"In my opinion, he has a strange view on things; but then again, he thinks the same of me".

We have been able to add the prefix "*re-*" to many of the verbs we have worked with. The same applies to *videre*.

Revise (from the Latin *revidere* "to look again") is a verb that means basically "to look over again", but adds the "in order to correct or improve" element

Revision then becomes the noun that means "either the act of revising or the result of that effort"

Revisionism refers to "the advocacy of revising; in Marxist socialism in the early 20th century, this referred to preferring an evolutionary as opposed to a revolutionary spirit"

Revisionist as a noun is "the person who practices revisionism"; as an adjective, this has taken on the connotation of "revising the way that history has been written"

Revisory is the adjective that means "having the power or purpose to revise"

Revisit as a simple verb means "to visit a place again", but has taken on the added meaning of "re-examining a previously discussed issue"

"As an English teacher, frequently my job was to ask my students to revise their original drafts."

"Word processing software certainly makes it much easier for students to complete a revision of their drafts with the guidance of a tech-savvy teacher."

"The revisionism practiced by factions in the Russian revolution was finally eliminated."

"Revisionist historians have brought to light many elements of our past that were not previously recorded, *viz.* Columbus' impact on indigenous peoples or the Japanese internment camps in the US during WW II".

"She was given revisory authority for the curriculum update meetings."

"The city council chose to revisit its decision on zoning."

Envision means literally "to picture to oneself"
"He envisions himself to be God's gift to womankind."

It's time to add a new prefix: *super-* meaning "over" or "above" or "in addition to".
Review these sentences and determine the meanings.
"The new principal showed a knack for being able to supervise the faculty."
"She honed her supervision skills by working closely with the new teachers."
"The supervisor on the construction project supervised four foremen."
    Supervise – verb meaning to "oversee" or "superintend"
    Supervisor – noun describing "the person who supervises" or "the administrative officer in charge of a particular school, business or governmental unit".
    Supervision – noun meaning "critical watching and directing".
        Vide: **Supervisory**

For this section, try envisioning the words that will flow from *dis-* or *di-*(apart) + *videre*. Literally, this combination means "to see apart" and for all practical purposes – to divide, to separate into classes or groups, to part, to distribute, to apportion.
    Division – noun meaning the act or process of dividing; the state of being divided; a method of organizing troops; a mathematical process of separating
    Divide – verb meaning to separate into parts; noun meaning a point or line of division, such as a dividing ridge between drainage areas.
    Divisor – noun – number by which a dividend is divided.
    Dividend – noun, a number to be divided; individual share of something divided, e.g. stock
    Divisive – adjective – tending to separate or divide; creating disunity or dissension
"The third grader struggled while trying to understand division."
"Let's divide my pizza into four pieces. I'm not hungry enough to eat eight."
"When the dividend 8 was divided by the divisor 4, the quotient was 2."
"The tactics used by the union leader had a divisive impact on the group."

This is not quite the same as *de-* (from, down, away) + *videre*.
This formed the word **devise**, to form in the mind by new combinations or applications of ideas or principles; to invent; to give by will – to bequeath (e.g. real estate)
    "He was always trying to devise a new way to solve problems."
BTW: What would a **subdivision** be?
Review (get it?):

View	Revisory	super-	Divide
Revise	Revisit	Supervise	Division
Revisionism	Envision	Supervisor	Divisor
Revisionist	Devise	Supervision	Dividend
			Divisive

Unit Four
Lesson 28

Latin offers us multiple ways "to see", all of which send additional words into English.

Specio, specere, {spay SAIR ray} *spexi, spectum* to look at, to watch, to observe

Specto, spectare, {spek TAR ray} *spectavi, spectatum* – to look at, to watch, to examine, to inspect

Note that the stems for both of these closely related but separate verbs are **spec-** or **spect-**

Obviously here, you must look closely at the words that flow directly from these stems. When you do, you will clearly see ...

Spectacle – noun, "something exhibited to view as unusual or notable"

Spectacled, *bespectacled* – adj. "having or wearing glasses or specs"

Spectacular adj. "striking, sensational; of or related to a spectacle"

Spectate verb – "to be present as a spectator at an event"

Spectator noun – "person who looks on or watches"

Specimen noun – "an individual, item or part considered typical of a group, class or whole"

"The bespectacled older gentleman made a spectacle of himself while spectating at the game."

"The spectators at the Super Bowl paid exorbitant prices for the tickets."

"The supervisor required a specimen from each employee for the drug testing."

The same application of prefixes impacts these verbs as well.

ad or *a* (to or toward) + *specere* lets us see a particular aspect of something.

Aspect - a position facing a particular direction; appearance to the eye or mind; the apparent position of a body in the solar system with respect to the sun

"The commission reviewed every aspect of the question."

Inspect – verb, to view closely in critical appraisal; to officially examine

"The custodial supervisor inspected the offices and hallways."

Vide: **inspection, inspector, inspective**

Respect – from *respicere* to look back at, to regard; verb – to consider worthy of high regard; to refrain from interfering with; noun – high or special regard, esteem, consideration; in relation to a particular thing

"The supervisor who closely inspected the work done by his employees earned their respect by his positive and supportive comments and directions."

Vide: **respectful, respectable, respective, respectively, irrespective**

"Rodney Dangerfield's complaint was that 'he didn't get no respect'".

Remember *dis* (away from)? Vide: *Disrespect, disrespectful , disrespectfully*

Perspective retrieves the "through" element. *Perspicere* literally meant "to see through" or "to look clearly". To an artist, the noun perspective refers to "the technique or process of representing on a plane or curved surface the spatial relation of objects as they might appear to the eye." Perspective can also refer to "point of view" or "the interrelation in which a subject or its parts are mentally viewed".

"Stan Dunlap called his educational consulting business Fresh Perspectives."

"When the five blind men approached the elephant, each one could only make contact with one part of it. One reached out and felt the trunk and based his 'vision' of the elephant from that perspective. The second grasped the tusk, the third the ear, the fourth the leg, and the fifth the tail. Imagine the discussion or argument that evolved from their sharing of perspectives."

Affixing the prefix *pro* (before) yields the English word ***prospect***. As a noun, this can mean "a mental consideration", "a place that commands an extensive view or a lookout", "a vision", "a likely candidate", or "a potential buyer". As a verb, prospect means "to explore an area, esp. for mineral deposits".

Vide: **prospective** (adj); **prospectus**

"The real estate agent identified me as a good prospect to buy the mansion."

Prefixing *intro* (inward) creates the word ***intro*spection** – noun meaning "a reflective looking inward"; "an examination of one's own thoughts and feelings".

Vide: **introspective**

"When I asked you to write a reflection on what you have learned in each lesson, I am essentially asking you to be introspective."

Let's add another prefix to your repertoire – *circum* which means "around"
***Circum*spect** then is an adjective meaning "looking around", "to be cautious, careful to consider all circumstances and possible consequences".

Vide: ***circum*spection**

"The investor was circumspect in reviewing the prospectus for stock offerings from the new company."

Review:

Spectacle	Aspect	Respectful	Perspective
Spectacled	Inspect	Respectfully	Prospect
Bespectacled	Inspection	Respectable	Prospective
Spectacular	Inspector	Respective	Prospectus
Spectate	Inspective	Respectively	Introspection
Spectator	Respect	Irrespective	Introspective
Specimen		Disrespect	*circum-*
		Disrespectful	Circumspect
		Disrespectfully	Circumspection

Assignment:
So, what new insights did this lesson bring you?
What *aspects* of this lesson were you able to connect to words from previous lessons?
In other words, from your *perspective*, what do you see now that you may not have seen before?

Unit Four
Lesson 29

Let's continue communicating with *"dicere"*, the Latin word for "to speak".

    Principal Parts: *dico, dicere*, {dee SAIR ray} *dixi, dictum*

    The basic **stems** are *dic-* or *dict-*. (Sorry, dixi- just hasn't made the *stem* cut.)

It is closely related to another Latin verb, *dicare*, which meant to proclaim or dedicate.

It is also related to the Latin noun *dictio* meaning "speaking" or "speech".

    Diction is one word that flows directly from the root. It is a noun that means "choice of words, esp. with regard to correctness, clearness or effectiveness"; "vocal expression"; "enunciation"; "pronunciation and enunciation of words in singing".

    Dictionary is the noun that means "a reference book that contains words, their forms, pronunciations, meanings, etymology, etc."

    Dictum is a noun that means "a noteworthy statement"; "a formal pronouncement of a principle, proposition or opinion"; "pledge"; Pl. **Dicta**.

    Dictate, as a verb, means "to speak or act domineeringly"; "to prescribe"; as a noun, "an authoritative rule, prescription or injunction".

    Dictator is the noun that describes "a person granted absolute emergency power" or "one holding complete autocratic control".

    Dictatorial, as an adjective, "of, relating to or befitting a dictator" or "ruled by a dictator" or "oppressive to or arrogantly overbearing to others".

    Dictation is the noun meaning "prescription" or "act or manner of uttering words to be transcribed" (more on this word later); "the performing of music to be reproduced by a student".

    "His precise diction was really appreciated by the audience."

    "Webster's dictionary is one of the most widely renowned for its clarity of definition."

    "The unexpected dictum from the prime minister shocked the assembly."

    "With an overwhelming majority of support, she should be able to dictate the terms of her new role."

    "Fidel Castro was Cuba's dictator for over half a century."

    "The new principal's dictatorial style did not sit well with the veteran faculty."

    "In the olden days, the 'boss' would call his secretary into his office to 'take dictation', which she would write using shorthand in her 'steno book'."

    Vide: **Dictatorship, Dictatorially**

Pre- meaning "before" or "earlier than" or "prior to" connotes the impact of timing. When prefixed to *-dict*, the English word ***predict*** means "to declare or indicate in advance"; "to foretell".

***Pre**dict*ion means "an act of predicting" or "something that is predicted"; "forecast".

    Vide: **predictable, predictability, predictive, predictor**

    "The meteorologist used computer models to predict the next day's weather."

    "His prediction about the outcome of the Super Bowl was spectacularly accurate."

Remember the prefix *ex-* or *e-* ? Place this in front of *–dict* and end up with **edict** – a noun meaning "a proclamation having the force of law", "an order or a command".

"Violation of the dictator's edict was punishable by death."

The prefix *ad-* or *a-* (meaning to or toward) creates **addict**. This can be a verb meaning "to devote oneself to something habitually" or as a noun to describe "one who is addicted to a substance".

Vide: **addiction, addictive**

While the prefix *inter-* normally means "between" or "among", **interdict** as a verb means "to forbid in a formal, authoritative manner" and as a noun "a prohibitory decree, a prohibition".

"The duke felt it necessary to interdict his citizens from assembling in the duchy square."

Vide: **Interdictive, Interdictor, Interdiction**

Indict {in DITE} verb that means" to charge with an offense" or "to criticize or accuse."

Indictment is the noun that is used to describe "the action or process of being indicted; a formal written statement framed by a prosecuting authority and found by a jury".

Vide: **indictable**

"The grand jury delivered the indictment against the mob leader, irrespective of his attorney's protestations of his client's innocence."

There is also a rarely used variant – **indite** – a verb which means "to make up or compose"; "to give literary or formal expression to" or "to put down in writing".

"She chose to indite her poem during spring break."

Closely related to this is the verb **indicate** – "to point out, to point at; to state or express briefly".   "He indicated a desire to cooperate."

Let's add a new prefix – *contra* – against, in opposition to, contrary, contrasting"
This creates the verb **contradict** which means "to assert the contrary of, to imply the opposite of"; "to take issue with"; "to deny".

Vide: **Contradiction, contradictory, Contradictable**

"This evidence clearly contradicts the testimony of the previous witness."

Review:

Diction	Predict	Addict	Contra-
Dictionary	Prediction	Addiction	Contradict
Dictum	Predictable	Addictive	Contradiction
Dicta	Predictability	Interdict	Contradictory
Dictate	Predictive	Indict	Interdictor
Dictator	Predictor	Indicate	Interdictive
Dictatorial	Edict	Indite	Interdiction
Dictation	Dictatorship	Dictatorially	Contradictable

Unit Four
Lesson 30

Just as we have many English words to describe similar needs, Latin had multiple ways to describe the acting of speaking.

Let's continue with *"sermocinare"*, {sair MO si nar ray} the Latin word for "to talk with, to converse, to hold a conversation". However, when utilized in English, it takes on a more familiar, unidirectional tone.

Principal Parts: *sermocinor, sermocinare, sermocinavi, sermocinatum*

The basic **stem** is *sermo-*

The noun form in Latin was *"**sermo**"* – n. "talk, conversation, dialog, discussion, ordinary speech"

<u>Sermon</u> – n. "a religious discourse usually delivered in public by a clergyman as part of a worship service"; "a speech on conductor duty"

<u>Sermonize</u> – v. "to compose or deliver a sermon"; "to speak didactically or dogmatically"; "to preach to or on at length"

<u>Sermonette</u> – n. "a short sermon"

Vide: <u>Sermonic</u>

"The preacher worked for days on his sermon for Easter."

"When the teacher got upset with her class, she tended to sermonize for the entire period."

"The abbreviated church service featured a sermonette instead of the lengthier sermon."

Loquor, loquere, {lo KWAIR ray} *loqui, locutus* "to talk, speak; say; mention"

Loquax is the Latin adjective that means "talkative"

The basic **stems** are *loquo-* and locu-

<u>Loquacious</u> adj. – "given to fluent or excessive talk; garrulous, talkative, wordy";

Vide: {lo KWAY shus} <u>Loquaciously, Loquaciousness, Loquacity</u>

"While she perceived herself as eloquent, many considered her loquacious."

Adding the prefix *"e-"* creates *"eloqui"* " to speak out". This yields the basic stems *eloquo-* and *elocu-*

<u>Elocution</u> n. "style of speaking"; "the art of effective public speaking"

Vide: {el lo KU shun} <u>Elocutionary, Elocutionist</u>

"Elocution used to be taught in high schools around the country."

<u>Eloquent</u> adj. – "marked by forceful and fluent expression"; "vividly or movingly expressive or revealing"

<u>Eloquence</u> n. – "discourse marked by force and persuasiveness"; "the art or power of using such discourse"; "the quality of forceful or persuasive expressiveness"

Vide: <u>Eloquently</u>

"He was such an eloquent orator that his audience gave him a rousing ovation"

"After kissing the Blarney Stone in Ireland, he was blessed with the gift of eloquence."

Any kind of speaking or talking is done with the mouth – Latin noun *os* — and there are many related terms. (*Os* is the nominative form of the noun and *oris* is the genitive or possessive form. More in Lesson 64.) The basic **stems** are *os-* and *or-*

Oral – adj. "uttered by the mouth or in words; spoken"; noun – "an oral examination (usually used in plural form *orals*) in which answers are given by spoken words rather than written words"

BTW, do not confuse **ORAL** with **VERBAL**, from the Latin word *verbum* which means **WORD**.

> Vide: **Orally, Orality**

"The dentist gave her a complete oral exam before she had to give her oral report."

Related to this is **Oracle** – n. "a person (as a priestess of ancient Rome or Greece) through whom a deity is believed to speak"

> Vide: **Oracular**

> "The Oracle of Delphi is perhaps the most widely known of all oracles in the ancient Greek world."

The oracle was typically a priestess, who had the job of **praying**.

The Latin word "to pray" was "orare", with **Principal Parts** *oro, orare, oravi, oratum*

> From *os / oris* comes the noun form – *oratio* "oration or speech".

Oration noun— "speaking, speech, language, oration, discourse, oratory"

Orate verb — "to speak in an elevated and often pompous manner"

Orator noun— "speaker"; "one who delivers as oration"; "one distinguished for skill and power as a public speaker"

Oratory (from the Latin *oratorium* where a speech is given) (NOTE the suffix -*ium*) noun— "the art of speaking in public eloquently or effectively"; "a place of prayer; a church"

Oratorical adj.— "of or related to, or characteristic of an oratory or oration"

> Vide: **Oratorically, Oratorio**

"He spent several weeks preparing his oration for the oratorical contest."

"The new boss tends to orate instead of communicating directly with his employees."

"He is quite the orator, always impressing his audiences."

"One of the events in a forensics or speech competition is called Original Oratory."

"Each year, the Elks Club sponsors an oratorical contest for high school students."

Review:

Sermon	Elocution	os, oris (mouth)	Oration
Sermonize	Elocutionary	Oral	Orate
Sermonette	Elocutionist	Orally	Orator
Sermonic	Eloquent	Verbal (word)	Oratory
Loquacious	Eloquence	Orally	Oratorical
Loquaciously	Eloquently	Orality	Oratorically
Loquaciousness		Oracle	Oratorio
Loquacity		Oracular	

Unit Four
Lesson 31

Consider the Latin noun "*lingua, linguae*", meaning "tongue" or (in a broader sense) "speech" or "language". The basic stem is "*ling-*". It takes off in several directions in English.

Lingual adj. "of or related to the tongue"; "in dentistry, the surface of the tooth next to the tongue"; "produced by the tongue"

Linguist or **Linguistician** n. "a person accomplished in language, esp. one who speaks several languages"; "a person who specializes in linguistics"

Linguistics n. "the study of human speech"; "the scientific study of language structure and meaning, including phonetics, phonology, morphology, syntax, and semantics"

Vide: **Lingua Linguistic Lingually** , **Linguistical, Linguistically**

Lingo n. "strange or incomprehensible speech"; "foreign language"; "special vocabulary of a particular field of interest, e.g. educationese"

Linguine {ling GWE nee} n. "narrow, flat pasta"

"The dental hygienist reported the lingual cavity to the orthodontist."

"He was a widely known linguist, reputedly fluent in eight languages."

"She has studied the linguistics of several indigenous peoples."

"Each profession seems to have its own lingo."

"Felix specified linguine to the server and insisted he not be given spaghetti."

Let's add a few new prefixes that are relevant to this term: *bi- tri- multi-*

Bi- from the Latin for "two"

   CAUTION: there is also *bi-* or *bio-* from the Greek which refers to "life"'

Tri- from the Latin *tres* and the Greek *treis* meaning "three"

Multi- from the Latin *multus* meaning "much" or "many"

Bilingual adj. "familiar with or able to use two languages"

Trilingual adj. "familiar with or able to use three languages"

Multilingual "containing or expressed in several languages"; "using or able to use several languages"

BTW, there is a comparable term from the Greek – "***polyglot***" – (from the Greek *poly-* meaning "many" and *glotto* meaning "language:) meaning "multilingual or speaking or writing several languages"; "a book (esp. the Bible) or a group containing or using several languages"

"As a renowned polyglot, he was fluent in every language spoken in Europe."

As we have see elsewhere, prefixing *non-* to a word makes it negative.

Nonlinguistic "Having been raised by wolves, he was nonlinguistic in civilization."

The Romans had several words for "**whisper**" *susurrare* or *insusurrare* meaning "to whisper, to rustle; to insinuate".

There was also the Latin noun ***susurrus*** "hum or whisper" which came directly into English.

> **Susurrus** {sue SUR rus} n. "hum or whisper"; "a whispering or rustling sound"
> > Vide: swarm
>
> **Susurration** {sue SUR ray shun} n. "a whispering sound"; "murmur"
>
> **Susurrus** adj. "full of whispering sounds"

"As the swarm of bees approached, the susurrus grew louder."

"A susurration floated quietly from the confessional."

"A susurrus murmur buzzed around the room after he announced his resignation."

At the other end of the vocal range was "**shout**" – as a verb *clamo, clamare, {kla MAR ray} clamavi clamatus* and as a noun *clamor, -oris.* These left the **stem** *clam-* which evolved through the French into these words in English:

> **Clamor** {KLAH mer} <u>noun</u>— "noisy shouting"; "a loud continuous noise"; "an insistent public expression either support or protest"

This is also a <u>verb</u> in English meaning "to make a din"; "to become loudly insistent"; "to utter or proclaim insistently and noisily"; "to influence by means of clamor"

Clamorous adj. "marked by confused din or outcry"; "tumultuous"; "vociferous (NEXT)"

> Vide: **Clamored, Clamoring, Clamorously**

"The clamor of the crowd about the new taxes could be heard for blocks."

"They intended to clamor the committee into their perspective."

"The clamorous marketplace intrigued the foreign visitors."

From here, we also get ***Ex*claim** and ***Excla*mation.**

"We heard him exclaim as he flew out of sight, (you know the rest)."

As you just saw, there was another Latin word for **Shout.** The verb *vociferare* meant "to cry out, to voice loudly, to scream". The companion noun was *vociferatio, -onis* meaning "clamor or shout".

Vociferous {vo SIFF er us} adj. "marked by or given to vehement insistent outcry"; syns: clamorous, strident, boisterous, obstreperous

Vociferate v. "to shout"; "to cry out loudly"

> Vide: **Vociferant, Vociferation, Vociferator**

"The students' vociferous outburst quickly got the principal's attention."

Review:

Lingua	Lingually	Nonlinguistic	Clamorously
Lingual	Linguistical	Susurrus	Exclaim
Linguist	Lingulstically	Susurration	Exclamation
Linguistician	*Bi-, Tri-, Multi-*	Susurrus	Vociferous
Linguistic	Bilingual	Clamor	Vociferate
Lingo	Trilingual	Clamorous	Vociferant
Linguine	Multilingual	Clamored	Vociferation
Linguistics	Polyglot	Clamoring	Vociferator

Unit Four
Lesson 32

Another aspect of the communication theme of this unit invites to work with "scribere", the Latin infinitive for "to write".

  Principal Parts: scribo, scribere, {SKREE burr ray} scripsi, scriptum
  The basic **stems** are ***scrib-*** or ***script-***.

Scribe noun – "an official or public secretary or clerk"; "a writer, specifically a journalist";
  verb— "to write"; to work as a scribe"
Scribble verb — "to write hastily or carelessly without regard to legibility or form"
Scribbler noun – "one that scribbles"; " a minor or insignificant author"
Scribal adjective – "of or related to a scribe"
          Vide: **scribed, scribing, scribbled, scribbling**
  "He was fired from his job as scribe because of his illegible scribbles."
  "He perceived himself to be another Hemingway, but the publishers saw him only as a scribbler."
  "The scribe for the tribe had his own scribal chambers."

  Scrip noun "a short writing, e.g. list or certificate"; "paper currency or token used in an emergency"
  Script n. "something written, text"; "an original document, manuscript" "a style of printed letters that resembles handwriting"; "written text for a stage play or film"; v. "to prepare a script for"; "to provide careful details for, e.g. a plan of action"
    Scripter noun – "scriptwriter"
    Scripture noun – "act or product of writing"; "books or a passage of the bible".
    Scriptural – adjective – "of, related to, or contained in a sacred writing"
    Scriptorium noun – "a copying room for the scribes in a medieval monastery"
  "After the earthquake, the military had to issue scrip to the villagers."
  "The script for the play contained detailed stage directions."
  "He was selected to be the scripter for the film version."
  "The Bible is frequently referred to as Holy Scripture."
  "The short play contained a beautiful scriptural interpretation."
  "The monk scribes worked in silence in the monastery's scriptorium."
{NOTE: ***manu*** is from the Latin word for hand, hence a hand-written ***manuscript***};
FYI: The noun form of the Latin verb "scribere" is "scriptio".

Review:	Scribe	Scribble	Scrip	Scripture
	Scribal	Scribbler	Script	Scriptura
	Scribed	Scribbled	Scripted	Scriptorium
	Scribing	Scribbling	Scripter	Manuscript

Unit Four
Lesson 33

Again, adding a prefix impacts the meaning of the offspring of the root.

A<u>scribe</u> {uh SKRIBE} verb – "to refer to a supposed cause, source or author"; "to attribute"; "to assign"; "to impute" (more on this word shortly); *ascribe* suggests an inferring of cause or authorship
> Vide: **A<u>scription</u>, A<u>scribed</u>, A<u>scriptive</u>**

"It seemed logical to ascribe authorship to the veteran author because of his successful track record."

Con<u>scribe</u> verb – "to enlist forcibly"; "to conscript"
> Vide: **Con<u>script</u>, Con<u>scription</u>, Con<u>scripted</u>**

"Even though there were many volunteers, the shortage of soldiers forced the army to conscribe hundreds of residents into military service."

De<u>scribe</u> verb – "to represent or give an account in words"
> Vide: **de<u>scription</u>, de<u>scriptive</u>**

"Words can hardly describe the beauty of the desert *vista*."
> Vide: **Described, Describing**

In<u>scribe</u> verb – "to write, engrave or print as a lasting record"; "to enroll"; "to draw within a figure, as to touch many points"
> Vide: **in<u>scription</u>**

"The students were told to inscribe a polygon within the circle."
> Vide: **Inscribed**

Pre<u>scribe</u> verb – "to lay down a rule"; "to write or give medical prescriptions"
> Vide: **Pre<u>script</u>, Pre<u>scription</u>, Pre<u>scriptive</u>**

"Based on her patient's symptoms, the doctor prescribed antibiotics."
> Vide: **Prescribed**

Sub<u>scribe</u> verb – "to write one's name underneath"; "to attest by signing"; "to enter one's name for a publication or service"
Sub<u>script</u> noun – "a distinguishing symbol written immediately below and to the right of a character, e.g. X_2 or Y_{sub3}"
> Vide: **Sub<u>scription</u>, Subscribed, Subscriber**

"Before he could subscribe to 'Math World', he had to figure out what a subscript was or they would not fulfill his subscription."

Tran<u>scribe</u> verb – "to write across"; "to make a written or typed copy of dictated or recorded material"; "to record for later broadcast"

Transcript noun – "a written, printed or typed copy of dictated or recorded material"; "an official or legal, often published copy of the proceedings, e.g. court reporting or a student's academic record"

      Vide: *Transcription, Transcriptionist*, **Transcribed**

"Before she could transmit the transcript, she had to transcribe the inscribed scriptural passage."

Circumscribe verb – "to define or mark off"; "to draw a line around"

      Vide: *Circumscription*

"After learning how inscribe a polygon in a circle, then students had to learn how to circumscribe a circle around a polygon."

      Vide: **Circumscribed**

Superscribe verb – "to write as a name or address on the outside"; "to write or engrave on the top or outside"

Superscript noun – "a distinguishing symbol written immediately above and to the right of a character, e.g. X^2 or Y^{super3}"; also an adjective

Superscription noun – "something written or engraved on the surface of, outside of or above something else"; "the act of superscribing"

"She chose to superscribe her address in the upper left corner of the outside of the envelope."

"The teacher wanted to be sure that her math students knew how to write a superscript number such as 3^3, or three cubed."

"The Envelope's superscription contained the return address."

Review:

Ascribe	Conscribe	Inscribe	Subscribe
Ascription	Conscript	Inscribed	Subscript
Ascribed	Conscription	Inscription	Subscription
Ascriptive	Conscripted	Prescribe	Subscribed
Circumscribe	Describe	Prescribed	Subscriber
Circumscription	Described	Prescript	Superscribe
Circumscribed	Describing	Prescription	Superscript
	Description	Prescriptive	Superscription
	Descriptive		

Now take a look at this graphical review ...
Is a good method for you to preserve your understanding of the content?

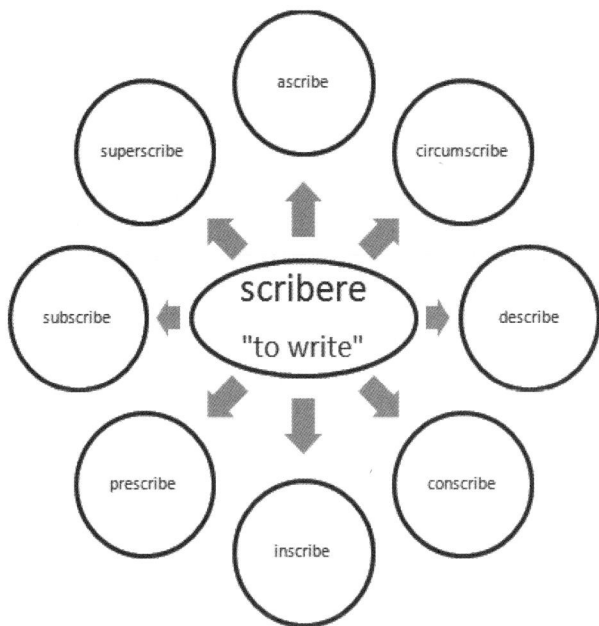

Unit Four

Lesson 34

Related to "write" is the Latin word "*notare*" which means "to write", "to mark, to brand" **Principal Parts**: noto, notare, notavi, notatum

The basic **stem** is not-.

Note verb – "to notice or observe with care"; "to record or preserve in writing"; "to make special mention of"; "to remark, indicate, show";   noun – "a condensed or informal record"; "a printed comment or reference set apart from the text"; "a written promise to pay a debt"

Notation noun – "note or annotation" ; "a system of characters, symbols, or abbreviated expressions in art, science, math or logic used to express technical facts or quantities"

Nota bene – Latin phrase that has come directly into English –"Note well"

>   Vide: **Notate**, **Notable**, **Notably,**   **Notary**

  "Be sure to note the inclusion of the substantial evidence to support their contention."

  "It is almost impossible to succeed as a scientist without a solid understanding of scientific notation."

Related to "write" is the Latin word "*annotare*" which means "to mark"

   Principal Parts: *annoto, annotare, annotavi, annotatum*

The basic **stem** is *annot-*.

Annotate verb – "to make critical or explanatory notes or comments"

Annotation noun – "a note added by way of comment or explanation"

>   Vide: **Annotated, Annotator**

  "The professor demanded that students annotate their theses."

  "An effective annotation can add real depth of insight to an essay or research paper."

Related to "write" is the Latin word "denotare" which means "to apply", "to indicate"

   Principal Parts: denoto, denotare, denotavi, denotatum The basic **stem** is *denot-*.

Denote verb – "to serve as an indication of"; "to make known, to announce"; "to stand for, to designate"; literally the dictionary definition of a word

Denotation noun – "a direct specific meaning as distinct from an implied or associated idea"

Denotative adjective – "tending to denote"; "relating to denotation"

  "His presence at the meeting denoted his tacit support."

  "Her denotation of the purpose of the meeting removed any doubt in their minds."

  "The denotative use of the technical jargon clarified the issues to be discussed."

Related to "write" is the Latin word "connotare" which means "to note with"

   Principal Parts: *connoto, connotare, connotavi, connotatum*

The basic **stem** is *connot-*.

Connote verb – "to be associated with or inseparable from consequences"; "to convey in addition to exact, explicit meaning"; connote adds the emotional component of the word

Connotation noun – "the suggesting of the meaning of a word apart from the thing it explicitly names or describes"; "implication"

> Vide: **Connoted, Connotative, Connotatively**

"The earthquake connoted personal tragedy and misery in addition to the obvious devastation."

"A warm connotation of comfort surrounded my old chair."

Be aware of the fact that there is another word loosely related to "write", relevant for its heritage in English. It is the Latin word "noscere" which means "to get to know, to investigate"; "to know, to be familiar with, to recognize"

Principal Parts: *nosco, noscere, novi, notum*

The related Latin noun *notitia* means "knowledge"

The basic **stems** are *not-* or *nos-* or *no-*

Know verb – "to perceive directly; to have direct cognition of, to have understanding or recognition of"

Knowledge noun – "acquaintance with or understanding of a science, art or technique; cognizance (*more on this word later*)"; "learning, scholarship, erudition"

Knowledgeable adjective – "having or exhibiting knowledge or intelligence, keen"

Notice verb – "to comment on, to review"; "to treat with attention or civility"; noun – "announcement"; "warning";"notification, often written, by one of the parties to an agreement"; "a short critical account or examination"

Noticeable adjective – "worthy of being noticed; capable of being noticed"

> Vide: **Knowing, Knowingly, Knowledgeably, Noticeably**

"'That's for me to know and you to find out' was a pejorative retort used by children in 'the olden days'."

"An extensive vocabulary provides an incredible knowledge base."

"Of all members of the team, she was the most knowledgeable of audiology."

"The notice of the upcoming meeting was posted for all to see."

"His nation's absence from the summit was noticeable."

Review

Note	Annotate	Connote	Knowledgeable
Notation	Annotation	Connotation	Notice
Nota Bene	Annotated	Connoted	Noticeable
Notate	Annotator	Connotative	Knowing
Notable	Denote	Connotatively	Knowingly
Notably	Denotation	Know	Knowledgeably
Notary	Denotative	Knowledge	Noticeably

Unit Four
Lesson 35 – **Review** Communication Verbs
"audire" "videre" "specere" "spectare" "dicere" "scribere" "notare"

In Unit Four, we have explored the Latin root words "audire", meaning "to hear", "videre", meaning "to see", "specere", meaning "to watch, to observe", "spectare", meaning "to look at, to inspect", "dicere", meaning "to speak, to talk", and "scribere", meaning "to write".

We have also examined the impact of adding a Latin preposition in front of several of these verbs to see how that can significantly change the meaning of the root word. Likewise, you have learned that many common suffixes can be affixed to the root word to expand that range of options for you. Now it's time to take a look back and see how things are fitting into your active vocabulary. If it's just not there for you yet, no problem! TAKE A LOOK BACK and be sure you have it.

Answers can be found on pages 89-92.

It's time to take a little deeper look at some of our recently added prefixes and suffixes

Prefixes

Contra- "against, opposite, contrasting, e.g. contradict"

Inter- "between, among, in the midst, e.g. interstellar"; "occurring between, e.g. international"; "shared by or involving two or more, e.g. interfaith"

Intro- 'inward, within, e.g. introspection, introduction"

Super- "over, above, in addition to"; "over and above", "higher in quantity, quality, or degree than"; "more than"'; "surpassing all others of its kind"; "placed or written above, e.g. superscript ^{super}"

Suffixes

-or - er -tor noun - "one who does a specific thing, e.g. supervisor, dictator, abductor, adductor, conductor, educator, inductor, producer, seducer, transducer

-ory noun – "a place for or something that serves for a specific purpose, e.g. observatory"; adjective – "related to, characterized by, e.g. revisory, contradictory, supervisory"

-ful adjective – full of, characterized by, having the qualities of, e.g. respectful"

-ible > -ibly or **–able > -ably** adjective > adverb – from "able to" e.g. *predictable* > how this ability is applied, e.g. *predictably*

-ly adjective "like in appearance, manner or nature, having the characteristics of, e.g. admittedly, audibly; "characterized by regular recurrence over time, e.g. hourly"; adverb "to a specified degree, e.g. relatively"

-ism noun - "act, process, practice, e.g. plagiarism"; "discrimination on the basis of a specific attribute – e.g. racism"; "doctrine or religion, e.g. revisionism"

-ist noun - "one that performs a specific action, e.g. unicyclist"; "one who advocates or subscribes to a particular doctrine, e.g. revisionist"; "one who specializes in a particular field or skill, e.g. audiologist"

-ity noun - "quality, state or degree, e.g. visibility"

-ium noun - "ending for many chemical elements, e.g. Helium"; "ending for a room or place, e.g. auditorium"

-ize verb - "to cause to conform or be like, e.g. audible-ize"; "to engage in a specific activity, e.g. visualize"; "to adopt or spread the manner of activity or the teaching of, e.g. Christianize"

-ization noun - "action, process or result of making, e.g. visualization"

-graph noun - from the Greek "*graphein*" "to write"; "something written or drawn, e.g. audiograph"; "instrument for making or transmitting records or images, e.g. videograph"

-graphic or **-graphical** written or transmitted in a specific way, e.g. videographic

-grapher a person who creates or transmits graphically created products, e.g. videographer

-graphy "writing or representation in a specified manner, e.g. videography"

Verbs

In the upcoming sections, identify the word that best completes the sentence or matches the definition. If you don't get it correct, just go back and look at the lesson. Look at the context of the sentence for clues about the correct form. Spelling???

Words from the root word "audire"

He was very nervous before his ___ in the ___ for a role in the upcoming play .

After the ___ completed the ___ of the company's financial records, he explained his findings of fraud to the Board of Directors.

The ___ adjusted the calibration of the ___ and determined that the man suffered from acute ___ deficiency; besides that he was almost deaf.

___ adjective – capable of being heard

Words from the root word "videre"

With access to ___ camera technology being so prevalent, many people consider themselves to be a competent ___ .

The architect's ___ plans challenged the contractor's skills.

___ adjective – capable of being seen

___ namely, that is to say, abbreviation of "Videlicet"

___ command for See:

Words from the root word "videre" and prefixes (re- en- super- dis-)

Word processing software makes it much easier for a student to ____ a draft of an essay.
When she returned to her home town for a reunion, she wished to ____ her old haunts.
He ____ himself to be God's gift to women.
The ____ on the construction project ____ ten bricklayers.
He was always trying to ____ a new way to solve problems.

____   adjective – describing a way of revising the way history was recorded
____   noun – the number by which a dividend is divided
____   verb – to see apart, to separate into classes or groups, to distribute

Words from the root word "specere", "spectare" and prefixes (ad- in- re- per- circum- intro- pro-)

The *be-*____ older gentleman made a ____ of himself while he was ____-*ing* at the game.
The commission on higher education reviewed every ____ of the evidence about student achievement and the need for remedial coursework for almost one third of incoming students.
The supervisor earned the ____ of his workers by carefully noting their successes and quietly guiding them to better performance where needed.
The realtor was seeking just the right ____ for the million dollar home.
The investor was ____ as she reviewed all circumstances surrounding the purchase.

____   adjective – filled with respect for or displaying that attitude towards
____   noun – a reflection looking inward; examination of one's own thoughts/feelings
____   verb – to view closely in critical appraisal; to officially examine, as in prior to purchasing a home

Words from the root word "dicere" and prefixes (ad- contra- e- in- inter- re- pre-)

His precise ____ helped him achieve a successful audition.
Just because she was a straight A student, she thought she could ____ classroom procedures.
The meteorologist used several computer models to ____ the following day's weather.
His ____ personality made it extremely difficult for him to quit smoking.
The grand jury handed down the formal ____ against the mob boss.

____   adjective – able to declare or indicate in advance
____   noun – an order or command; a proclamation having the force of law
____   verb – to assert the contrary of, to imply or state the opposite of, to deny

Words from the root word "scribere" and prefixes (a- circum- con- de- in- pre- sub- trans-)

Since the young ___ didn't really 'get it', he simply _____ in the _____ while he was in the _____.

Words can hardly ____ the beauty of the desert vista.

The students were told to ____ a polygon within the circle.

Next, they had to _____ the polygon with a round figure.

___ or __ verb – to enlist forcibly, usually into military service

___   verb – to write or give medical prescriptions

___   noun – a written, printed or typed copy of dictated or recorded material

___   verb – to write, engrave or print as a lasting record

Words from the root word "notare" and prefixes (an- contra- e- in- inter- re- pre-)

It is almost impossible to succeed as a scientist without a solid understanding of scientific ___.

An effective _____ can add real depth of insight to an essay or research paper.

A warm _____ of comfort surrounded my old chair.

Her ____ of the purpose of the meeting removed any doubt in the minds of the other participants.

_____   verb – "to make critical or explanatory notes or comments"

_____   verb – "to be associated with or inseparable from consequences"; "to convey in addition to exact, explicit meaning"; "to imply as a logical connotation"

_____   verb – "to serve as an indication of"; "to make known, to announce"; "to stand for, to designate"

Words from the root word "noscere"

Of all members of the team, she was the most _____ of audiology.

His nation's absence from the summit was _____.

An extensive vocabulary provides an incredible _____ base.

The _____ of the upcoming meeting was posted for all to see.

_____   verb – "to perceive directly; to have direct cognition of, to have understanding or recognition of"

_____   verb – "to comment on, to review"; "to treat with attention or civility";

_____   noun – "announcement"; "warning";"notification, often written, by one of the parties to an agreement"; "a short critical account or examination"

Previously, you saw a summary of many of the suffixes used throughout the first units. As you think about the definition or usage for each that has stuck with you, which of them correlates with the following descriptions?

Suffixes

____ or ____ or ____ noun - "one who does a specific thing, e.g. supervisor, dictator, abductor, adductor, conductor, educator, inductor, producer, seducer, transducer

____ > ____ adjective > adverb – from "able to"

____ noun - act, process, practice, prejudice or discrimination on the basis of a specific attribute, doctrine or religion

____ noun - ending for many chemical elements, ending for a room or place

____ verb - to cause to conform or be like, to engage in a specific activity, to adopt or spread the manner of activity or the teaching of

____ noun - something written or drawn, instrument for making or transmitting records or

____ usually an adjective that means capable of, fit for, worthy of tending, given, or liable to

____ adjective that means tending, given, or liable to that performs or tends toward an indicated action

____ noun meaning act or process, result of an act or process, state or condition

Consider writing a short essay incorporating some of the terms related to this unit on communication as a method of reinforcing your understanding.

Answers

Words from the root word "audire"

He was very nervous before his <u>audition</u> in the <u>auditorium</u> for a role in the upcoming play.
After the <u>auditor</u> completed the <u>audit</u> of the company's financial records, he explained his findings of fraud to the Board of Directors.
The <u>audiologist</u> adjusted the calibration of the <u>audiometer</u> and determined that the man suffered from acute <u>aural</u> deficiency; besides that he was almost deaf.

<u>audible</u>   adjective – capable of being heard

Words from the root word "videre"
With access to <u>video</u> camera technology being so prevalent, many people consider themselves to be a competent <u>videographer</u>.
The architect's <u>visionary</u> plans challenged the contractor's skills.

<u>visible</u>   adjective – capable of being seen
<u>viz</u>.   namely, that is to say, abbreviation of "Videlicet"
<u>Vide:</u>   command for <u>See:</u>

Words from the root word "videre" and prefixes (re- en- super- dis-)

Word processing software makes it much easier for a student to <u>revise</u> a draft of an essay.
When she returned to her home town for a reunion, she wished to <u>revisit</u> her old haunts.
He <u>envisions</u> himself to be God's gift to women.
The <u>supervisor</u> on the construction project <u>supervised</u> ten bricklayers.
He also tried to <u>devise</u> a new way to solve problems.

<u>Revisionist</u>	adjective – describing a way of revising the way history was recorded
<u>Divisor</u>	noun – the number by which a dividend is divided
<u>Divide</u>	verb to see apart, to separate into classes or groups, to distribute

Words from the root word "specere", "spectare" and prefixes (ad- in- re- per- circum- intro- pro-)

The bespectacled older gentleman made a spectacle of himself while he was spectating at the game.

The commission on higher education reviewed every aspect of the evidence about student achievement and the need for remedial coursework for almost one third of incoming students.
The supervisor earned the respect of his workers by carefully noting their successes and quietly guiding them to better performance where needed.
The realtor was seeking just the right prospect for the million dollar home.
The investor was circumspect as she reviewed all circumstances surrounding the purchase.

respectful   adjective – filled with respect for or displaying that attitude
     towards
introspection   noun – a reflection looking inward; an examination of one's own
     thoughts and feelings
inspect   verb – to view closely in critical appraisal; to officially examine, as
     in prior to purchasing a home

Words from the root word "dicere" and prefixes (ad- contra- e- in- inter- re- pre-)

His precise diction helped him achieve a successful audition.
Just because she was a straight A student, she thought she could dictate classroom
     procedures.
The meteorologist used several computer models to predict the following day's
     weather.
His addictive personality made it extremely difficult for him to quit smoking.
The grand jury handed down the formal indictment against the mob boss.

predictable   adjective – able to declare or indicate in advance
edict   noun – an order or command; a proclamation having the force of
     law
contradict   verb – to assert the contrary of, to imply or state the opposite of,
     to deny

Words from the root word "scribere" and prefixes (a- circum- con- de- in- pre- sub- trans-)

Since the young scribe didn't really 'get it', he simply scribbled in the scriptures while he was in the scriptorium.
Words can hardly describe the beauty of the desert vista.
The students were told to inscribe a polygon within the circle.
Next, they had to circumscribe the polygon with a round figure.

Conscribe or conscript   verb – to enlist forcibly, usually into military service
Prescribe   verb – to write or give medical prescriptions
Transcript noun – a written, printed or typed copy of dictated or recorded material
Inscribe   verb – to write, engrave or print as a lasting record

Words from the root word "notare" and prefixes (an- contra- e- in- inter- re- pre-)

It is almost impossible to succeed as a scientist without a solid understanding of
scientific notation.
An effective annotation can add real depth of insight to an essay or research paper.
A warm connotation of comfort surrounded my old chair.
Her denotation of the purpose of the meeting removed any doubt in the minds of
the other participants.

Annotate   verb – "to make critical or explanatory notes or comments"
Connote verb – "to be associated with or inseparable from consequences"; "to
convey in addition to exact, explicit meaning"; "to imply as a logical connotation"
Denote   verb – "to serve as an indication of"; "to make known, to announce"; "to
stand for, to designate"

Words from the root word "noscere"

Of all members of the team, she was the most knowledgeable of audiology.
His nation's absence from the summit was noticeable.
An extensive vocabulary provides an incredible knowledge base.
The notice of the upcoming meeting was posted for all to see.

Know   verb – "to perceive directly; to have direct cognition of, to have
understanding or recognition of"
Notice   verb – "to comment on, to review"; "to treat with attention or civility";
noun – "announcement"; "warning";"notification, often written, by one of the
parties to an agreement"; "a short critical account or examination"

Suffixes

-or - er -tor   person who does things
-ible > -ibly   adjective > adverb – from "able to"
-ism   noun - act, process, prejudice or discrimination on the basis of a specific
        attribute, doctrine or religion
-ist   noun - one who performs a specific action, one who advocates or
        subscribes to a particular doctrine, one who specializes in a particular field or
        skill
-ium   noun - ending for many chemical elements, ending for a room or place
-ize   verb - to cause to conform or be like, to engage in a specific activity, to
        adopt or spread the manner of activity or the teaching of
-graph   noun - something written or drawn, instrument for making or transmitting
        records or images
-ible or **-able**   usually an adjective that means capable of, fit for, worthy of
        tending, given, or liable to
-ion   noun meaning act or process, result of an act or process, state or condition

Congratulations!!

You have cemented and inter-connected 188 words into your
active vocabulary through this unit.

Words of Wisdom

Four minutes a day to a richer and more powerful vocabulary
Unit Five

In Unit Five, the focus is on words related to human mental activity – thinking, feeling, dreaming etc.

ENJOY!

Unit Five
Lesson 36

Now, look at *"putare"*, the Latin word for "to think" or "to consider".
  Principal Parts: *puto, putare,* {pooh TAH ray} *putavi, putatum*
  The basic **stem** is *put-*

Putative {PEW tuh tive} adjective – "commonly accepted or supposed"; "assumed to exist or have existed"
        Vide: **Putatively** adverb
  "He was the putative mob boss in southern New Jersey."

Adding the prefix *"im-"* tends to point the finger of blame.
Impute verb – "to lay the responsibility or blame for, often unjustly"; "to credit to a person or a cause, to attribute"; "syn. ascribe"
Imputation noun – "attribution, ascription, accusation, insinuation"
        Vide: **Imputative, Imputatively**
  "The defendant imputed the crime to his partner."
  "The imputation that he is a fraud has no basis in fact."

Dispute verb – from the Latin *disputare* "to discuss" – verb "to engage in argument"; "to call into question"; "to struggle against, to oppose"; "to contend over, to contest"; noun – "a verbal controversy, a debate"; "a quarrel"
Disputation noun "the action of disputing"; "a verbal controversy"; "an academic exercise in oral defense of a thesis by formal logic"
Disputable adjective – "capable of being disputed; debatable; questionable"
        Vide: **Disputed, Disputable, Disputably, Disputer, Disputant, Disputatious**
  "There always seemed to be some dispute between the brothers."
  "Her disputation of her Master's Thesis was very logically explained."
  "His logic was disputable and deemed incredible by his supervisors."
Indisputable adjective – "not capable of being disputed; unquestionable"
  "The evidence given the jury was indisputable."

Repute verb – "to think over, to reckon up, to consider a thing to be as specified"; noun – "estimation in the view of others, reputation"
Reputation noun (from the Latin noun *reputatio*) "overall quality of character as judged by people in general"; "a good name"
Reputable adjective – "enjoying good repute, held in esteem"; "employed widely by good writers"
Reputed adjective – "having a good repute, reputable"; "being such according to reputation or popular belief"
Reputedly adverb – "according to reputation or general belief"
        Vide: **Reputably**

"She was viewed to be woman of ill repute."
"Guard your reputation like gold."
"He worked diligently to maintain a reputable business."
"She was reputed to be the best orator on the debate team."
"He was reputedly an embezzler, but no one ever proved it."

Depute verb – [dee PYUT] "delegate"
Deputy noun – "a person appointed as a substitute with the power to act"
　"Sheriff Andy deputed Barney Fife to be his deputy."
Disrepute verb – "lack or decline of good reputation; held in low esteem"
Disreputable adjective – "not reputable"
　　　　Vide: *Disreputability, Disreputableness, Disreputably*
　"After his actions, the name 'Madoff' was held in disrepute."
　"The ambulance-chasing attorney's actions were considered disreputable in the legal community."

Now, look at "**cogitare**", the Latin word for "to think", "to consider", "to meditate".
　Principal Parts: *cogito, cogitare, cogitavi, cogitatum*
　The basic **stem** is *cogit-*

Cogitate verb – "to ponder or meditate deeply or intently"
Cogitation noun – "the act of cogitating"; "meditation"; "a single thought"
Cogitative verb – "of or relating to cogitation"; "capable of or given to cogitation"
"Cogito, ergo sum" – "I think, therefore I am" Rene Descartes – "the philosophic principle that one's existence is demonstrated by the fact that one thinks"
　"Sometimes, I just like to get away by myself and cogitate about the future chapters of my book."
　"Personally, I find cogitation good for the spirit."
　"As evidenced by her pensive countenance, she was in a particularly cogitative mood."

Adding the prefix *in-* adds a definite negative tone.
Incogitant adj. "thoughtless, inconsiderate"
　"His incogitant remark left her in tears."

Review:

Putative	Repute	Disrepute	Cogitate
Impute	Reputation	Disreputable	Cogitation
Imputation	Reputable	Disreputability	Cogitative
Dispute	Reputed	Disreputableness	Incogitant
Disputation	Reputedly	Disreputably	*"Cogito, ergo sum"*
Disputable	Reputably	Depute	
Indisputable	Disrepute	Deputy	

Unit Five
Lesson 37

Similar to *"cogitare"*, now let's look at **"cognoscere"**, the Latin word for "to get to know", "to learn", "to investigate", "to discover", "to understand". "Cognoscere" was assembled from "co" + "gnoscere".

Principal Parts: *cognosco, cognoscere, cognovi, cognitum*
The basic **stem** is *cogni-*

Cognize   verb – "to know"; "to understand"
Cognition   noun – "act or process of knowing including both awareness and judgment"; "the mental process of knowing, including aspects such as awareness, perception, reasoning, and judgment"
Cognitive   adjective – "of or relating to cognition"; "based on or capable of being reduced to empirical factual knowledge"
Cognizant   adjective – "knowledge of something, esp. through personal experience"
Cognizable   adjective – "capable of being known"; "capable of being judicially heard and determined"
Cognizance   noun – "knowledge, awareness"; "notice, acknowledgement"; "jurisdiction"
   Vide: **cognoscible**, cognitive science, cognitive dissonance
   "The goal of this book is to help you cognize roots and stems."
   "A variety of different 'brain games' may improve cognition and memory function."
   "Alcohol can seriously impair cognitive function."
   "The goal of this book is to help you increase your cognizance of roots and stems."
   "Based on his experiences as a soldier in Viet Nam, he was quite cognizant of the impact of war on children."
   "Many great insights are cognizable if only one can open the mind to experiencing them."
   "After reading this book, your cognizance of roots and stems should be enhanced."

Adding the prefix "re-" and a variety of suffixes impacts the meaning.
Recognize verb – "to acknowledge formally or to take notice of in some definite way"; "to know or identify from past experience"
Recognition n. "acknowledgement"; "knowledge or feeling that someone or something present has been encountered before"; "special notice or attention"
Recognizance noun "an obligation of record entered into before a court"
Recognizable adj. "can be recognized"
   Vide: **recognized, recognizing, recognizability, recognizably**
   "His appearance had changed so much I could barely recognize him."
   "It is about time her efforts were given appropriate recognition."
   "Because of his status in the community, he was released from jail on a personal recognizance bond."

"Though Lucille tried to go incognita, she was easily recognizable because of her red hair."

Adding the prefix "*pre*"- gives you a foretaste of what is to come – from the Latin "*praecogniscere*" "to know beforehand".
Precog**nition** n. "clairvoyance relating to an event of state not yet experiences"
Precog**nitive** adj. "clairvoyant" (fr. *clair* or "clear" + *yoyant* from *videre* "to see")
   "After predicting the upcoming disaster, he was widely acknowledged for his precognition."
   "Although some doubted her abilities, she was alleged to have credible precognitive skills."

Incog**nito** NO, not the little town of Cognito in Mexico --- adj. "with one's identity concealed"; n. "one appearing or living incognito"; "the state of assumed identity of one living or traveling incognito"; Vide: **in**cog**nita** (used only of a woman)
Incog**nizance** noun "the state of lack of awareness or consciousness"
Incog**nizant** adjective "lacking awareness of consciousness"; usually followed by "of"
   "While he traveled incognito, she was unable to travel incognita."
   "His incognizance of his surroundings left him vulnerable to the wandering bandits."
   "She was so self-absorbed as to be incognizant of the feelings he had for her."

Meta- or **Met-** prefix, from the Greek "after, with, among"; "occurring or situated after ..."; "used with the name of a discipline to designate a new but related discipline designed to deal critically with the original one"
Metacog**nition** n. essentially "cognition about cognition" or "thinking about thinking"; "contains 3 basic elements: *developing* a plan of action, *maintaining/monitoring* the plan, *evaluating* the plan"
Metacog**nitive** adj. refers to a learner's automatic awareness of their own knowledge and their ability to understand, control and manipulate their own cognitive processes
   "The importance of Metacognition in student learning has been clearly demonstrated."
   "I try to incorporate metacognitive components into all my assignments."

Review:

Cognize	Recognition	Precognition	*meta-* or *met-*
Cognition	Recognitive	Precognitive	Metacognition
Cognitive	Recognizance	Incognito	Metacognitive
Cognizant	Recognizable	Incognita	
Cognizable	Recognized	Incognizance	
Cognizance	Recognizing	Incognizant	
	Recognizability		
	Recognizably		

Unit Five
Lesson 38

The Romans definitely understood "thinking" and had several words to describe the process. Likewise, they were aware of "feelings" and used the verb *sentire* as one way to express it.

Let's start with *"sentire"*, the Latin word for "to feel". Depending on the context, it was also used for "to perceive" "to notice" or "to sense".

Principal Parts: *sentio, sentire, sensi, sensum*

The basic **stem** is **sent**- but it may also surface as ***sens***-.

As you have seen with other Latin verbs, there is also a noun counterpart – *sensus,* a masculine noun meaning, among other things, "sensation, sense" or "faculty or power of perceiving, perception, sentiment, inclination, or state of mind".

From these roots, we have multiple words in English.

<u>Sense</u> n. "a meaning conveyed or intended"; "faculty of perceiving by sense organs"; "conscious awareness or rationality, usu. used in pl. 'senses'"; "a definite but often vague or nebulous awareness or impression": "a capacity for effective application of the powers of the mind, intelligence, showing good judgment"

"I got the sense of what he meant."

"Her sense of smell of was acute."

"He finally came to his senses."

"I got the sense that he was serious about leaving."

"Of all the choices, this one makes the most sense."

<u>Sensible</u> adj. (from the Latin adj. *sensibilis*) "perceptible as real or material through the senses, capable of receiving sensory impressions, receptive to external influences"; "having good sense or sound judgment"; "practical, rational, reasonable"

"Her distress was sensible from her facial expression."

"His decisions about the future of the company were quite sensible."

"Before her first day as a waitress, everyone told her to wear sensible shoes."

<u>Sensitive</u> adj. "delicately aware of the feelings and attitudes of others, thoughtful and sympathetic"; "readily affected or changed by various agents"; "concerned with highly classified government information, secret or confidential"; "touchy"

"He was amazingly sensitive to the feelings of his employees."

"The folder of military secrets was labeled 'Sensitive'."

"Bringing up his past made you realize how sensitive he was about it."

Vide: <u>Sensate</u> adj. <u>Sensitize</u> v., <u>Sensitization</u> n.

<u>Sensation</u> n. "the process of sensing, awareness due to stimulation of a sense organ"; "a state of excited interest or feeling, the cause of such a feeling"

"He became aware of a burning sensation in his arm."

"His batting average of over .500 made him an overnight sensation."

<u>Sensational</u> adj. "outstanding, exceedingly or unexpectedly great"; "emphasizing lurid details, giving too much emphasis to the lurid detail of something"

"The theatre group's performance of 'Phantom' was sensational."

"The ads for the show only emphasized the sensational aspects."

Sensationalism n. "use of shocking material, the practice of emphasizing the lurid aspects of something".

"He felt he had to stoop to sensationalism to draw a crowd."

Sensationalize v. "to present in a sensational manner, exaggerate details, to place excessive emphasis on the most shocking and emotive aspects of a subject".

"The media sensationalized the story of the kidnapping."

Vide: **Sensationalization**

Sensibility n. "ability to receive and respond to sensations and stimuli"; "ability to feel, the capacity for being affected emotionally or intellectually"

"Her friends appreciated her sensibility to their feelings."

Sensory adj. "of or related to the senses, conveying nerve impulses from the sense organs to the nerve centers"

"The car accident damaged many of her sensory organs."

Sensual adj. "relating to gratification of the senses or the indulgence of a sense appetite, fleshly"; "voluptuous"; "deficient in moral, spiritual or intellectual interests"

"She lived a very sensual lifestyle."

Vide: **Sensualize, Sensualization**

Sensuous adj. (**Sensuously** adv.) "having strong sensory appeal"; "characterized by sense impressions or imagery aimed at the senses"; "enjoying or appreciating pleasurable stimulation of the senses, causing pleasurable stimulation of the senses."

"Watching a sunset on a sandy beach can be a truly sensuous experience."

> ***So what's the difference?*** *Sensuous* was reputedly invented by the poet Milton, because he wanted to avoid the sexual connotations of the word *sensual*. The consensus is that **sensual** emphasizes gratification or indulgence of the physical appetites while **sensuous** emphasizes aesthetic pleasure.

Sentiment n. "an attitude, thought or judgment prompted by feeling"; "a predilection, a specific view or notion, opinion"; "a romantic or nostalgic feeling verging on sentimentality"; "a general, underlying mental feeling, an emotion"; "a literary device designed to produce an emotional response in the reader"

"Can sentiment 'get in the way' of a good decision?"

Vide: **Sentimentality, Sentimentalism, Sentimentalize, Sentimentalization**

What a wealth of options from a root word ... but there's more.

Review:

Sense	Sensation	Sensory	Sentiment
Sensible	Sensational	Sensual	Sentimentality
Sensitive	Sensationalism	Sensualize	Sentimentalism
Sensate	Sensationalize	Sensualization	Sentimentalize
Sensitize	Sensationalization	Sensuous	Sentimentalization
Sensitization	Sensibility	Sensuously	

Unit Five
Lesson 39

Well, my sentiment is that Lesson 38 was a good start, but my *sense* is that there are more options. Let's explore.

Assent {AS sent} v. "to agree to something, esp. after thoughtful consideration"; "to concur"; n. "acquiescence, agreement"
Assentation {AS sen TAY shun} n. "ready assent, esp. when insincere or obsequious (*marked by a fawning attentiveness*)"
      Vide: **Assentor** or **Assenter**
  "After giving this a great deal of thought, I assent to your proposal."
  "After a long pensive pause, he gave his assent to the option at hand."
  "His assentation was prompt, but sounded obsequious and insincere."
Using the prefix *dis* "away or apart", the Romans created *dissentire*, (to feel apart).
Dissent v. "to differ in opinion, to withhold assent"; n. "difference or opinion; a religious nonconformity; a justice's nonconcurrence with the majority opinion".
Dissenter n. "one who dissents"
Dissenting adj. "differing in opinion with the majority"
Dissentious adj. "characterized by dissent or dissension"
Dissension n. "disagreement, esp partisan and contentious quarrelling; discord"
Dissensus n. "difference of opinion"; ant. "consensus"
  "Thought that is silenced is always rebellious. Majorities, of course, are often mistaken. This is why the silencing of minorities is necessarily dangerous. Criticism and dissent are the indispensable antidote to major delusions." Alan Barth
  "The dissenter is every human being at those moments of his life when he resigns momentarily from the herd and thinks for himself." Archibald Macleish
  "The justice filed the only dissenting opinion on the case."
  "The sergeant was concerned about dissension within the ranks."
  "This group was so argumentative that they could only arrive at dissensus."

Using the prefix *con* "with", the Romans created *consentire*, (to feel with).
Consent v. "to give assent or approval; to agree"; n. "compliance with or approval of what is done or proposed by another; agreement".
Consenting adj. "differing in opinion with the majority"
Consensus n. "general agreement; unanimity of opinion"; ant. "dissensus"
Consensual adj. "existing by mutual consent without a written agreement"
Consentaneous adj. "expressing agreement, done or made by consent of all"
      Vide: **Consenter Consented Consentingly Consensually**
  "Without his consent, the project cannot begin."
  "It was done between two consenting adults."
  "The jury finally reached consensus on convicting the accused."
  "Even though there was nothing in writing, their mutual approval was consensual."
  "The committee finally reached consentaneous resolution."

We have worked with the prefix *in-* previously. Here it also casts a negative tone.

In*sen***sate** {in SEN sate} adj. "lacking sense or understanding; foolish"; "lacking humane feeling, brutal"

In*sen***sible** adj. "imperceptible"; "incapable or lacking feeling"; "unconscious"; "lacking emotional response, apathetic, indifferent, unaware"

In*sen***sitive** adj. "not responsive or susceptible"; "lacking feeling or tact"

> Vide: **Insensibility Insensibly**

"His approach to raising children was totally insensate."

"He was so emotionally drained by the encounter as to be insensible to the chaos."

"His remarks showed just how insensitive he really is."

The other negative prefix is *non-* which gives us …

Non*sen***se** or **Non-***sen***se** n. "words or language having no meaning or conveying no intelligible ideas"; "an instance of absurd action"

> Vide: **Nonsensical Nonsensically**

"I like nonsense. It wakes up the brain cells." *Dr. Seuss*

Let's add a new prefix: *ultra-* originally meaning "situated beyond" and now denting "beyond in space, beyond the limits of".

Ultra*sen***sitive** adj. "beyond sensitive"

"His third degree burns left him ultrasensitive to human contact."

Extra*sen***sory** adj. "residing beyond or outside of the ordinary senses"

"She claimed strong powers of extrasensory perception."

Review:

Assent	Dissension	Consenter	Insensibly
Assentation	Dissensus	Consented	Nonsense
Assentor	Consent	Consentingly	Non-sense
Assenter	Consenting	Consensually	Nonsensical
Dissent	Consensus	Insensate	Nonsensically
Dissenter	Consensual	Insensible	Ultrasensitive
Dissenting	Consentaneous	Insensibility	Extrasensory
Dissentious		Insensitive	

Assignment:

Are you comfortable being able to explain these new terms? Can you use them in a sentence? Since life is all about choices, which of these words do you think you will aggressively include in your active vocabulary?

Unit Five
Lesson 40

It is definitely important to think and to feel, but it is also important "to dream".

"We grow great by dreams. All big men are dreamers. Some of us let these great dreams die, but others nourish and protect them; nurse them through bad days till they bring them to the sunshine and light which comes always to those who sincerely hope that their dreams will come true."
Woodrow Wilson

"Trust the dreams, for in them is hidden the gate to eternity."
Kahil Gibran

"Hopes are but the dreams of those who wake."
Pindar

Let's start with "somniare", the Latin word for "to dream".
Principal Parts: *somnio, somniare, somniavi, somniatum*
The basic **stems** are *somn-* or *somno-*
The noun form is *somnium,* "a dream; a day-dream or a fantasy".

Somnolence n. "the quality or state of being drowsy; sleepiness"
Somnolent adj. "of a kind likely to induce sleep; inclined to or heavy with sleep; drowsy"
   "During the overly lengthy sermon, I was overcome with somnolence."
   "This was the most somnolent sermon I have ever struggled through."

There is also a variant stem – *somnambul-* which yields:
Somnambulism – adding the stem *ambul-* from the Latin verb *ambulare* "to walk" gives us the noun for "sleepwalking"
Somnambulant – adj. "walking or addicted to walking while asleep"
Somnambulist – adj. "a person who walks while sleeping"
Somnambulate – v. "to walk when asleep"
   "My sister suffered with somnambulism, but at least she learned to prepare her clothes for school while she was sleepwalking."
   "Her somnambulant meanderings were the talk of the family."
   "She was a true somnambulist."
   "I must admit that when I was younger, there were nights when I would somnambulate as well."

Adding our negative friend *in-* shows another nocturnal concern. In fact, the Romans had the word *insomnis* to describe this condition. In English, that becomes …
Insomnia n. "prolonged and usu. abnormal inability to obtain adequate sleep"
Insomniac n. "a person who suffers with insomnia"; adj. "describing someone with insomnia"

"I wonder which is worse as a condition of the night: insomnia or somnambulism?"
"Providing sleep aids for insomniacs is a multi-billion dollar business"

"Nothing happens unless first we dream."   **Carl Sandberg**

"Some men see things as they are and say 'Why?' I dream of things that never were and 'Why Not?'"   **George Bernard Shaw**

"Every great dream begins with a dreamer. Always remember, you have within you the strength, the patience, and the passion to reach for the stars to change the world."   **Harriet Tubman**

"Dream as if you'll live forever; live like you'll die today."   **James Dean**

"When a dream takes hold of you, what can you do? You can run with it, let it run your life, or let it go and think for the rest of your life about what might have been."   **Patch Adams**

There is another Latin verb meaning *to dream – dormitare* – but that usually happens when you sleep, which is the main topic for Lesson 41.

Somnolence
Somnolent
Somnambulism
Somnambulant
Somnambulist
Somnambulate
Insomnia
Insomniac

Unit Five
Lesson 41

It is definitely important to dream, but that usually happens when you sleep. The Romans had several words that have left their mark on English.

Dormire means "to sleep" while *dormitare* means "to dream"

> "To sleep, perchance to dream –
> Ay, there's the rub." Hamlet, III   **William Shakespeare**

Shakespeare saw the connection ... and the rub.

From *dormire* and the *dorm-* stem, we get ...

Dormant – adj. "marked by suspension of activity, temporarily devoid of external activity"; "asleep, inactive, sluggish"

Dormancy – n. "the quality or state of being dormant"

From the participial *dormitus*, the Romans had *dormitorium* which became

Dormitory – n. "a room for sleeping; a residence hall" and its slang term **dorm.**

If you set a window vertically in a sloping wall usu. over a sleeping area, you have a **dormer.**

"The Vesuvius volcano has been dormant since 1944."

"The dormancy of the volcano is under close scrutiny by the volcanologists."

"While most people on campus still call it a dormitory, the administrators refer to it as a residence hall."

"When the architect designed the house, he incorporated dormers in all the second story sleeping areas."

In addition to *somnus* for "sleep", to describe "sleepiness", the Romans had the noun *sopor* and the verb *sopire* which has crawled into English as ...

Sopor n. "abnormally deep sleep or a stupor which is difficult to get rid of; often caused by drugs".

Soporific – adj. "causing or tending to cause sleep, tending to dull awareness or alertness" or its cousin ...

Soporiferous – adj. "soporific" {Later you will learn about *facere*, "to make"}

"The drugs left him in a sopor."

"The minister's sermon ended up being more soporific than inspirational."

> Vide: **Soporiferousness**

As a verb, this was *sopire* "to make to sleep; to lull to sleep; to stupefy"

This yields only one word in English, and even it is rarely used nowadays...

Sopite v. "to put or lull to sleep"

Well, it's time to cast aside this pall of sopor and WAKE UP!

Oh, there's a word for that ... Latin *excitare* "to rouse, to stir, to raise up; to excite"

> The **stem** is *excit-*

OK, you caught me. The root word in Latin was *cito, citare* "to rouse", but we will come back to that in a future lesson. In the mean time, adding the prefix *ex-* meaning "out of" or "up" or "former" rouses you UP.

Excite v. "to call to activity"; "to rouse to an emotional response, to arouse"; "to energize, to stimulate"
Excitable adj. "capable of being roused to a state of excitement or irritability"; "capable of being activated by and reacting to stimuli"
Excitement n. "something that excites or rouses; the action or state of being excited"
Excitation n. "the disturbed or altered condition resulting from stimulation of an individual, organ, tissue or cell"

      Vide: **Excited Exciting Excitement Excitation Exciter**

  "I was very excited to hear from my good friend."
  "The class was easily excitable waiting for the visit from the fireman."
  "The excitement in the delivery room was palpable."
  "The Beach Boys picked up a good vibration that included an excitation."

Review:

Dormant	Sopor	Excite
Dormancy	Soporific	Excitable
Dormitory	Soporiferous	Excitement
Dormer	Soporiferousness	Excitation
Dorm	Sopite	Exciter

Unit Five
Lesson 42

One of the key human mental processes is learning. As you might expect, Latin offered several words that have left an imprint on English.

One key verb was *studeo, studere,* {stew DAIR ray}. I imagine you can see what flowed from that. The Latin noun was *studium,* the adjectical from was *studiosus,-a, -um* and the adverbial form was *studiose*. Just a quick glance at the endings associated with this root word gives you a clue about how Latin used word structure so extensively. We will take a closer look at that in Units Six and Seven.

In the mean time, the basic **stem** is *stud*-.

Study verb "to engage in study, to undertake formal study of a subject (e.g. vocabulary)"; "to meditate, to reflect, to endeavor, to try"; "to consider attentively in detail"; noun "a state of contemplation, reverie"; "careful examination or analysis of a phenomenon, development or question"; "a branch or department of learning"; "a building or room devoted to study or literary pursuits"
>   Vide: **Studying, Studies**

Studied – v. "past tense of study"; adjective – "careful considered or prepared; thoughtful, knowledgeable, learned {LURN ed}"
>   "He was truly a studied poet."
>   "To truly study a subject, the learner must be actively engaged."
>   "As learners, you are currently actively engaged in the study of vocabulary that has come from Latin roots and stems."
>   "Effective study of a topic incorporates reflection so as to achieve the maximum metacognitive benefit."
>   "Biology is a fascinating field of study."
>   "As was his custom, after dinner he retired to the study to smoke his cigar."

Student – noun "a person who studies or learns"
>   "When I was a principal, I liked to reward students who tried to do their very best, regardless of the achievement grades."

Studious – adjective "assiduous in the pursuit of learning"
>   "For being a new student, he was impressively studious."

Studio – noun "a working place for a painter, sculptor, photographer, artist"
>   "The cleanliness of his studio directly reflected his art."

Loosely related is ... **Astute** {uh STOOT} "having or showing shrewdness or perspicacity (*having acute mental vision or discernment*)"; "crafty, wily, shrewd"
>   "She provided multiple astute insights into the discussion."

Disco, discire, didici, "to learn, to hear of, to get to know, to ascertain"
   The **stems** are *disc-* and *did-*
The English word disciple ("a follower of a teacher") comes from *discipulus* which evolved from *disco.* Strangely enough the well-loved disco dance halls of the 70's and 80's did NOT come from this word, but rather a shortened form of *discotheque.* Obviously, it took great **discipline** ("training that corrects, molds or perfects the mental faculties or moral character"; "field of study") to be a good student of a teacher.
   "She showed great discipline in pursuing her learning of audiology."

The *did-* stem actually evolved through Latin from the Greek word *didaskein* "to teach".
It left us only the **didactic** family, the adjective meaning "designed or intended to teach"; "intended to convey instruction and information as well as pleasure and entertainment".
The related noun is **didact,** "a didactic person" and the plural version **didactics** meaning "systematic instruction, pedagogy"
   Vide: **Didactical, Didactically, Didacticism**
   "For a pleasant person, he tended to be overly didactic in his conversations."
   "He was viewed as a perpetual didact by his colleagues."

There is also *Cognosco, cognoscere cognovi, cognitum* "to learn, to get to know" but you have already learned that (remember **Cognition, Cognitive, Recognition, Precognition, Incognito, Metacognitive, etc.)**

Review:

Study	Student	Disciple	Didactics
Studying	Studious	Discipline	Didactical
Studies	Studio	Didactic	Didactically
Studied	Astute	Didact	Didacticism

Assignment:
What part of this lesson makes most sense to you as you reflect on your study of vocabulary?

Unit Five
Lesson 43

What would human life be like without love? As you might expect, Latin offered several words that have left an imprint on English.

The verb that just about every new Latin student learns is *amo, amare, amavi, amatus*. The noun form of "love" is *amor, amoris*. The adjectival forms are *amabilis* meaning "lovely" and *amicabilis* meaning "friendly". Finally, the Latin noun *amicus* meant "lover or friend", *amica* "a female friend or lover or mistress" while *amiculus* meant "dear friend". (*Lesson 45 will explain conjugations of verbs and Lesson 64 declensions of nouns and adjectives in more detail, but again observe the endings of words carefully.*)

The **stems** are **amo-** and **ama-** and **ami-**

Amigo n. "casual or slang term for friend; also fr. Spanish"
"It was good to reacquaint myself with my old high school amigo."
Amiable adj. "generally agreeable, being friendly, sociable and congenial"; "good natured"
"He was quite an amiable chap."
> Vide: **Amiably, Amiability**
Amicable adj. "characterized by friendly good will"; "neighborly, friendly"
> Vide: **Amicably, Amicability**
"Shoveling my driveway was an amicable gesture from my young neighbor."
Amorous adj. "strongly moved by love, esp. sexual love"; "being in love, enamored"
"Be warm, but pure; be amorous, but be chaste." Lord Byron
Amour n. "fr. the French, casual or slang term for love"; "a love affair"
"L'amour, toujours l'amour – Love, always love!"
Amorist n. "a devotee of love, one who writes about romantic love"
> Vide: **Amatory, Amaurosis**
"Her diary clearly defined her as an amorist."
Amicus curiae – "friend of the court"; "a professional not a party to judicial proceedings but permitted by the court to advise it"
"He earned his status as amicus curiae by successfully advising the court on numerous previous occasions."

Two other noun forms are interesting: *caritas* which has come to us as "charity" and *studium* (knowing) which we just saw in Lesson 42.
"Philosophers ponder whether it is possible to love someone without really knowing them."

They also used the verb d*iligo, diligere, dilexi, dilectum* — "to esteem, to love".
Diligence n. "persevering application"; "the attention and care legally required of a person"

Diligent adj. "characterized by steady, earnest and energetic effort"; "painstaking"
>Vide: **Diligently**

"The legal department had to perform due diligence prior to the acquisition."

"He was a diligent student who loved learning."

The Romans also covered the other end of the spectrum: *Contemno, contemnere, contempsi, contemptum* "to hate". Hate was represented by the noun *odi, osum* and hatred by *odium, odi* or *inimicitia.*

English inherited these words:

Contempt n. "the act of despising, the state of mind of one who despises"; "lack of respect or reverence for something"; "willful disobedience to or open disrespect of a court, judge or legislative body"

Contemptible adj. "worthy of contempt"

Contemptuous adj. "manifesting, feeling or expressing contempt"
>Vide: **Contemptibly, Contemptibility, Contemptuously, Contemptuousness**

"I have nothing but contempt for you."

"The judge called him one of the most contemptible felons with whom he had ever dealt."

"His inconsiderate actions towards the court were contemptuous."

Odious adj. "exciting or deserving hatred or repugnance"
>Vide: **Odiously, Odiousness, Odium**

"His treatment of women was odious."

Review:

Amigo	Amour	Contempt	Odious
Amiable	Amorist	Contemptible	Odiously
Amiable	Amatory	Contemptuous	Odiousness
Amiability	Amaurosis	Contemptibly	Odium
Amicable	Amicus curiae	Contemptibility	
Amicable	Diligence	Contemptuously	
Amicability	Diligent	Contemptuousness	
Amorous	Diligently		

Lesson 44 – **Review** Mental Activities Verbs
"putare" "cogito" "cogniscere" "sentire" "assentire" "somniare" "dormire" "amare"

In Unit Five, we have explored the Latin root words related to some mental functions. There are more, but this was a good place to start. Take a look back at them now and make sure they will stay with you. We added two more affixes, so let's start there. Answers: 116 >

Prefixes
_____- or _____- prefix, from the Greek "after, with, among"; "occurring or situated after …"; "used with the name of a discipline to designate a new but related discipline designed to deal critically with the original one"

_____- originally meaning "situated beyond" and now denoting "beyond in space, beyond the limits of"

Words from the root word "putare" + *im-, dis-, indis-, re-*

verb – "to lay the responsibility or blame for, often unjustly"; "to credit to a person or a cause, to attribute"; "syn. ascribe" _____

   "The _____ that he is a fraud has no basis in fact."

verb – from the Latin *disputare* "to discuss" – verb "to engage in argument"; "to call into question"; "to struggle against, to oppose"; "to contend over, to contest"; noun – "a verbal controversy, a debate"; "a quarrel" _____

   "The evidence given the jury was _____."

noun (from the Latin noun *reputatio*)– "overall quality of character as judged by people in general"; "a good name" _____
   "She was viewed as a woman of ill _____."
   "He worked diligently to maintain a _____ business."
   "He was _____ (adv.) an embezzler, but no one ever proved it."
   "The ambulance-chasing attorney's actions were considered _____ in the legal community."

Words from the root word "cogitare" + *in-*
Verb – "to ponder or meditate deeply or intently" _____
   "As evidenced by her pensive look, she was in a particularly _____ mood."
   Adjective "thoughtless, inconsiderate" _____

Words from the root word "cognoscere" + re- + pre- + in- + meta-

noun – "act or process of knowing including both awareness and judgment"; "the mental process of knowing, including aspects such as awareness, perception, reasoning, and judgment" _____

adjective – "knowledge of something, esp. through personal experience" ____
_____

"Alcohol can seriously impair _____ function."

n. "acknowledgement"; "knowledge or feeling that someone or some thing present has been encountered before"; "special notice or attention" _____

adj. "can be recognized" _____

"His appearance had changed so much I could barely _____ him."
"Because of his status in the community, he was released from jail on a personal _____ bond."

"Though she tried to go _____, she was easily _____ because of her red hair."

n. "clairvoyance relating to an event of state not yet experiences" _____

"Although some doubted her abilities, she was alleged to have credible ____
_____skills."

adjective "lacking awareness of consciousness"; usually followed by "of" _____
_____

n. essentially "cognition about cognition" or "thinking about thinking"; "contains 3 basic elements: *developing* a plan of action, *maintaining/monitoring* the plan, *evaluating* the plan" _____
"I try to incorporate _____ components into all my assignments."

Words from the root word "sentire"

n. "a meaning conveyed or intended"; "faculty of perceiving by sense organs"; "conscious awareness or rationality, usu. used in pl. 'senses'"; "a definite but often vague awareness or impression": "a capacity for effective application of the powers of the mind, intelligence, showing good judgment" _____
"Of all the choices, this one makes the most _____."

"Before her first day as a waitress, everyone told her to wear _____ shoes."

adj. "delicately aware of the feelings and attitudes of others, thoughtful and sympathetic"; "concerned with highly classified government information, secret or confidential, not to be revealed"; "touchy". _____

"She was highly _____ to most perfumes."

n. "the process of sensing, awareness due to stimulation of a sense organ"; "a state of excited interest or feeling, the cause of such a feeling" _____
"His batting average of over .500 made him an overnight _____."

"The ads for the show only emphasized the _____ aspects."

n. "use of shocking material, the practice of emphasizing the lurid aspects of something". _____

"The media _____ the story of the kidnapping."

n. "ability to receive and respond to sensations and stimuli"; "ability to feel, the capacity for being affected emotionally or intellectually". _____

adj. "of or related to the senses, conveying nerve impulses from the sense organs to the nerve centers". _____

adj. "relating to gratification of the senses or the indulgence of a sense appetite, fleshly"; "voluptuous"; "deficient in moral, spiritual or intellectual interests". _ _____

"Watching a sunset on a sandy beach can be a truly _____ experience."

n. "an attitude, thought or judgment prompted by feeling"; "a predilection, a specific view or notion, opinion"; "a romantic or nostalgic feeling verging on sentimentality"; "a general, underlying mental feeling, an emotion"; "a literary device designed to produce an emotional response in the reader" _____

Words from the root word "sentire" + as- + dis- + con- + in- + non- + ultra- + extra-

n. "ready assent, esp. when insincere or obsequious (*marked by a fawning attentiveness*)" _____

"After a long pensive pause, he gave his _____to the option at hand."

v. "to differ in opinion, to withhold assent"; n. "difference or opinion; a religious nonconformity; a justice's nonconcurrence with the majority opinion". _____

"The justice filed the only _____ opinion on the case."
"The sergeant was concerned about _____ within the ranks."
"Congress was so argumentative that they could only arrive at _____."

v. "to give assent or approval; to agree"; n. "compliance with or approval of what is done or proposed by another; agreement". _____
adj. "differing in opinion with the majority" _____
adj. "existing by mutual consent without a written agreement" _____

"The jury finally reached _____ on convicting the accused."

adj. "lacking sense or understanding; foolish"; "lacking humane feeling, brutal"
_____

"He was so emotionally drained by the encounter as to be _____ to the chaos."
"His remarks showed just how _____ he really is."

n. "words or language having no meaning or conveying no intelligible ideas"; "an instance of absurd action" _____ or _____
"I like _____. It wakes up the brain cells." *Dr. Seuss*

adj. "beyond sensitive" _____
"His third degree burns left him _____ to human contact."

adj. "residing beyond or outside of the ordinary senses" _____
"She claimed strong powers of _____ perception."

Words from the root word "somnolare" + in-

n. "the quality or state of being drowsy; sleepiness" _____
"This was the most _____ sermon I have ever struggled through."

n. – adding the stem *ambul-* from the Latin verb *ambulare* "to walk" gives us the noun for "sleepwalking" _____
adj. "describes a person who walks while sleeping" _____

"Her _____ meanderings were the talk of the family."

"I must admit that when I was younger, there were nights when I would ____ as well."

n. "prolonged and usu. abnormal inability to obtain adequate sleep" _____
   "I wonder which is worse as a condition of the night: _____ or _____?"
   "Providing sleep aids for _____ is a multi-billion dollar business"

Words from the root word "dormire" "sopor" & "excitare"

adj. "marked by suspension of activity, temporarily devoid of external activity"; "asleep, inactive, sluggish" _____

   "The _____ of the volcano is under close scrutiny by the volcanologists."
   "While most people on campus still call it a _____, the administrators refer to it as a residence hall."
   "When the architect designed the house, he incorporated _____ in all the second story sleeping areas."

n. "abnormally deep sleep or a stupor which is difficult to get rid of; often caused by drugs". _____

   "The minister's sermon ended up being more _____ than inspirational."

v. "to call to activity"; "to rouse to an emotional response, to arouse"; "to energize, to stimulate" _____

   "I was very _____ to hear from my good friend."
   "The _____ in the delivery room was palpable."
   "The Beach Boys picked up a good vibration that included an _____."

Words from the root word "studere" & "discere"

   "To truly _____ a subject, the learner must be actively engaged."
noun "a person who studies or learns" _____
   "When I was a principal, I liked to reward _____ who tried to do their very best, regardless of the academic grades."
adjective "assiduous in the pursuit of learning" _____
   "The cleanliness of his _____ directly reflected his art."

Adj. "having or showing shrewdness or perspicacity (*having acute mental vision or discernment*)"; "crafty, wily, shrewd" _____

n. "training that corrects, molds or perfects the mental faculties or moral character"; "field of study" "required to be a good student of a teacher". _____

"She showed great _____ in pursuing her learning of audiology."

adjective meaning "designed or intended to teach"; "intended to convey instruction and information as well as pleasure and entertainment" _____

"For a pleasant person, he tended to be overly _____ in his conversations."

Words from the root word "amare" & "diligere" & "contemnare"

adj. "generally agreeable, being friendly, sociable and congenial"; "good natured"

_____

"He was quite an _____ chap."

adj. "characterized by friendly good will"; "neighborly, friendly" _____

"Shoveling my driveway was an _____ gesture from my young neighbor."

adj. "strongly moved by love, esp. sexual love"; "being in love, enamored" ___

_____

n. "persevering application"; "the attention and care legally required of a person"

_____

"He was a _____ student who loved learning."

n. "the act of despising, the state of mind of one who despises"; "lack of respect or reverence for something"; "willful disobedience to or open disrespect of a court, judge or legislative body" _____

adj. "manifesting, feeling or expressing contempt" _____

"The judge called him one of the most _____ felons with whom he had ever dealt."

adj. "exciting or deserving hatred or repugnance" _____

Answers:

Meta- or **Met-** prefix, from the Greek "after, with, among"; "occurring or situated after …"; "used with the name of a discipline to designate a new but related discipline designed to deal critically with the original one"
ultra- originally meaning "situated beyond" and now denting "beyond in space, beyond the limits of"

Words from the root word "putare" + *im-, dis-, indis-, re-*

verb – "to lay the responsibility or blame for, often unjustly"; "to credit to a person or a cause, to attribute"; "syn. ascribe" ***Impute***
The <u>imputation</u> that he is a fraud has no basis in fact.
verb – from the Latin *disputare* "to discuss" – verb "to engage in argument"; "to call into question"; "to struggle against, to oppose"; "to contend over, to contest";
noun – "a verbal controversy, a debate"; "a quarrel" ***Dispute***
The evidence given the jury was <u>indisputable</u>."
noun (from the Latin noun *reputatio*)– "overall quality of character as judged by people in general"; "a good name" ***Reputation***
She was viewed as a woman of ill <u>repute</u>.
He worked diligently to maintain a <u>reputable</u> business.
He was <u>reputedly</u> (adv.) an embezzler, but no one ever proved it.
The ambulance-chasing attorney's actions were considered <u>disreputable</u> in the legal community.

Words from the root word "cogitare" + *in-*

verb – "to ponder or meditate deeply or intently" ***Cogitate***
As evidenced by her pensive countenance, she was in a particularly <u>cogitative</u> mood.
adj. "thoughtless, inconsiderate" ***Incogitant***

Words from the root word "cognoscere" + *re- + pre- + in- + meta-*

noun – "act or process of knowing including both awareness and judgment"; "the mental process of knowing, including aspects such as awareness, perception, reasoning, and judgment" ***Cognition***
adjective – "knowledge of something, esp. through personal experience" ***Cognizant***
Alcohol can seriously impair <u>cognitive</u> function.
n. "acknowledgement"; "knowledge or feeling that someone or some thing present has been encountered before"; "special notice or attention" ***Recognition***

adj. "can be recognized" **_Recognizable_**

His appearance had changed so much I could barely recognize him.

Because of his status in the community, he was released from jail on a personal recognizance bond.

Though she tried to go incognito, she was easily recognizable because of her red hair.

n. "clairvoyance relating to an event of state not yet experiences" **_Precognition_**

Although some doubted her abilities, she was alleged to have credible precognitive skills.

adjective "lacking awareness of consciousness"; usually followed by "of" **_Incognizant_**

n. essentially "cognition about cognition" or "thinking about thinking"; "contains 3 basic elements: _developing_ a plan of action, _maintaining/monitoring_ the plan, _evaluating_ the plan" **_Metacognition_**

"I try to incorporate metacognitive components into all my assignments."

Words from the root word "sentire"

n. "a meaning conveyed or intended"; "faculty of perceiving by sense organs"; "conscious awareness or rationality, usu. used in pl. 'senses'"; "a definite but often vague awareness or impression": "a capacity for effective application of the powers of the mind, intelligence, showing good judgment" **Sense**

"Of all the choices, this one makes the most sense."

"Before her first day as a waitress, everyone told her to wear sensible shoes."

adj. "delicately aware of the feelings and attitudes of others, thoughtful and sympathetic"; "readily affected or changed by various agents"; "concerned with highly classified government information, secret or confidential, not to be revealed"; "touchy". **Sensitive**

"She was highly sensitive to most perfumes."

n. "the process of sensing, awareness due to stimulation of a sense organ"; "a state of excited interest or feeling, the cause of such a feeling" **Sensation**

"His batting average of over .500 made him an overnight sensation."

"The ads for the show only emphasized the sensational aspects."

n. "use of shocking material, the practice of emphasizing the lurid aspects of something". **Sensationalism**

"The media sensationalized the story of the kidnapping."

n. "ability to receive and respond to sensations and stimuli"; "ability to feel, the capacity for being affected emotionally or intellectually". **Sensibility**

adj. "of or related to the senses, conveying nerve impulses from the sense organs to the nerve centers". **Sensory**

adj. "relating to gratification of the senses or the indulgence of a sense appetite, fleshly"; "voluptuous"; "deficient in moral, spiritual or intellectual interests". **Sensual**

"Watching a sunset on a sandy beach can be a truly sensuous experience."

n. "an attitude, thought or judgment prompted by feeling"; "a predilection, a specific view or notion, opinion"; "a romantic or nostalgic feeling verging on sentimentality";

"a general, underlying mental feeling, an emotion"; "a literary device designed to produce an emotional response in the reader" **Sentiment**

Words from the root word "sentire" + *as-* + *dis-* + *con-* + *in-* + *non-* + *ultra-* + *extra-*

{AS sen ta shun} n. "ready assent, esp. when insincere or obsequious (*marked by a fawning attentiveness*)" **Assentation**
   "After a long pensive pause, he gave his <u>assent</u> to the option at hand."
v. "to differ in opinion, to withhold assent"; n. "difference or opinion; a religious nonconformity; a justice's nonconcurrence with the majority opinion". **Dissent**
   "The justice filed the only <u>dissenting</u> opinion on the case."
   "The sergeant was concerned about <u>dissension</u> within the ranks."
   "Congress was so argumentative that they could only arrive at <u>dissensus</u>."
v. "to give assent or approval; to agree"; n. "compliance with or approval of what is done or proposed by another; agreement". **Consent**
adj. "differing in opinion with the majority" **Consenting**
adj. "existing by mutual consent without a written agreement" **Consensual**
   "The jury finally reached <u>consensus</u> on convicting the accused."
{in SEN sate} adj. "lacking sense or understanding; foolish"; "lacking humane feeling, brutal" **Insensate**
   "He was so emotionally drained by the encounter as to be <u>insensible</u> to the chaos."
   "His remarks showed just how <u>insensitive</u> he really is."
n. "words or language having no meaning or conveying no intelligible ideas"; "an instance of absurd action" **Nonsense** or **Non-sense**
   "I like <u>nonsense</u>. It wakes up the brain cells." *Dr. Seuss*
adj. "beyond sensitive" **Ultrasensitive**
   "His third degree burns left him <u>ultrasensitive</u> to human contact."
adj. "residing beyond or outside of the ordinary senses" **Extrasensory**
   "She claimed strong powers of <u>extrasensory</u> perception."

Words from the root word "somnolare" + *in-*

n. "the quality or state of being drowsy; sleepiness" **Somnolence**
   "This was the most <u>somnolent</u> sermon I have ever struggled through."
– adding the stem *ambul-* from the Latin verb *ambulare* "to walk" gives us the noun for "sleepwalking" **Somnambulism**
– adj. "a person who walks while sleeping" **Somnambulist**
   "Her <u>somnambulant</u> meanderings were the talk of the family."
   "I must admit that when I was younger, there were nights when I would <u>somnambulate</u> as well."

n. "prolonged and usu. abnormal inability to obtain adequate sleep" **Insomnia**
   "I wonder which is worse as a condition of the night: <u>insomnia</u> or <u>somnambulism</u>?"
   "Providing sleep aids for <u>insomniacs</u> is a multi-billion dollar business"

Words from the root word "dormire" "sopor" & "excitare"

adj. "marked by suspension of activity, temporarily devoid of external activity"; "asleep, inactive, sluggish" **Dormant**

"The <u>dormancy</u> of the volcano is under close scrutiny by the volcanologists."

"While most people on campus still call it a <u>dormitory</u>, the administrators refer to it as a residence hall."

"When the architect designed the house, he incorporated <u>dormers</u> in all the second story sleeping areas."

n. "abnormally deep sleep or a stupor which is difficult to get rid of; often caused by drugs". **Sopor**

"The minister's sermon ended up being more <u>soporific</u> than inspirational."

v. "to call to activity"; "to rouse to an emotional response, to arouse"; "to energize, to stimulate" **Excite**

"I was very <u>excited</u> to hear from my good friend."

"The <u>excitement</u> in the delivery room was palpable."

"The Beach Boys picked up a good vibration that included an <u>excitation</u>."

Words from the root word "studere" & "discere"

"To truly <u>study</u> a subject, the learner must be actively engaged."

noun "a person who studies or learns" **Student**

"When I was a principal, I liked to reward <u>students</u> who tried to do their very best, regardless of the academic grades."

adjective "assiduous in the pursuit of learning" **Studious**

"The cleanliness of his <u>studio</u> directly reflected his art."

Adj. "having or showing shrewdness or perspicacity (*having acute mental vision or discernment*)"; "crafty, wily, shrewd" **Astute**

n. "training that corrects, molds or perfects the mental faculties or moral character"; "field of study") to be a good student of a teacher **discipline**

"She showed great <u>discipline</u> in pursuing her learning of audiology."

adjective meaning "designed or intended to teach"; "intended to convey instruction and information as well as pleasure and entertainment" **didactic**

"For a pleasant person, he tended to be overly <u>didactic</u> in his conversations."

Unit Six
Lesson 45

Ready for a little break?
This lesson will not require you to absorb and remember lots of details, but I do want you to understand some of the big picture of this Latin language that I have been throwing at you. Let's start by working through the conjugation of verbs in Latin. Actually this is what really helped me understand the structure and grammar of English, so take from this lesson what works for you.

As I have mentioned, a great deal of Latin relies on the **endings** of words. This may stem from the fact that the Romans did not put spaces between words when they etched their edicts in stone (or even when they wrote them on parchment). This meant that they needed a fairly consistent visual cue about the content of their writings.

Nearly every first year Latin student had to memorize the conjugation of the verb *amo, amare* which you saw in Lesson 43. Let's look at it in detail.

It started with **Present** <u>Tense</u>, **Active** <u>Voice</u>, **Indicative** <u>Mood</u> and worked through **Singular** <u>Number</u> and then went to **Plural** <u>Number</u> by stepping up through First Person, Second Person and Third Person. **Stems**: *am-* or *amo-* or *ama-*. This is what it looked like and what it meant. Closely observe the endings.

am**o**	"I love" (or "I am loving" or "I do love")
am**as**	"You love (Singular)" (or "you are loving" or "you do love")
am**at**	"He, she or it loves" (or … you got it, right?)
	(the "it" is probably for other verbs)
ama**mus**	"We Love" (etc.) *(Remember **mittimus** ???)*
ama**tis**	"You love (plural)" (etc.)
ama**nt**	"They love"

Repeat after me: amo, amas, amat, amamus, amatis, amant

Good! That's takes care of present tense. But what if it happened yesterday?
Imperfect Tense, **Active** Voice, **Indicative** Mood

ama**bam**	"I loved"
ama**bas**	"You loved (singular)"
ama**bat**	"He or she loved"
ama**bamus**	"We loved"
ama**batis**	"You loved (plural)"
ama**bant**	"They loved"

amabam, amabas, amabat, amabamus, amabatis, amabant
But what about tomorrow?

Future Tense, **Active** Voice, **Indicative** Mood:

ama**bo**	"I shall love"
ama**bis**	"You will love (sing.)"
ama**bit**	"He or she will love"
ama**bimus**	"We shall love"
ama**bitis**	"You will love (pl.)"
ama**bant**	"They will love"

OK, but what if is over and done with?

Perfect Tense, **Active** Voice, **Indicative** Mood:

ama**vi**	"I have loved"
ama**visti**	"You have loved (sing.)"
ama**vit**	"He or she has loved"
ama**vimus**	"We have loved"
ama**vistis**	"You have loved (pl.)"
ama**verunt**	"They have loved"

How about if it had already been over by then?

Pluperfect Tense, **Active** Voice, **Indicative** Mood:

ama**veram**	"I had loved"
ama**veras**	"You had loved (singular)"
ama**verat**	"He or she had loved"
ama**veramus**	"We had loved"
ama**veratis**	"You had loved (plural)"
ama**verant**	"They had loved"

Well, how about if it will be over in the future?

Future Perfect Tense, **Active** Voice, **Indicative** Mood:

ama**vero**	"I shall have loved"
ama**veris**	"You will have loved (sing.)"
ama**verit**	"He or she will have loved"
ama**verimus**	"We shall have loved"
ama**veritis**	"You will have loved (pl.)"
ama**verint**	"They will have loved"

Do you get the impression that the Romans liked precision in their use of language? Well, so much for the Active Voice. Here is a condensed version of the Passive Voice.

All of these will be **Passive** Voice and **Indicative** Mood

Present Tense: "I am loved", "you are loved", "He or She is loved", etc.

	Singular	Plural
1st	am**or**	ama**mur**
2nd	am**aris**	ama**mini**
3rd	am**atur**	ama**ntur**

Imperfect Tense: "I was loved", "you were loved", etc.

	Singular	Plural
1st	am**or**	ama**mur**
2nd	am**aris**	ama**mini**
3rd	am**atur**	ama**ntur**

Future Tense: "I shall be loved" etc.

	Singular	Plural
1st	ama**bor**	ama**bimur**
2nd	ama**beris**	ama**bimini**
3rd	ama**bitur**	ama**bantur**

In order to get to the Passive Voice of the Perfect, Pluperfect and Future Perfect, you must add afterwards the relevant verb of "to be" –

sum, es, est, sumus, estis,sunt   AND

the appropriate gender ending generally –*us* for male, -*a* for female, & -*um* for neuter to the Perfect Infinitive, in this case *amatus (-a, -um)* or plural *amati (-ae, -a)*

Perfect Tense: "I have been loved" etc.

	Singular	Plural
1st	ama**tus (-a, -um) sum**	ama**ti (-ae, -a) sumus**
2nd	ama**tus es**	ama**ti estis**
3rd	ama**tus est**	ama**ti sunt**

e.g. *amata est* = "She has been loved"

Pluperfect Tense: "I had been loved"

	Singular	Plural
1st	ama**tus (-a, -um) eram**	ama**ti (-ae, -a) seramus**
2nd	ama**tus eras**	ama**tus eratis**
3rd	ama**tus erat**	ama**tus erant**

e.g. *amatus eram* = "I (a boy) had been loved"

e.g. *amata eras* = "You (a girl) had been loved"

Future Perfect Tense: "I shall have been loved" etc.

	Singular	Plural
1st	ama**tus (-a, -um) ero**	ama**ti (-ae, -a) erimus**
2nd	ama**tus eris**	ama**tus eritis**
3rd	ama**tus erit**	ama**ti erunt**

e.g. *amatae erunt* = "They (girls) have been loved"

e.g. *amatus erit* = "It (neuter???) will have been loved"

AND THAT'S JUST THE **INDICATIVE** MOOD! (the most common, used to express facts and opinions or to make inquiries; most of the statements you make or you read are in the indicative mood.)

At least the **SUBJUNCTIVE** (a grammatical mood that expresses doubts, wishes, and possibilities) only has four tenses.   Think **IF** (among others)

	IF I love	IF I loved	IF I have loved	IF I had loved
Sing	Present	Imperfect	Perfect	Pluperfect
1st	amem	amarem	amaverim	amavissem
2nd	ames	amares	amaveris	amavisses
3rd	amet	amaret	amaverit	amavisset
Plural				
1st	amemus	amaremus	amaverimus	amavissemus
2nd	ametis	amaretis	amaveritis	amavissetis
3rd	ament	amarent	amaverint	amavissent

And now for the IMPERATIVE ... and YES, you MUST do this! Think **COMMAND**!

Present – 2nd person

| ama | (a MA) | (you sing. Implied) | Love (someone) |
| amate | (a MA tay) | (you pl. implied) | Love (someone) |

Future – 2nd and 3rd person

| amato | (a MA toe) | (you sing. Implied) | (You will) love (someone) |
| amato | (a MA toe) | (he or she implied) | (They will) Love (someone) |

Future – 3rd person

| amatote | (a ma TOE tay) | (you sing. Implied) | (You will) love (someone) |
| amanto | (a MON toe) | (they implied) | (They will) Love (someone) |

In the Principal Parts of the various verbs I have included so far, I have frequently included the present infinitive, in this case *amare.* There are several other infinitives for you to be aware of:

Present	**Perfect**	**Future**
To love	To have loved	To love (in the future)
amare	*amavisse*	*amaturum (-am, -um) + esse(to be)*

There are also several **PARTICIPLES** to note. A participle can be a verb or an adjective (participial phrase). It is a derivative which can be used in compound tenses or voices, or as a modifier. Participles often share properties with other parts of speech, in particular adjectives and nouns.

Present	Perfect
Loving	Will be loving
amans (-ntis)	*amaturus (-a, -um)*

OK, that's a good start. You may have noticed that not all of the verbs we have seen ended with –*are*. Typically Latin verbs that end in –*are* are from the **First Conjugation** (e.g. *amare, spectare, sermocinare, putare*). Verbs that end with –*ere* are from the **Second Conjugation** (e.g. *videre, ducere, dicere, scribere*).   Verbs ending in –*ire* are usually from the **Third Conjugation** e.g., *specire,regere* [*to rule* which you will see later]), but some are from the **Fourth Conjugation** (e.g. *dormire, audire, sentire*) .

So what is this **CONJUGATION** stuff? I imagine by analyzing it, you have identified the **con-** prefix and the –*ion* suffix. That leaves the root word *iugo, iugare (note the 1st conjugation verb)* "to join" or "to marry".

Conjugation n. "a schematic arrangement of the inflectional forms of a verb"; "a class of verbs having the same types of inflectional forms".

Imagine the bigger picture of learning Latin – memorizing all the verbs and verb forms and "inflectional forms". Those inflectional forms are essentially the endings for the various words.

BTW Note also that the verb wasn't *jugo*, but instead *iugo*. The Latin language did not have the letter "j".

So, what do you remember from all this. REFLECT on it (imperative)!

Review: **CONJUGATION, Mood, Voice, Tense, Person, Number**

Unit Six
Lesson 46

Well, that was probably more than you wanted to know about Latin verbs. Aren't you glad you didn't have to memorize all of those endings? Actually, Latin can be a fascinating language. Once I had grown very comfortable with it, learning French, Spanish and Italian was easy. As you have already seen, there are many words that have moved directly from Latin into English and still more that have morphed somewhat and become part of the 600,000 or so words in English. In this Unit, we will spend some time with actions, such as making, holding, putting, cutting, covering, extending, and following.

There were several Latin verbs for "to make". Let's start with *facio, facere, feci, factum* "to make, form, do or perform".

The most direct descendent is the English word "**fact**", a noun meaning "the quality of being actual; a piece of information presented as having objective reality".

The adjectival form is **factual** [FAK chew uhl] "of or relating to facts; based on fact".
   "Their presentation was completely factual."

This would make a **factualist** (noun) "a person dedicated to facts" and probably one addicted to **factualism**.
         Vide: **facticity**
   "Unfortunately, he presented his opinion as fact."

There is also **facticious** [fak TIH shus] adjective "produced by humans rather than by natural forces."
   "The oil companies may have created a factitious demand by spreading rumors of shortage."

All of the making and producing has to happen somewhere, so why not in a **factory,** a noun referring to "a building with facilities for manufacturing".

Facility— noun "something designed, built, installed to serve a particular purpose".
Also in the last definition is the word **manufacturing** from *facere* and *manu* "by hand", or literally, "making something by hand"; "to make into a product suitable for use from raw materials".
   "We understand that the word *manufacture* can also mean to make something using machinery or equipment, even though it originally meant only *by hand.*"
         Vide: **manufacturer**
Question: What would **remanufactured** mean?

There is even the suffix –*factive* which means "making or causing". The Romans combined this with the **stem** *putre-* meaning "rotten" yielding the noun **putrefaction** [pyew truh FAK shun], "the process of making rotten; decomposition of organic matter; corruption" or the verb **putrefy** "to make rotten".
   "Putrefaction is a natural process that occurs when organic material decays."

Working from the Latin verb *olere* meaning "to smell", we end up with **_olfaction_**, the noun meaning "a sense of smell; the act or process of smelling" and the related adjective **_olfactory_** "related to or connected with the sense of smell".

"My olfactory nerves were offended by the smell of the putrefying garbage."

There is also the Latin verb *fabrico* or *fabricor, fabricare, fabricavi, fabricatum* "to fashion, to craft, to construct". The basic **stem** is **_fabr_**-.

One Latin noun form is *fabricator* "a fashioner, an artificer [from *ars* 'art' and *facere* who 'makes art']", while *fabrica* is "craft, art, construction" and *fabricatio* for "manufacture or fabrication".

These flow almost directly into English.

Fabric – n "a structure, a building; the arrangement of physical components in relation to one another"; "cloth or a material that resembles cloth".

Fabricate – v. "to invent, to create; to construct, to manufacture, esp. from diverse and standardized parts; to create or invent, to make up as in for the purpose of deception".

Fabrication – n. "the act or process of fabricating; the product of fabrication".

Vide: **Fabricant** – n. "manufacturer"

"A self does not amount to much, but no self is an island; each exists in a fabric of relations that is now more complex and mobile than ever before."

Jean-Francois Lyotard

"I can't believe he would fabricate such a story."

"Blacksmiths, welders, boilermakers and millwrights are all in the business of fabrication."

Assignment: What will be the best way for you to capture what you have learned from this lesson? Do you want to fabricate a graphical representation of the words? Or would you prefer a verbal reflection?

Review:

Fact	Manufacture	Putrefaction
Factual	Manufactured	Putrefy
Factualist	Manufacturing	Olfaction
Factualism	Manufacturer	Olfactory
Facticity		Fabric
Facticious	Remanufactured	Fabricate
Factory		Fabrication
Facility		Fabricant

Unit Six
Lesson 47

This could easily be a wedding lesson because we'll be working with words that mean "to have" and "to hold".

Let's start with *habeo* "to hold, to hold onto, to have, possess"; "to retain"
    Principal Parts: *Habeo, habere, habui, habitum*
    The **stem** is: *hab-*
These are the most obvious of the words from this root.

Habit n. "the prevailing disposition (*more later on this word*) or character of a person's thoughts and feelings; mental makeup"; "a settled tendency or usual pattern of behavior"; "a behavior pattern acquired by frequent repetition"
Habitual [ha BIT chew uhl] adj. "having the nature of a habit"; "customary"
Habitable adj. "capable of being lived in or on; suitable for habitation"
        Vide: **Habitually Habitualness Habitably Habitability Habitableness**
Habitant n. "inhabitant or resident"
    "Well, maybe just this once, but don't plan to hold onto it and make a habit of it."
    "I'm worried about my daughter's boyfriends. They're all sons of habitual drunkards." James Thurber *(read it fast)*
    "The scientists determined that the planet was not habitable for humans."
    "The census was designed to count all the habitants of the country."

Habituate [ha BIT chew ate] v. "to make used to something; to accustom"; "to cause habituation or the development of a habit"
Habituation n. "the process of habituating or creating a habit"
    "Studying vocabulary daily is an excellent way to habituate the learning process."
    "One of my goals in writing this book is your habituation of learning new vocabulary words every day."

The stem also goes a slightly different direction.
Habitat n. "the place or environment where a plant, animal or person naturally or normally lives and grows"
Habitation n. "the act of inhabiting; occupancy"; "a dwelling place, residence, settlement, colony"
    "Habitat for Humanity tries to create decent, affordable housing for people who need it."
    "The early settlers worked to establish suitable habitation in the wilderness."

Prefixing our old friend *"in-"* adds a new group to our family based on *inhabitare*.
Inhabit v. "to occupy as a place of settled residence; to live in, to dwell"
Inhabited adj "lived in; having inhabitants"

*In*habitable adj. "capable of being lived in or inhabited"
*In*habitant or *In*habiter n. "a person who occupies a particular place regularly, routinely, or for a period of time"
> Vide: *in*habitation
> "Only dedicated scientists inhabit the regions around the earth's poles."
> "The camp in the swamp did not look inhabited or even inhabitable for that matter."
> "He was the only inhabitant on the desert island."

If you are feeling negative about it, you can always add *un-* and get **un*in*habited** or **un*in*habitable.**
> "The camp looked uninhabited, or even uninhabitable, for that matter."

In Latin, this evolved to *habilitare* "to habilitate"
Habilitate "to make fit or capable, as in for making one able to function in society"
> Vide: **Habilitated Habilitating Habilitation**
> "The Cerebral Palsy Association hopes to habilitate each child with CP."

*Re*habilitate [REE huh BIL lih tate] v. "to restore to a former capacity; to reinstate"
Re*hab*ilitated adj. "returned or restored to a former capability"
Re*hab*ilitation n. "the process of restoring to a former capacity level"
Re*hab* slang
> Vide: *Re*habilitating *Re*habilitant *Re*habilitative *Re*habilitator
> "After tearing his ACL, the athlete had to rehabilitate his knee."
> "After six months, his knee was fully rehabilitated."
> "Craig Rehabilitation Center in Denver is nationally recognized as effective."

Review:

	Habitableness	Inhabit	Rehabilitate
Habit	Habitant	Inhabited	Rehabilitated
Habitual	Habitat	Inhabitable	Rehabilitating
Habitually	Habitation	Inhabitant	Rehabilitant
Habitualness	Habilitate	Inhabiter	Rehabilitative
Habitable	Habilitated	Inhabitation	Rehabilitator
Habitably	Habilitating	Uninhabited	
Habitability	Habilitation	Uninhabitable	

Assignment:
Find the best way of connecting all these related words into your active vocabulary. Which word from this list do you think will be the most difficult for you to remember?

Unit Six
Lesson 48

Habere is not the only word for "to hold". There is also *teneo, tenere, tenui, tentum* "to hold, to keep fixed"; "to occupy, to own"; "to contain, to maintain".

The basic **Stem** is *ten-*, but it also shows up in English as *tain-* or *–tain*.

As with our other roots, there is a plethora of words that flow from this root.

Tenable [TEN uh bull] adj. "capable of being held, maintained or defended; defensible, reasonable"

> Vide: **Tenability   Tenableness   Tenably**

"His position in the debate was clearly tenable."

Tenet n. "a principle, belief, or doctrine generally held to be true; one held true by members of an organization"

"One of the key tenets of Rotary is 'Service Above Self'."

Tenacious [teh NAY shus] adj. "not easily pulled apart; persistent in maintaining or adhering to something valued or habitual"

Tenacity (teh NAAH si tee) n. "the quality or state of being tenacious; syn. courage"

> Vide: **Tenaciously   Tenaciousness**

"She was tenacious in her defense of her client."

"His tenacity in his support of his cause was admirable."

> This stem can also go a different direction.

Tenant n. "one who holds or possesses real estate"; "one who has the occupancy or temporary possession of lands or tenements of another"

Tenancy n. "temporary possession or occupancy of something that belongs to another"

> Vide: **Tenantless   Tenantable**

"The landlord explained the lease agreement to the new tenant."

"He wished to end his tenancy when his landlord sold the building."

Tenement n. "a dwelling, a house used as a dwelling, a residence; apartment, flat"

"The tenement building was dilapidated."

> OR, prefixing *un-* can send it negative.

Untenable adj. "not able to be defended"; "not able to be occupied"

> Vide: **Untenability**

"When he realized his position in the argument was untenable, he conceded defeat."

OK, one more for the road:

Tenaculum n. "a slender, sharp, pointed hook attached to a handle used mainly in surgery for seizing and holding parts such as arteries."

"Nurse, hand me that sharp, pointy thing, you know, the tenaculum."

Contain v. "to keep within limits; to control, to restrain, to check, to halt"

Contained v. past tense or adj. "restrained, calm"

Container n. "one or something that contains; a receptacle for holding goods"

Containerization n. "a shipping method or process in which a large amount of material is packaged into large standardized containers"

"She could hardly contain her enthusiasm about the new vehicle."
"The firefighters contained the fire to the first floor."
"He purchased a dozen, blue, plastic storage containers."
"Containerization has changed the way most goods are shipped between continents aboard the huge container ships."
> Vide: **Containerize   Containerless   Containment**

Abstain v. from *abstinere* "to refrain deliberately and often with an effort of self-denial from an action or practice"
"On his doctor's advice, he chose to abstain from alcohol."
> Vide: **Abstainer   Abstinence   Abstinent   Abstention**

Detain   v. "to hold or keep in as if in custody; to withhold; to refrain from proceeding"
"The Border Patrol was ordered to detain any illegal immigrants."
> Vide: **Detainee   Detainment   Detainer   Detention**

Maintain   from *manu* "hand" and *tenere* "to hold" –v. "to keep in an existing state; to preserve from failure or decline"; "to sustain against opposition or danger, to uphold and defend"
"Failure to properly maintain a purchase may void the warrantee."
> Vide: **Maintainer Maintainable   Maintainability   Maintenance**

Retain   from *retinere* v. "to keep in possession or use; to keep in mind or memory";"to keep in one's pay or service; to employ by paying a retainer"
Retainer n. "a fee paid to a lawyer or professional advisor for services rendered"
Retention n. "act or state of retaining"; "ability to retain things in mind"
> Vide: **Retained   Retentive   Retentiveness   Retentively   Retentivity**

"When the school proposed retaining their child, the couple retained an attorney by giving him a retainer."
"His abnormal retention of fluids caused his doctor great concern."
The next lesson adds two more pre-fixed variations of *tenere*. Can you think of them?

Review:	*tenere* "to hold"		Tenaculum
Tenable	Tenantable	Containerize	Maintained
Tenability	Untenable	Containerization	Maintenance
Tenableness	Untenability	Containerless	Maintainable
Tenably	Abstain	Containment	Maintainability
Tenacious	Abstained	Detain	Retain
Tenaciously	Abstainer	Detained	Retained
Tenaciousness	Abstinence	Detainment	Retainer
Tenacity	Abstention	Detainer	Retention
Tenant	Contain	Detention	Retentiveness
Tenancy	Contained	Maintain	Retentively
Tenantless	Container	*Manu*	Retentivity

Unit Six
Lesson 49

You were right – they are **SU*STAIN*** and **A*TTE*NUATE**.

Su*stain* from *sustinere* "to hold up or sustain" v. "to give support or relief to"; "to supply with sustenance, to nourish"; "to prolong"; "to support as true, legal or just"

Su*stain*able adj. "capable of being sustained"; "relating to a lifestyle using sustainable methods"

"In order to qualify for a grant, the applicant must show how they will sustain their project once grant funding ends."

"It is considered socially responsible to practice sustainable living practices."

Vide: **Su*stain*ed Su*stain*edly**   **Su*stain*er**   **Su*stain*ability Su*sten*ance**

A*tte*nuate -from *attenuare* v. "to make thin or slender" "to lessen the amount, force, magnitude or value of"; adj. "tapering to a long slender point"

A*tte*nuator n. "a device for reducing the amplitude of an electrical signal"

"She needed to attenuate the probe to get it inserted properly."

"Once he saw the problem, he installed the attenuator in the radio transmitter."

Closely related to holding is grasping, from the Latin verb ***prehendo*** "to take hold of, to grasp, to catch, to seize, to accost"; "to take in, to comprehend" *prehendo prehendere prehendi prehensum* and *prendo prendere prendi prensum* "to lay hold of , seize, grasp; to catch, detain, arrest; to take in", mentally or by the senses. Several words come directly from this root (***prehen***-) and many others from its "pre-fixed" cousins.

Prehensile adj. "adapted for seizing or grasping, esp. by wrapping around"; "gifted with mental grasp or moral or aesthetic perception"

Prehension n. "act of taking hold or grasping, seizing"; "mental understanding, comprehension"

Vide: **Prehen**sility

"Howler monkeys have incredibly strong prehensile tails."

"She demonstrated a clear prehension of the complicated issue."

Ad + prehendere = apprehendere apprehensus "seize (upon), grasp, cling to, lay hold of; apprehend; embrace; overtake"

Apprehend v. "to arrest, seize"; "to become aware of, to perceive"; "to grasp the meaning with understanding, to understand"

Apprehensible adj. "capable of being apprehended"

Apprehension n. "act or power of perceiving or comprehending; conception"; "seizure by legal process, arrest"; "suspicion or fear of future evil, foreboding"

Vide: **Apprehen**sive **Apprehen**sively **Apprehen**siveness

"The marshals were able to apprehend him regardless of his disguise."

"The mathematical model was challenging, but apprehensible."

"The criminal was apprehensive about his upcoming apprehension."

Com + prehendere = comprehendere "to grasp"

Com*prehend* v. "to grasp the nature, meaning or significance of; to understand"

***Comprehen*sion** n. "act or action of grasping with the intellect, understanding"; "the act or process of comprising, the faculty of capability of including"

***Comprehen*sive** adj. "covering completely or broadly; inclusive"; "having or exhibiting a wide mental grasp"

***Comprehen*sible** or ***Comprehen*dible** adj. "able to be understood"

***Compri*se** v. "to be made up of"; "compose, constitute"

Vide: **Comprehen*sibility**

"They didn't seem to comprehend the gravity of their situation."

"When I taught English, I included numerous puns in my presentations to check for student comprehension."

"The Master's Level Comprehensive exams checked their understanding of the whole range of their course of studies."

"The most incomprehensible thing about the world is that it is at all **comprehensible**."

Albert Einstein

"A typical APA citation is simple in that in-text citations usually comprise two elements: a *signal phrase* or pointer in the body of the paper, and a *parenthetical*."

Add the prefix *in-* and turn it all negative.

***Incom*prehensible** adj. "not able to be understood"

"The mid school student's behavior was incomprehensible.

Reprehend v. "to voice disapproval, to censure"; "to criticize"

Reprehensible adj. "worthy of or deserving reprehension"; "culpable"

Vide: **Reprehension Reprehensive**

"As a principal, there were many occasions when I had to reprehend students."

"The attacker's treatment of his victims was reprehensible."

Repri*se n. "a recurrence or resumption of an action"; "a musical repetition"

Repri*sal n. "the act or practice in international law of resorting to force short of war in retaliation for damage or loss suffered"

"The reprise in the song was delightful."

"Victims of domestic violence are often afraid to do anything to stop their attackers for fear of reprisal."

Review:

Sustain	Attenuator	Apprehensively	Comprise
Sustainable	Prehensile	Apprehensiveness	Reprehend
Sustained	Prehension	Comprehend	Reprehensible
Sustainedly	Prehensility	Comprehension	Reprehension
Sustainer	Apprehend	Comprehensive	Reprehensive
Sustainability	Apprehensible	Comprehensible	Reprise
Sustenance	Apprehension	Comprehendible	Reprisal
Attenuate	Apprehensive	Comprehensibility	

You should be at a point now in your comfort with many prefixes and suffixes that I shouldn't have to provide additional definition or example sentence for many of them. If you are not sure, simply check a dictionary or on-line for details. Or, you can just "trust the force" and work on your hunches about the meaning.

Not related to *tenere* but very similar in appearance is *tendere*. This root word, however, has enough descendents to make this into a second lesson.

Tendo tendere tetendi tensum   *"to stretch out, to extend"; "to pull tight or draw"*
The **stems** are **ten-, tend-, tens-, tet-** and they yield three dozen or so direct descendents.

Tend v. "to pay attention, to apply oneself"; "to exhibit an inclination or tendency"; "to conduce (remember *ducere* ?)"

        Tendance n. "watchful care, short for attendance"
Tendency n. "a proneness to a particular thought or action"
Tendentious adj. "marked by a tendency in favor of a particular point of view; biased"

        Vide: **Tendentiou**sly **Tendentiou**sness
   "As humans, we tend to associate with those who share our own tendentious predilections."
   "The basketball player had a tendency to fail to follow through with his hand on his free throw shots."

Tender adj. "having a soft or yielding texture; delicate; fragile; succulent"; "immature, young"; "fond, loving; considerate, solicitous"; "gentle, mild; dear or precious". V. "to make tender"; "to make an offer or proposal for acceptance". N. "a supply ship employed to provide provisions to a larger boat"; "a car attached to a steam locomotive for carrying a supply of fuel and water"

        Vide; **Tender**ly **Tender**ness **Tender**ize v. **Tender**izer **Tender**ization
   "She was a tender young thing, who tendered her offer to work on the tender so she could be near her tender sailor." *(a little overkill, but I think you get the idea)*

Tenon n. "a projecting member in a piece of wood or other material for insertion into a mortise to make a joint"

Tenor n. "the drift of something spoken or written"; "an exact copy of a writing, a *transcript* (remember *scriptere*?"; "the voice part next to the lowest in four part chorus; the highest adult male singing voice"; "habitual condition, character"

   "It takes a skilled carpenter to make a successful mortise and tenon joint."
   "I gathered from the tenor of the note, that the newest tenor in the chorus had a seriously flawed tenor about him when it came to the ladies."

        Vide: **Tenor**ist

Tense n. "a distinction of form in a verb to express distinctions of time or duration of the action or state it denotes (confer or cf. Lesson 34)"; adj. "stretch tight, made taut; rigid"; "feeling or showing nervous tension"; v. "to become tense"

Vide: **Tens**ely **Tens**eness **Tens**ed **Tens**ing

Tension n. "the action of being stretched or the degree of being stretch to stiffness; the stress resulting from the elongation of an elastic body"; "the state of latent hostility existing between two individuals or groups"; "inner striving, unrest or imbalance often with physiological indication of emotion"

Vide: **tensile tensive tensity tensional tension**less

"The tension between the two teams was obvious once they *perceived* the tension of the rope in their tug of war."

Tent n. "a collapsible shelter of fabric stretched and *sustained* (remember *sustinere*?) by poles used for camping outdoors or as a temporary building"

Vide: **tent**less **tent**like

"The campers found it very difficult to put up the tent in the mud with the onslaught of down-pouring rain."

Tenure Tenured n. & adj. "the act, right, manner or term of holding something e.g. a landed property, position or office"; "a status granted to a teacher after a trial period that gives protection from summary dismissal"

"Imagine how different the American education system would be if we did not have tenure."

Tenuous [TEN you us] adj. "having little substance or strength; flimsy, weak, shaky"

"His argument was tenuous at best, completely *untenable* at worst."

Tensiometer n. "a device for measuring tension; an instrument for determining the moisture content of soil"

"Modern farm tractors often carry an on-board tensiometer connected to GPS and a base computer for tracking moisture needs around the farm."

Tetanus n. "an acute infectious disease characterized by toxic spasm of muscles, esp. the jaw; sometimes called 'lockjaw' because of its symptoms"

Vide: **tetany tetanic tetanize**

"The DPT injection given to most children should prevent development of diphtheria, pertussis and tetanus."

Review:

Tend	Tenderize	Tensing	Tentlike
Tendance	Tenderizer	Tension	Tenure
Tendency	Tenderization	Tensile	Tenured
Tendentious	Tenon	Tensive	Tenuous
Tender	Tenor	Tensity	Tensiometer
Tendentiously	Tense	Tensional	Tetanus
Tendentiousness	Tensely	Tensionless	Tetany
Tenderly	Tenseness	Tent	Tetanic
Tenderness	Tensed	Tentless	Tetanize

Unit Six
Lesson 51

Adding prefixes to the *tendere* root **extends** the list dramatically. You will notice the effect as you identify 74 new words in this lesson and the next.

Attend v. "literally, to tend to"; "to pay attention to; to look after, to take charge of"; "to wait for"; "to go to (~ school)"
Attendance n. "the act of attending"; "the person or number of persons at an event"
Attendant n. "accompanying, waiting or following as a result or to perform service"; "an employee who waits on customers"; "something that accompanies, concomitant"
Attendee n. "a person who is present on a given occasion or at a given place"
> Vide: **Attender**
"If you intend to attend a championship event, be prepared to pay dearly for it."
"Attendance in school is mandatory until the age of sixteen."
"He found a quiet satisfaction in his role as attendant to the philanthropist."
"I plan to be an attendee at next year's annual vocabulary convention."

Attention n. "the act or state of attending, esp. through applying the mind to an object of sense of thought"; "observation, notice, attentiveness"
Attentive adj. "mindful, observant"; "heedful of the comfort of others, solicitous"
> Vide: **Attentional Attentively Attentiveness**
"Class, focus your attention on the dissected frog."
"He was quite attentive to her needs."

Contend v. "to strive or vie in contest or rivalry or against difficulties; to argue"; "to struggle for, to contest"; "to *maintain* or assert"
Contender n. "one who contends"; "a competitor for a championship or high honor"
"It was impressive to watch her contend for the highest honors in science."
"I coulda been a contender." *Marlon Brando*, 'On the Waterfront'

Détente [day TAUNT] n. "the relaxation of strained relations or tensions, as in between nations; a policy promoting this"; "a period of detente"
"Détente between two superpowers armed with nuclear weapons is a good thing."

Extend v. "to spread or stretch forth"; "to unbend"; "to exert to full capacity"; "to make an offer of, to proffer"; "to cause to be longer, to prolong"
> Vide: **Extendable Extendible Extendibility Extended Extendedly Extendedness Extender**
"I wish to extend a warm welcome to all of you."
Extension n. "the enlargement in scope or operation"; "the stretching or unbending operation around a joint"; "an increase in length of time"
> Vide: **Extensive Extensional Extensionality Extensity**

"Sorry, I cannot grant you an extension for your research paper."
Exten**sible** adj. "capable of being extended"
> Vide: **Ex**ten**sibility**

"This portion of your project is non-extensible (or not extensible)."
Extent n. "the range over which something extends, the scope"; "magnitude"
Exten**uate** v. "to try to lessen the seriousness or extent of by making partial excuses; to mitigate"
> **Ex**ten**uating Ex**ten**uator Ex**ten**uatory Extenuation**

"The extent of the damage from the earthquake was almost *incomprehensible*."
"The lawyer tried to mitigate the damages by saying there were extenuating circumstances that needed to be considered."

Intense   adj. "existing in an extreme degree"; "marked by or expressive of great zeal, energy, determination or concentration"; "exhibiting strong feeling or earnestness of purpose"; "deeply felt"
Inten**sive** adj. "highly concentrated; tending to strengthen or increase"
Inten**sity** n. "extreme degree of strength, force, energy"; "magnitude of a quantity per unit"
> Vide: **In**ten**sion In**ten**sely In**ten**seness In**tens**ify In**tens**ifier**
> **In**tens**eness In**tens**ification**

"Feelings about controversial issues such as abortion are often intense."
"She just completed an intensive course in breakthroughs in *audiology*."
"The intensity of the earthquake was measured at 7.5 on the Richter scale."

Intent n. "the act or fact of intending; purpose"; "the state of mind with which an act is done; volition"; "meaning, significance, *connotation*"
> Vide: **In**tent**ly**

"The jury was asked to decide the intent of the accused."
Inten**tion** n. "determination to act in a certain way"; "import, significance"; "purpose with respect to marriage"
> Vide: **In**ten**tional In**ten**tionality In**ten**tionally**

"The prospective father-in-law intentionally asked about the young suitor's intentions."
Intend n. "to direct the mind on; to signify, to mean"; "to have in mind as a purpose or goal, to plan"
> Vide: **In**tend**ed In**tend**ance In**tend**ant In**tend**ing In**tend**ment**

"I wondered why the intense contender intended to extend his stay."

Review of keywords: **attend contend détente extend intend**
*The complete word **review** of "tendere" + at- con- de- ex- and in- will be at the end of Lesson 52.*

Portend v. "to give an omen or anticipatory sign of; to bode"
Portent n. "something that foreshadows a coming event; an omen"; "prophetic indication or significance"
>   Vide: **Portent**ous **Portent**ously **Portent**ousness
  "The gathering dark clouds did not portend well for a peaceful afternoon."

Pretend v. "to give a false appearance of being, possessing or performing"; "to make believe, to feign"; "to claim, represent or assert falsely"
Pretender n. "one who pretends"; "one who makes a false or hypocritical show"
>   Vide: **Pretend**ed

Pretentious adj. "characterized by pretension"; "making usu. unjustified or excessive claims"; "expressive of affected, unwarranted, or exaggerated importance, worth or stature"
>   Vide: **Pretentious**ly   **Pretentious**ness

Pretension n. "an allegation of doubtful value, pretext"; "vanity, pretentiousness"
Pretense n. "a claim made or implied but not supported by fact"; "a mere ostentation"' "make believe, fiction"; "false show"
  "I love to watch children pretend to be their heroes."
  "Since he wasn't a legitimate royal heir, he was considered a pretender to the throne."
  "The smaller the understanding of the situation, the more pretentious the form of expression." John Romano
  "True glory strikes root, and even extends itself; all false pretensions fall as do flowers, nor can any feigned thing be lasting." Marcus Tullius Cicero
  "His claim to be a duke was only a pretense."

Let's add a new prefix – from the Greek "**hyper-**"meaning "above, beyond, super"
Hypertension n. "abnormally high blood pressure"
Hypertensive adj. "characterized by or due to hypertension"; n. "a person with hypertension"
  "When the doctor diagnosed his hypertension, the patient agreed to take the appropriate medicine."
  "The doctor diagnosed her as hypertensive."

While we're at it, let's add another new prefix – from the Greek "**hypo-**" meaning "under, beneath, down" – basically the antonym for *hyper*.
Hypotension n. "abnormally low blood pressure"
Hypotensive adj. "characterized by or due to hypotension"; n. "a person with hypotension, or low blood pressure"

"Since his blood pressure was chronically low, the doctor *prescribed* medication for his hypotension."

All right – let's visit math land for a minute…
Hypotenuse n. "the side of a right triangle that is opposite the right angle"
"The hypotenuse of a right triangle is equal to the square root of the sum of the squares of the other two legs."

Review:

Attend	Extendedly	Intensive	Portentous
Attendance	Extendedness	Intensify	Portentously
Attendant	Extender	Intensifier	Portentousness
Attendee	Extension	Intensification	
Attender	Extensive		Pretend
Attention	Extensional	Intent	Pretender
Attentional	Extensionality	Intently	Pretended
Attentive	Extensity	Intention	Pretentious
Attentively	Extensible	Intentional	Pretentiously
Attentiveness	Extensibility	Intentionality	Pretentiousness
	Extent	Intentionally	Pretension
Contend	Extenuate		Pretense
Contender	Extenuating	Intend	
	Extenuator	Intended	Hyper
Détente	Extenuatory	Intendance	Hyertension
	Extenuation	Intendant	Hyertensive
Extend		Intending	
Extendable	Intense	Intendment	Hypo
Extendible	Intensely		Hypotension
Extendibility	Intenseness	Portend	Hypotensive
Extended	Intension	Portent	Hypotenuse

Unit Six
Lesson 53

Well, so far in this unit we have **made** and **held**. Now it's time **to put** or **to place** or **to arrange** using the Latin verb *ponere*. *Pono ponere posui positum* provides us several stems: **pon- pos- posit-**

These next four lessons add almost 150 words to your tally.

Ponder v. "to weigh in the mind, to contemplate"
Ponderable adj. "significant enough to be worth considering"; "appreciable"
       Vide: **Ponder**ed **Ponder**er **Ponder**ing
  "I prefer to ponder as I wander."
  "I like to pose ponderable questions."
Posit v. "to dispose or set firmly"; "to assume or affirm the existence of, to postulate"; "to propose an explanation, suggest"
       Vide: **Posit**ed
  "Darwin posited the theory of evolution."
Position n. "the act of placing or arranging; a point of view adopted and held to"
v. "to put in proper position, to locate (*more on this later*)"
       Vide: **Posit**ioned **Posit**ioning **Posit**ional
Positive adj. "formally laid down or imposed, prescribed"' "fully assured, confident"; "incontestable"; "having more protons than electrons"
       Vide: **Posit**ively **Posit**iveness **Posit**ivity
Post n. as in "post office"; v. "to publish, announce or advertise"
  "Her position was that altruism was better than selfishness."
  "He was positive that the negative electrode was *reversed*."
  "They posted their moving sale poster juxtaposed to the 'Post No Bills' Sign."
Pose (also related to *pausare* "to stop, rest or pause" & n. *pausa* "a pause") "v. "to present for consideration or attention [~ a question]"; "to place or put in place"; "to affect an attitude or character, usu. to impress"; n. "a sustained posture for artistic effect"; "an attitude, role or characteristic assumed for effect"
Posture n. "a position or bearing of the body whether characteristic or assumed for a special purpose"; "the pose of a model"; "a conscious mental or outward behavioral attitude "
       Vide: **Pose**d **Pos**ing **Pos**er   **Postur**ed **Postur**ing **Postur**er **Postur**al
  "She posed as a princess to impress the handsome stranger."
  "His normal posture was quite erect."

Appose v. "to place in juxtaposition or proximity"
Apposite adj. "highly pertinent or appropriate; relevant; proximate"
Apposition n. "a grammatical construction in which two usu. adjacent nouns with one element serving to define the other"
       *Appos*itive *Appos*itional *Appos*itionally

"I will appose this sentence adjacent to the definition."

"She made an apposite contribution to the debate."

"'John the Baptist' is a good phrase to demonstrate words in apposition."

Component n. "literally, placed with"; "a constituent part; ingredient"; "math – either member of an ordered pair of numbers"

        Vide: **Compon**ential

"There were multiple components in the scientific compound."

Compose v. "to form by putting together, to fashion, to constitute"; "to create by mental or artistic labor"; "to free from agitation, to calm, to settle"

Composite adj. "made up of distinct parts"; "combining the typical or essential characteristics of individuals making up the group"; n. "a compound; a solid material which is composed of two or more substances in which each substance retains its identity while contributing desirable qualities to the whole"

Compositor n. "a typesetter"

Composition n. "the arrangement or production of type or typographic characters laid out for printing"; "an intellectual creation, e.g. a piece of writing"

        Vide: **Compos**er **Compos**itional **Compos**itionally

Compost n. "a mixture that consists largely of decayed organic material; a mixture, a compound"; v. "to convert (plant debris) to compost"

Compound v. "to put together parts to create a whole"; n. "composed from the union of separate elements, ingredients or parts"; "a sentence having two or more main parts"

"Once he had composed himself, he set about trying to compose a fugue."

"The pot-holed road required five tons of composite road base."

"With desktop publishing so readily available, there are simply not as many jobs available for compositors."

"The students had to create an expository composition."

"The rooftop gardener decided to compost his organic garbage, much to the chagrin of his neighbors."

"IF you wish to see a compound sentence, then look at this one."

Review:

Ponder	Positive	Postured	Compose
Ponderable	Positively	Posturing	Composite
Pondered	Positiveness	Posturer	Compositor
Ponderer	Positivity	Postural	Composition
Pondering	Post	Appose	Compositional
Posit	Pose	Apposite	Compositionally
Position	Posture	Apposition	Compost
Positioned	Posed	Appositive	Compound
Positioning	Posing	Appositional	
Positional	Poser	Appositionally	

Well, that was a good start, but there are many more prefixes available for *ponere*.

Depone   [dee POAN] from *deponere* meaning "to put down"; v. "to testify"

Deponent   n. "one who gives evidence"

Depose   v. "to remove from a throne or high position"; "to testify to under oath or affidavit"

Deposal   n. "the act of deposing from office"

Deposit   [dee PAWS it] n. "money deposited in a bank or as a pledge or down payment"; v. "to place for safekeeping or as a pledge"; "to let fall (e.g. sediment)"

Depositary   n. "person to whom something is entrusted"

Depository   n. "a place where something is deposited for safekeeping"

Deposition   n. "an act of removing from a position of authority"' "testifying before a court, a declaration; testimony taken down in writing under oath"

   Deposed   **Deposit**ed   **Deposit**ing   **Deposit**or

"The defense attorneys needed to depone the key witness."

"The deponent was credible in his testimony."

"The peasants stormed the castle to depose the king at the same time as the lawyer began to depose the witness."

"She handed the deposit to the depositary in the depository."

"The lawyer completed the deposition of a very hostile witness."

Depot   n. "a place for storing goods, motor vehicles or military supplies; a cache"; "a building for railroad or bus passengers of freight"

"The passengers departed the bus and entered the depot"

Dispose   v. "to give a tendency, to incline, to arrange"; "to put in place, to set in readiness, to arrange"; "to settle a matter finally"

Disposal   n. "the power or authority to dispose of"; "an orderly placement of distribution"; "regulation, distribution"

Disposable   adj. "subject to or available for disposal"; "remaining to an individual after deduction of taxes"; "designed to be used once and then thrown away"

Disposition   n. "final arrangement"; "transfer to the care or possession of another"

   Disposed   **Dispos**ing   **Dispos**er   **Dispos**itional   **Dispos**itive   **Dispos**ure

"The lawyer helped dispose of the assets of the estate."

"When I grew up, it was rare to find a garbage disposal in a home."

"This age of disposable products requires a great deal of disposable income."

"Nothing in human nature is so God-like as the disposition to do good to our fellow-creatures." Samuel Richardson

Exponent   n. "a symbol written above and to the right of a mathematical expression[2] to indicate the operation of raising to a power[2]"; "one who practices or exemplifies"

Exponential   adj. "involving a variable in an exponent"; "expressible by an exponential function"

Exponentiation n. "the act or process of raising a quantity to a power"

Vide: **Expon**entially

"The math whiz was a real exponent of incorporating exponential figures in his compounds, such as 10^5."

"Understanding exponentiation helps young math students appreciate the 'powers' of math."

Expose v. "to deprive of shelter, protection or care"; "to make accessible to a particular action or condition"; "to make known, to bring to light"

Vide: **Expos**ed **Expos**ing **Expos**er

Exposé [ex po ZAY] n. "a formal statement of facts"; "an exposure of something discreditable"

Exposit   v. "to expound"

Exposition n. "setting forth of the meaning or purpose"; "a discourse designed to explain what is difficult to understand"; "a public exhibition or show"

Exposure n. "condition of being exposed"; "the condition of being at risk for financial loss": "the condition of being unprotected, e.g. from the weather"

Expound v. "to set forth, to state' to defend with argument"; "to explain by setting forth in careful and often elaborate detail"

Vide; **Expos**itory n. "containing exposition, (~ writing)"

"The newspaper published a blistering exposé of corruption in local government."

"Exposition Park in Los Angeles includes the L.A. Memorial Coliseum."

"As he began to exposit on the financial exposure the city was facing, the *commissioner* cut him off before he could provide details."

"One of my college professors loved to expound on his theories, specifically the 'Law of Demand and then Supply' that he thought oil companies were using."

Let's add a new prefix *hydro-* or *hydr-* from the Greek for "water"

Hydroponics n. "literally to place in water"; "the growing of plants in nutrient solutions"   Vide: **Hydro**ponic **Hydro**ponically

"A friend of mine has an entire hydroponic garden in which she does not use the traditional soil method for growing vegetables."

Review:

Depone	Deposed	Disposing	Exposé
Deponent	Deposited	Disposer	Exposit
Depose	Depositing	Dispositional	Exposition
Deposal	Depot	Dispositive	Exposure
Deposit	Dispose	Disposure	Expound
Depositor	Disposal	Expose	Hydroponics
Depositary	Disposable	Exposed	Hydroponic
Depository	Disposition	Exposing	Hydroponically
Deposition	Disposed	Exposer	

Unit Six

Lesson 55

We're about half way through our additional prefixes with *ponere,* so let's continue.

***Impo**se* v. "to establish or apply by authority"; "to place or set"; "to force into the attention or company of another"
***Impo**sition* n. "something imposed, e.g. a levy or tax"; "an excessive or uncalled for requirement or burden"; "deception"

> ***Impo**sed* ***Impo**sing* ***Impo**ser*

***Impo**sture* n. "the act or practice of deceiving by means of an assumed character or name"; "an instance of imposture"
***Impo**und* v. "to shut up in as in a pound, to confine"; "to seize and hold in the custody of the law"

> Vide: ***Impo**undment*

"Frank Abagnale, Jr. used imposture as a way of life, convincing people he was everything from an airline pilot to a doctor."

"The deputy showed the *mittimus* to the Warden indicating that the prison was to impound the scofflaw for ten years."

***Interpo**se* v. "to place in an intervening position"; "to intrude"; "to throw in between parts of a conversation or argument"

> Vide: ***Interpo**sition* ***Interpo**ser*

"He was so rude that he felt he could interpose his comments at any time."

Time for another prefix *juxta-* from the Latin for "near"

***Juxtapo**se* v. "literally to place near"; "to place side by side"
***Juxtapo**sition* n. "the act or an instance of placing two objects adjacent to one another"

> ***Juxtapo**sed* ***Juxtapo**sing* ***Juxtapo**sitional*

"The juxtaposition of the two images – one of the warlord's face and the other of the atomic explosion – created an indelible impression on the viewers of his unsavory nature."

***Oppo**se* v. "literally to place against"; "to place opposite or against something"; "to offer resistance to, e.g. combat, resist, withstand"
***Oppo**sable* adj. "capable of being opposed or resisted"; "capable of being placed against one or more of the remaining digits of a hand or foot"
***Oppo**sition* n. "the act of setting over or against"; "hostile or contrary action or condition"; "a political party opposing and set to replace the party in power"
***Oppo**site* adj. "set over against something that is at the other end or side"; "diametrically different"

> ***Oppo**sed* ***Oppo**ser* ***Oppo**sing* ***Oppo**sitely* ***Oppo**siteness* ***Oppo**sitional*

"If you take that stand, then philosophically I must oppose you."

"Not all animal species have 'opposable thumbs' with the thumb capable of bending so that it can touch all the other digits on the hand."

"The report from the African country said that the opposition was ready to take over control of the country."

"She is such a contrarian that she shall *exposit* the opposite of whatever you say."

Preponderate adj. "to exceed in weight; or influence, power or importance; to exceed in numbers"; "to outweigh"; adj. "preponderant"

Preponderant adj. "having superior weight, force or influence"; "having greater prevalence; dominant"

Preponderance n. "superiority in weight, power, influence, strength, number or quantity"; "majority"

> **Prepon**derancy

"The preponderate influence by the lobbyists caused distrust among the citizens."

"The evidence from the defense was considered preponderant by the jury."

"The debate judge said the affirmative team presented an overwhelming preponderance of evidence."

Preposition n. "a function word that typically combines with a noun phrase to form a phrase (prepositional phrase) which usually expresses a modification or predication"

Prepositive adj. "put before; prefixed"

> **Prepos**itional **Prepos**itionally

" 'With, by and after' are all prepositions and when they 'take an object', a prepositional phrase is created."

"The prefixes explained throughout this book have frequently become prepositions in English."

BTW in one of the many quirks in English, change the pronunciation slightly and change [PREP o zih shun] to [PREE po zih shun], a verb which means "to position something ahead of something else".

"I had to preposition the preface before the word."

ALWAYS note the context of the word in its sentence.

Review:

Impose	Interposition	Opposite	Preponderant
Imposition	Interposer	Opposed	Preponderance
Imposed	Juxtapose	Opposer	Preponderancy
Imposing	Juxtaposition	Opposing	Preposition n.
Imposer	Juxtaposed	Oppositely	Preposition v.
Imposture	Juxtaposing	Oppositeness	Prepositive
Impound	Juxtapositional	Oppositional	Prepositional
Impoundment	Oppose	Oppositionist	Prepositionally
Interpose	Opposable	Preponderate	

Unit Six
Lesson 56
We're heading down the *ponere* + home stretch.

Propone   v. "to propose, to propound"
Proponent   n. "one who argues in favor of something; an advocate"
    Proponed **Propon**ing
  "He proponed a neighborhood park for the site."
  "I am an avid proponent of effective recycling programs."

Propose   v. "to form or put forward a plan or intention"; "to make an offer of marriage"; "to recommend someone to fill a place or vacancy; to nominate"; "to offer a toast"
Proposal   n. "an act of putting forward or stating something for consideration"; something proposed, a suggestion"; "an offer of marriage"
Proposition   n. "something offered for consideration or acceptance"
    Proposed **Propos**ing **Propos**itus
Propound   v. "to offer for discussion or consideration"
  "He picked a romantic setting as the place to propose to his sweetie."
  "The real estate developer submitted his proposal to the zoning board."
  "The godfather offered a proposition that couldn't be refused."
  "Who could imagine that he would propound such an idea?"

Repose   v. "to lie at rest; to lie dead"; "to take a rest"; "to remain quiet or concealed"; n. "rest in sleep, sometimes after exercise"; "peace, tranquility, quiescence"
Reposit   v. "to deposit, to store"; "to put back in place, to restore"
Reposition   n. "the act of repositing"; v. "to change the position; to revise the marketing strategy so as to make more money"
Repository   n. "a place, room or container where something is deposited or stored"; "a place or region richly supplied with a natural resource"
    Reposed **Repos**ing **Repos**eful   **Repos**ited **Repos**iting
  "When he lies in repose, it's hard to tell if he is alive or dead."
  "It's time to reposit the Christmas decorations."
  "Our company must reposition itself in the market."
  "That part of the state is a rich coal repository."

Suppose   v. "to lay down tentatively as a hypothesis, assumption or proposal"; "to hold as an opinion, to believe"; "to think probable or in keeping with the facts, to conceive, to imagine"; "to have a suspicion of, to presuppose"; "to conjecture"
Supposed   adj. "pretended, alleged"; "held as an opinion, believed, or mistakenly believed, understood"
Supposition   n. "something that is supposed"; "hypothesis"

Supposititious adj. "fraudulently substituted"; "spurious; illegitimate"
Suppository n. "a solid but readily meltable cone or cylinder of medicated material usu. for insertion into a bodily passage or cavity"

Supposing, ***Suppos***itious

"I suppose you are going to want more proof than what I have given you."
"He was supposed to have been more reliable than he has been."
"After examining the data, my current supposition is that the ice melted."
"The jury viewed his claim as supposititious."
"The doctor prescribed use of a suppository to treat his patient's hemorrhoids."

Unimposing adj. "lacking in impressiveness"
"All in all, the results of the test are unimposing."
Unopposed adj. "without opposition"
"When the other candidate withdrew from the race, she was left to run unopposed."
Unposed adj. "not arranged for pictorial purposes, natural"
"The candid pictures were unposed and the people looked very comfortable."
Presuppose v. "to suppose beforehand"' "to require as an antecedent in logic or fact."

Vide: ***Presuppos***ition ***Presuppos***itional

"To presuppose someone's beliefs based on their outward appearance is a clear indication of an underlying bias."

Review of the key prefixed verbs related to *ponere*. Prefer a graphical view???

Appose	Expose	Oppose	Suppose
Compose	Hydroponics	Preponderant	
Depose	Impose	Propose	
Dispose	Interpose	Repose	

Propone	Propound	Repositing	Unopposed
Proponent	Repose	Suppose	Unposed
Proponed	Reposit	Supposed	Presuppose
Proponing	Reposition	Supposition	Presupposed
Propose	Repository	Supposititious	Presupposition
Proposal	Reposed	Suppository	Presuppositional
Proposition	Reposing	Supposing	
Proposed	Reposeful	Suppositious	
Proposing	Reposited	Unimposing	

Complete Review - *ponere +*

Ponder
Ponderable
Pondered
Ponderer
Pondering
Posit
Position
Positioned
Positioning
Positional
Positive
Positively
Positiveness
Positivity
Post
Pose
Posture
Posed
Posing
Poser
Postured
Posturing
Posturer
Postural

Appose
Apposite
Apposition
Appositive
Appositional
Appositionally

Compose
Composite
Compositor
Composition
Compositional
Compositionally
Compost
Compound

Depone
Deponent
Depose
Deposal
Deposit
Depositor
Depositary
Depository
Deposition
Deposed
Deposited
Depositing
Depot

Dispose
Disposal
Disposable
Disposition
Disposed
Disposing
Disposer
Dispositional
Dispositive
Disposure

Expose
Exposed
Exposing
Exposer
Exposé
Exposit
Exposition
Exposure
Expound
Hydroponics
Hydroponic
Hydroponically

Impose
Imposition
Imposed
Imposing
Imposer
Imposture
Impound
Impoundment

Interpose
Interposition
Interposer

Juxtapose
Juxtaposition
Juxtaposed
Juxtaposing
Juxtapositional

Oppose
Opposable
Opposite
Opposed
Opposer
Opposing
Oppositely
Oppositeness
Oppositional
Oppositionist

Preponderate
Preponderant
Preponderance
Preponderancy
Preposition
Prepositive
Prepositional
Prepositionally

Propone
Proponent
Proponed
Proponing
Propose
Proposal
Proposition
Proposed
Proposing
Propound

Repose
Reposit
Reposition
Repository
Reposed
Reposing
Reposeful
Reposited
Repositing

Suppose
Supposed
Supposition
Supposititious
Suppository
Supposing
Suppositious

Unimposing
Unopposed
Unposed

Presuppose
Presupposed
Presupposition
Presuppositional

Ready for a challenge? The left column lists the prefixes we have seen so far. The center column includes the root word (usually a verb) and the right the suffixes. Mentally draw a line from each prefix through each root word and connect relevant suffixes. See if you can remember some of the many words that apply. Note also which combinations don't yield a valid word. If you get about a thousand words, you're doing extremely well. If not, look at the Unit & Lesson by each root word.

ENJOY!

Prefixes	Root words	Suffixes
A-	*Amare 5-43*	-able -ible
Ad-	*Assentire 5-39*	-ability -ibility
Ab- Ap- At-	*Audire 4-25*	-al -ally
Bi- tri- multi-	*Clamare 4-31*	-ance -ence
Circum-	*Cogitare 5-37*	-ancy -ency
Col- Com- Con- Cor-	*Cognoscere 5-37*	-ant -ent
Contra-	*Dicere 4-29*	-ary -ory
Cum-	*Dorminare 5-41*	-ate
De-	*Ducere 3: 14-23*	-ed
Dis- Di-	*Facere 6-46*	-ent -ant
Ex- E-	*Habere 6-47*	-er -or
Extra- Extro-	*Insurare 4-31*	-ful
Hydro-	*Loquere 4-30*	-ing
Hyper-	*Mittere 2: 8-13*	-ion
Hypo-	*Noscere 4-34*	-ious -iously
Im-	*Notare 4-34*	-iousness
In-	*Ponere 6: 53-56*	-ism -ist
Inter-	*Prehendere 6-49*	-ity
Intra- Intro-	*Putare 5-36*	-ium
Juxta-	*Scribere 4: 32-33*	-ive
Meta-	*Sentire 5-38*	-ize -ization
Non-	*Sermocinare 4-30*	-less
O- Op-	*Somniare 5-4-*	-ly
Per-	*Specere 4-28*	-ment
Pre-	*Spectare 4-28*	-ness
Pro-	*Studere 5-42*	-ous -ously
Post-	*Tendere 6: 50-52*	-ousness
Re-	*Tenere 6-49*	-uous -uousness
Sub- Suf- Sus-	*Vertere 1: 1-7*	
Ultra-	*Videre 4: 26-27*	
Un-	*Vociferare 4-31*	

Unit Six
Lesson 57

The last four lessons have given you numerous ways to spin off from just one Latin verb for "to place". As you have probably guessed, there is at least one more word with all of its attendant variations – *loco, locare, locavi, locatus.* The basic meaning in Latin was "to place or to arrange". It also was used in the phrase "to give (a girl) in marriage to", as well as "to contract" or "to hire out". It was even used for "to let" as in "to allow" or "to lease". With this much flexibility in Latin, you can see how it allows multiple uses in English.

Related to this is the noun form, *locus*, which may look familiar for you math fans. *Locus* and its plural form, *loci,* refer to a place or point (pl. places or points).

The person who "let out property" was the *locator* and *locatum* was the "something let out". *Locatio (locationis)* was the "letting out or the leasing".

As you read the previous paragraphs, you undoubtedly were able to identify the stem: **loc-** From it, we get the following direct descendents.

Locus n. "a place where something is situated or occurs"; "the center of activity, attention or concentration"
   "The focus of the locus was on the crocus."

Local n. "a person from this place"; "a local or particular branch, lodge or chapter of an organization"; adj. "characterized by or related to a position in space, relating to a particular place"

 Locale n. "a place or locality, esp. when viewed in relation to a particular event or characteristic"; "site, scene (the ~ for the story)"
        Vide: **Locally   Localism   Localist   Localize   Localization**
   "The bumper sticker almost shouted 'Don't hassle me—I'm a local!'"
   "The director and producer identified the ideal locale for their film."

Locate v. "to establish oneself or one's business in a particular location, to settle"; "to set or establish in a particular place"; "to find or fix the place esp. In a sequence, to classify"

Location v. "a position or site occupied or available for occupancy or marked by some distinguishing feature"; "a tract of land designated for a particular purpose"
        Vide: **Located   Locating   Locater   Locator   Locatable Locative**
   "Using MapQuest or Google Earth, you can locate just about any address."
   "The realtor's mantra is 'location, location, location'."

Your turn – try to think of some of the prefixes that will be applicable to this root.

Allocate from *allocare* v. "to apportion for a specific purpose or to particular persons or things, to distribute"; "to set apart or earmark, to designate"
Allocation n. "a designated portion set aside for a specific purpose"
        Vide: *Al*locable *Al*locatable *Al*locator *Al*located *Al*locating

"If you prefer, you may allocate the parcels of land for each person."
"The allocation set aside for reforestation was too small to be effective."

Bilocation n. "the state or ability to be in two places at one time"
"As a gifted prestidigitator, he was able to convince his audience that he possessed bilocation."

Collocate v. "to set or arrange in place or position, esp. to set side by side"; "to occur in conjunction with something"
Collocation n. "the act or result of arranging or placing together, specifically a noticeable arrangement or conjoining of *linguistic* elements"; "in *Linguistics*. a co-occurrence of lexical items, as *perform* with *operation* or *commit* with *crime*".
      Vide: **Collocated Collocating Collocational**
"The convention planners chose to collocate the breakout sessions after the keynote address."
"Collocation indicates that some word pairings are more appropriate than others, such as GET <u>*a job*</u> and DO <u>*homework*</u> and ASK <u>*permission.*</u>"
Which of these verbs goes best with each task?
BREAK   HAVE   TAKE ... *a break   a leg   a headache.*
    (BREAK a leg   HAVE a headache   TAKE a break)

Delocalize v. "to free from the limitations of locality, specif. to remove from a particular position"; "to broaden the scope of something, to make it more global
      Vide: **Delocalization**
"International business and trade have definitely delocalized our little planet."

Dislocate v. "to put out of place"; "to force a change in usual status, to disrupt"
      Vide: **Dislocated Dislocating Dislocation**
"When I fell off the roof, I dislocated my shoulder."

Relocate v. "to locate again; to establish in a new place" Vide: **Relocation**
"Many people have had to relocate with the weakened economy."

Review:

Locus	Located	Allocator	Dislocated
Local	Locating	Allocated	Dislocating
Locale	Locater	Allocating	Dislocation
Locally	Locator	Bilocate	Relocate
Localism	Locatable	Bilocation	Relocated
Localist	Locative	Collocate	Relocating
Localize	Allocate	Collocation	Relocation
Localization	Allocation	Delocalize	
Locate	Allocable	Delocalization	
Location	Allocatable	Dislocate	

Unit Six
Lesson 58

For this lesson, let's explore "to cut". Latin offers two verbs for that meaning: *Seco secare secui sectum* (1st conjugation – to cut, cut off, amputate). There is also *caedo caedere cecidi caesum* (3rd – to cut, to strike, to carve, to cut down, to wound to kill). *Caedere* obviously takes **cut** to a different level, which we will explore in Lesson 59.

By this point in your studies, you are looking at these verb forms and detecting the stems. So, let's build on your insights

Section n. "the action or instance of separating by cutting; a part cut off"; "a very thin slice [as of tissue] suitable for microscopic examination"; "a distinct part or portion of something written"; v. "to cut or separate into sections" + many more meanings

Sector n. "a geometric figure bounded by two radii & the included arc of a circle"; v. "to divide into or furnish with sectors" +

> Vide: **Sectioned Sectioning Sectional Sectionalism Sectionalist Sectile Sectorial**
> "Please prepare a section of this tissue for further examination."
> "I use a piece of round pizza to show students what a sector looks like."

One of the added benefits to identifying roots and stems comes when you study modern Romance languages. The roots and stems often show up in Italian, French and Spanish. The difference is usually in the endings of the words. Occasionally, a word from one of those languages will become Anglicized and used exactly as it is in the other language. Here is one example.

Secateur from the French n. "shears"

Math fans, listen up. This Cut's for you.

Secant n. "a straight line cutting a curve at two or more points; a straight line drawn from the center of a circle through one end of a circular arc to a tangent from the other end of the arc; a trigonometric function"

Bisect v. "to divide into two usu. equal parts"

> Vide: **Cosecant   Bisection Bisectional Bisectionally Bisector**
> "One of the key ingredients in learning trigonometry is understanding the role of a secant."
> "The teacher explained that bisecting a sector creates two equal sectors."

Science fans – your turn

Dissect v. "to separate into pieces; to expose the several parts of an animal for scientific examination"; "to analyze and interpret minutely"; "to make a dissection"

> Vide: **Dissected Dissecting Dissection Dissector Dissect**
> "After the class dissected the frog, the teacher had them dissect the process to enhance their *metacognitive* abilities."

Prosector (from the Greek prefix *pros-* meaning "in front of") n. "a person who makes dissections for anatomic demonstrations"

"Someone who becomes very proficient at dissecting may wish to pursue a career as a prosector."

Resect v. "to perform resection on"
Resection n. "the surgical removal of part of an organ or structure"
        Vide: **Resectable Resectability**

"The doctor said that the next step was to resect the cancerous portion of the lung."

"Recovering from a bowel resection can be a painful and debilitating experience."

Intersect v. "to cut across"; "to pierce by passing through or across"; "to meet and cross at a point"
Intersection n. "a place or area where two or more things intersect"

"Math fans know that an intersection can also refer to the set of points common to two geometric configurations"

Section	Secateur	Dissect	*Pros-*
Sector	Secant	Dissected	Prosector
Sectioned		Dissecting	
Sectioning	Bisect	Dissection	Resect
Sectional	Bisection	Dissector	Resection
Sectionalism	Bisectional	Intersect	Resectable
Sectionalist	Bisectionally	Intersection	Resectability
Sectile	Bisector		
Sectorial			

Unit Six
Lesson 59

For this lesson, let's cut into *caedo caedere cecidi caesum* (3rd – to cut, to strike, to carve, to cut down, to wound to kill). *Caedere* obviously takes **cut** to a deeper level.

One word comes directly into English.
Caesura [see ZYUR uh] n. "a break, an interruption"; "a literary term, referring, in poetry, to a pause that occurs naturally when a line is spoken usu. a break in the flow of sound in the middle of a line of verse"; "a pause marking a rhythmic point of division in a melody"; "usu. marked by || and usually occurs at a period or comma"
    "The proper study of mankind || is man." Alexander Pope, *An Essay on Man*
        Vide: **Caesural Caesuras Caesurae** (this ending is explained in Unit 7)

As this verb became Anglicized, the *ae* became *i* and the stem became **cis-**.

*Circum***cise** v. "to cut around, typically to cut off the prepuce of a male"
    "Many cultures have a great deal of ritual when it is time to circumcise a boy."
        Vide: *Circum***cis**ion *Circum***cis**ed *Circum***cis**ing

*Con***cise** adj. "cut short, brief"; "marked by brevity of expression or statement"; "free from all elaboration and superfluous detail"
        Vide: *Con***cis**ely *Con***cis**eness *Con***cis**ion
    "The winners at the awards ceremony were asked to keep their comments concise."

*In***cise** v. "to cut into"; "to carve figures or letters into, to engrave; to carve an *inscription*"
*In***cis**ion n. "a cut or gash; a wound made esp. in surgery by incising the body"; "the act of incising or the state of being incised"
*In***cis**or n. "a front tooth esp. adapted for cutting; one of the cutting teeth in mammals between the canines when they are present"
        Vide: *In***cis**ed *In***cis**ing *In***cis**ive *In***cis**ively *In***cis**iveness
    "The surgeon needed to incise just below the umbilicus."
    "His incision was very precise."
    "I went to the dentist because I had chipped one of my incisors."

*Ex***cise** v. "to cut out"; "to remove by excision"; "an additional tax"
*Ex***cis**ion n. "the process of cutting out"; "surgical removal or *resection*"
        Vide: *Ex***cis**ed *Ex***cis**ing *Ex***cis**ional *Ex***cis**able
    "I'm glad the dentist chose to excise my rotten incisor rather than circumcising it."
    "The excision of my incisor was much less painful than I had imagined."

Precise adj. "exactly or sharply defined or stated"; "minutely exact"; "strictly conforming to a pattern, standard or convention"

Precision n. "the quality or state of being precise or exact"; "the accuracy with which a number can be represented"; "relevance"; adj. "marked by precision of execution"

Précis [pray SEE] n. "a concise summary of essential points, statements or facts"

> Vide: ***Precisely   Preciseness   Precisionist***

"The lathe operator ground the widget to the precise specifications."

"It is a pleasure to see an artifact created with such precision."

"After his lengthy oration, the presenter ended with a clever précis."

Review:

Caesura	Concise	Incising	Excisional
Caesural	Concisely	Incisive	Excisable
Caesuras	Conciseness	Incisively	Precise
Caesurae	Concision	Incisiveness	Precision
Circumcise	Incise	Excise	Précis
Circumcision	Incision	Excision	Precisely
Circumcised	Incisor	Excised	Preciseness
Circumcising	Incised	Excising	Precisionist

Assignment: Have you figured the precise meanings of these various terms? How will you use them to incorporate them into your active vocabulary?

Unit Six
Lesson 60

This lesson will cover *tegere,* the Latin verb for "to cover". *Tego tegere texi tectum*
The Romans also used it to mean "to roof over, to clothe, to protect and to conceal".
There are several words that spin directly from this stem.

Tegmen n. "a superficial layer or cover, usu. of a plant or animal part"; more at
thatch
>Pre-med fans – here you go... This tegmentum's for you ...

Tegmentum n. "an anatomical covering, esp. part of the ventral midbrain above the
substantia nigra formed of longitudinal white fibers with arched *transverse* fibers and
gray matter"
>Vide: **Tegmental Tegument Tegmina** (more on this form in Unit 7)
>"The vet had to *resect* the tegmen before he could *excise* the ulcer."
>"The neurosurgeon had never seen tegmentum so badly scarred."

Integument n. "something that covers or encloses; an enveloping layer (as in skin,
membrane, or husk) of an organism or one of its parts"
>Vide: **Integumentary**
>"The dermatologist studied the digital integument *intensely*, so as to avoid making
a rash judgment."

Detect v. "to discover the true character of"; "to discover or determine the
existence, presence, or fact of (~ alcohol)"; "to demodulate"; "to work as a detective"
Detection n. "the act of detecting"; "the process of demodulating"
Detective adj. "fitted for used in detecting something"; n. "one engaged in or
employed in detecting lawbreakers or getting information that is not readily or
publicly accessible"
>Vide: **Detectable Detectability Detector**
>"The arresting officer said he could detect alcohol on the driver's breath."
>"The smoke detection system worked perfectly in alerting the *inhabitants*."
>"His *appositional* name was Mike Hammer, private detective."

Protect v. "to shield or to take precautions against harm or attack"
Protection n. "supervision and support of one who is smaller and weaker";
"immunity from prosecution purchased by criminals through bribery"; "money
extorted by racketeers posing as a protective association"; "the freeing of producers
of a country from foreign competition in their home market by restrictions (high
duties or tariffs) on foreign competitive goods"
Protectionism n. "advocacy of governmental economic protection for domestic
producers through restrictions in the form of duties on foreign competitors"
Protectorate n. "government by a protector"; "the relationship of superior authority
assumed by one power or state over a dependent one"

Protégé [***Protégée*** *(f.)*]   n. "one who is protected or trained or whose career is furthered by a person of experience, prominence or influence"

Vide: ***Protect**ive **Protect**iveness **Protect**ionist **Protect**ionism   **Protect**ant **Protect**or **Protect**ress   **Protect**oral **Protect**ory **Protect**able **Protect**ability*

"The motto of many police departments is 'To Serve and Protect'."

"The older brother provided adequate protection for his little sister when they *traversed* the rough neighborhoods."

"There have been periods in America's history when our government has adopted a policy of protectionism."

"The Protectorate in British history refers to the period 1653–59 during which the Commonwealth of England, Scotland and Ireland was governed by Lords Protector, Cromwell."

"Some people believe that Donald Trump appears to want to identify and nurture a protégé, but others remain skeptical."

Review:

Tegmen	**Detect**	**Protect**	**Protectant**
Tegmentum	**Detection**	**Protection**	**Protector**
Tegmental	**Detective**	**Protectorate**	**Protectress**
Tegument	**Detectable**	**Protégé**	**Protectoral**
Tegmina	**Detectability**	**Protégée**	**Protectory**
	Detector	**Protective**	**Protectable**
		Protectiveness	**Protectability**
		Protectionist	
		Protectionism	

Unit Six
Lesson 61

So far in this unit, we have looked at a variety of actions, primarily having to do with everything from holding to covering. When you're finished holding, it's time "to go". The Latin verb for "to go" was irregular and didn't fit the neat mold that we have seen previously.

The principal parts are: *eo, ire, ivi* and *itum*. There are not words in English that flow directly from the root, but when you add a prefix, we get many options.

Adding a variant of *ad-* or "to" produced the verb *ambeo, ambire, ambivi, ambitum* leaving the meaning "to go around". From here we find a few words. Observe the variation from one suffix to another.

Ambient adj. "existing or present on all sides; encompassing"; n. "an encompassing atmosphere, environment"

Ambience n. "a feeling or mood associated with a particular place; atmosphere"

Ambit n. "circuit, a compass"; "the bounds or limits of a place or district"; "the sphere of action, expression or influence, scope"

Ambition n. "an ardent desire for rank, fame or power; a desire to achieve a particular end"; "the object of ambition"

> Vide: **Amb**iance **Amb**itious **Amb**itiously **Amb**itiousness

"Ambient lights are used to project various colors onto the wall behind a TV, computer or gaming system, because they can add emotion and enhance the viewing experience."

"My favorite restaurant has a very relaxing ambience."

"Could a certain similarly named sleep aide be aimed at changing the ambience of an *insomniac's* night?"

"He fell within the ambit of a group of dedicated scientists."

"She cited her ambition as a key to achieving her level of success."

When the Romans wanted "to go out of", they used *ex – exeo, exire, exivi, exitum*.

Exit n. "departure from a stage"; "a way out of an enclosed space or place"; "death" v. "to go out or depart; to leave"; "to die"

Exeunt n. "a stage direction for actors meaning 'they all leave'"

If one person leaves, then the person behind must "follow" – *sequor sequire sequivi secutus* meaning "to come or go after, to follow, to chase, to pursue".

Sequence n. "a continuous or connected series"; "continuity of progression"; "a subsequent development, a consequence, a result"; v. "to arrange in a sequence"

Sequential adj. "of or related to or following in sequence, serial"

Sequel n. "consequence, result; a subsequent development"; "the next installment, esp. in a literary or cinematic work continuing the course begun in a preceding one"

> Vide: **Sequenced Sequencing Sequencer Sequentially Sequacious**

"The numbers on the raffle tickets were printed in sequence."
"Sometimes, children have difficulty remembering sequential instructions."
"The film was so involving that *attendees* could hardly wait for the sequel."

Let's add two more prefixes: *con-* and *sub-*.

Con*sequence* n. "a conclusion drawn through logic, an *inference*"; "something produced by a cause or necessity following a given set of circumstances"; "importance with respect to power to produce an effect, a moment"; "the appearance of importance, self importance"

Con*sequent* n. "a *deduction*, the conclusion of a conditional sentence"; "the second term in a ratio"; adj. "following as a result or effect"; "observing a logical sequence, rational"

Con*sequent*ial adj. "of the nature of a secondary result, indirect, consequent; having significant consequences, important"

Vide: **Con*sequent*iality Con*sequent*ialness Con*sequent*ially Con*sequent*ly**
"Some children struggle in understanding the consequences of their actions."
"The identity thief failed to consider the consequent jail time for her crime."
"His inappropriate behavior resulted in consequential punishment."

Adding our little negative friend *in-* reverses the meaning.

In*con*sequential adj. "illogical, irrelevant, of no importance, unimportant"

Vide: **In*con*sequence In*con*sequent In*con*sequently In*con*sequentiality**
"His attempted heroic actions ended up being inconsequential."

Con- + *sequor* usually *denotes* a logical result of an action.
Sub- + *sequor* usually *indicates* that one thing happens after another, with no direct causal relationship.

Sub*sequence* n. "a subsequent event"; "a mathematical sequence that is part of another sequence"

Sub*sequent* adj. "following in time, order or place"; can also be used as a preposition meaning "at a time later or more recent than, since" usually accompanied by "to"; can also be a noun

Vide: **Sub*sequent*ly** adv.
"Subsequent to the hunter's arrival, the flight of geese flew in."

Review

Ambient	Sequential	Consequence	Inconsequent
Ambience	Sequel	Consequent	Inconsequently
Ambit	Sequenced	Consequential	Inconsequentiality
Ambition	Sequencing	Consequentiality	*Sub-*
Ambiance	Sequencer	Consequentialness	Subsequence
Ambitious	Sequentially	Consequentially	Subsequent
Ambitiously	Sequency	Consequently	Subsequently
Ambitiousness	Sequacious	Inconsequential	
Sequence	*Con-*	Inconsequence	

Unit Six
Lesson 62

After all that "going" and "following", it's time "to sit".
Sedo, sedere sedivi seditum yield the stem *sed-*.

The English word **sit** comes from this as do the following:
Sedentary adj. "settled, not migratory, doing or requiring much sitting"
   "His sedentary lifestyle left him with weakened muscles."

Sedate v. "to dose with sedatives"; adj. "keeping quiet, steady attitude or peace; unruffled"
Sedation n. "the *inducing* of a relaxed easy state by the use of sedatives"; "a state resulting from sedation"
Sedative adj. "tending to calm, moderate or tranquilize nervousness or excitement"; n. "a sedating agent or drug"
   Vide: **Sedated Sedating Sedately Sedateness**
   "The doctor needed to sedate the violent, unruly patient."
   "The patient was in a deep state of sedation."
   "The preacher's monotone *sermon* had a sedative effect on the congregation."

Settling down a bit more gives us this family of words.
Sediment n. "the matter that settles to the bottom of a liquid"; "material deposited by water, wind or glaciers"
Sedimentary adj. "of, related to, or containing sediment"; "formed by or from deposits of sediment"
   Vide: **Sedimentable Sedimentation Sedimentology Sedimentologically**
   "At the bottom of my coffee cup was a disgusting layer of sediment."
   "In the canyon, it's easy to see the hundreds of layers of sedimentary rock deposited in this former lake-bed over millions of years."

Subside v. "to sink or settle to the bottom; to tend downward, to descend"; "to let one settle down (~ into a chair)"; "to become quiet or less, to abate"
Subsidy n. "money granted from one state to another; a grant by a government or entity to assist an enterprise deemed advantageous to the public"
Subsidize v. "to purchase the assistance of by payment of a subsidy; to aid or promote with public money"
Subsidiary n. "furnishing aid or support"; "of secondary importance"; "in business matters, is an entity that is controlled by a separate higher entity; a company for which a majority of the voting stock is owned by a holding company"

   Vide: *Subsidies Subsidized Subsidizing Subsidization Subsidizer*
   Subsidiarily Subsidiaries

"Once all the publicity subsides, peace will return to our small town."

"The government still provides subsidies to tobacco growers."

"Medicare Part B was designed to subsidize seniors for their medical care."

"It's interesting to observe the conglomerates trying to take over smaller companies to make them a wholly owned subsidiary."

Review:

Sedentary	**Sediment**	**Subside**
Sedate	**Sedimentary**	**Subsidy**
Sedation	**Sedimentable**	**Subsidize**
Sedative	**Sedimentation**	**Subsidies**
Sedated	**Sedimentology**	**Subsidized**
Sedating	**Sedimentologically**	**Subsidizing**
Sedately		**Subsidization**
Sedateness		**Subsidizer**
		Subsidiarily
		Subsidiaries

BTW, have you noticed the use of "**e.g.**" Make sure you know that this is the abbreviation of the Latin phrase *exempla gratia*, which means "**for example**" or "for the sake of an example".

This is not to be confused with **etc.,** the abbreviation for the two word Latin phrase *et cetera*, in which *et* means "and" *cetera* means "other things".

> *Note* that this is NOT *ect.*

Unit Six
Lesson 63   REVIEW
"facere" "habere" "tenere" ponere" "locare" "secare"
"caedere" "tegere" "ambire" "sequare" "ire" "sedere"

Think back and try to put into your own words what you learned about the conjugation of Latin verbs.

What does **CONJUGATION** mean?
Remember the three **MOODS** for verbs (Latin or English)???
What is the difference between **ACTIVE** and **PASSIVE VOICE**?
Explain **TENSE of VERBS** in your own words. What are some examples?
What does **PERSON** indicate?
NUMBER?

Which words from this root best explain or complete the following?

Facere – to make
The adjectival form of FACT is _____ "of or relating to facts; based on fact".
Manufacture comes from two Latin words meaning _____ & _____.
Adding the Latin verb for "**rotten**" to a form of *facere* gives us the English word

_____.

_____ v. "to invent, to create; to construct, to manufacture, esp. from diverse and standardized parts; to create or invent, to make up as in for the purpose of deception".
Another variation of *facere* describes the sense of smell.
    "My _____ nerves were offended by the smell of the putrefying garbage."

Habere – to have
_____ n. "the prevailing disposition or character of a person's thoughts and feelings; mental makeup"; "a settled tendency or usual pattern of behavior"; "a behavior pattern acquired by frequent repetition"
"A place where people live" --   "The early settlers worked to establish suitable _____ in the wilderness."

Which words based on ***inhabitare*** will best complete the following?
    "The camp in the swamp did not look _____ or even _____ for that matter."
Think negative ...
    "The camp looked _____, or even _____, for that matter."
Add the prefix *re-*
_____ n. "the process of restoring to a former capacity level"

160

Tenere – to hold, to keep fixed

_____ adj. "capable of being held, maintained or defended; defensible, reasonable"

"She was _____ in her defense of her client."

_____ n. "one who holds or possesses real estate"; "one who has the occupancy or temporary possession of lands or tenements of another"

Think negative …

"When he realized his position in the argument was _____, he conceded defeat."

Add the prefix con-

"_____ has changed the way most goods are shipped between continents aboard the huge _____ ships."

Use the prefix ab-

"On his doctor's advice, he chose to _____ from alcohol."

Use the prefix de-

_____ v. "to hold or keep in as if in custody; to withhold; to refrain from proceeding"

Use the prefix main-

_____ from manu "hand" and tenere "to hold" – v. "to keep in an existing state; to preserve from failure or decline"; "to sustain against opposition or danger, to uphold and defend"

Use the prefix re-

"His abnormal _____ of fluids caused his doctor great concern."

Use the prefix sub- or sus-

"In order to qualify for a grant, the applicant must show how they will _____ their project once grant funding ends."

Use the prefix at-

_____ v. "to make thin or slender" "to lessen the amount, force, magnitude or value of"; adj. "tapering to a long slender point"

Prehendere – to lay hold of , seize, grasp

_____ n. "act of taking hold or grasping, seizing"; "mental understanding, comprehension"

"Howler monkeys have incredibly strong _____ tails."

Use ad Apprehendere "seize (upon), grasp, cling to, lay hold of; apprehend; embrace; overtake"

_____ v. "to arrest, seize"; "to become aware of, to perceive"; "to grasp the meaning with understanding, to understand"

"The mathematical model was challenging, but _____."

Use the prefix com- **comprehendere** "to grasp"

_____n. "act or action of grasping with the intellect, understanding"; "the act or process of comprising, the faculty of capability of including"
    "The most _____thing about the world is that it is at all _____."
        Albert Einstein
Add the prefix *in-* and turn it all negative.
_____adj. "not able to be understood"
Make it bad by using the prefix *re-*
_____ adj. "worthy of or deserving reprehension"; "culpable"
Use a variant to get "paybacks".
    "Victims of domestic violence are often afraid to do anything to stop their attackers for fear of _____."

tendere "to stretch out, to extend"; "to pull tight or draw"
    "The basketball player had a _____ to fail to follow through with his hand on his free throw shots."
_____ adj. "having a soft or yielding texture; delicate; fragile; succulent"; "immature, young"; "fond, loving; considerate, solicitous"; "gentle, mild; dear or precious".
    "I gathered from the _____ of the note, that the newest _____ in the chorus had a seriously flawed _____ about him when it came to the ladies."
    "The _____ between the two teams was obvious once they *perceived* the _____ of the rope in their tug of war."
    "Imagine how different the American education system would be if we did not have _____."
_____ adj. "having little substance or strength; flimsy, weak, shaky"

Add prefixes to *tendere*
At-
_____adj. "mindful, observant"; "heedful of the comfort of others, solicitous"
    "I plan to be an _____ at next year's annual vocabulary convention."
Con-
_____ n. "one who contends"; "a competitor for a championship or high honor"
De-
    "_____ between two superpowers armed with nuclear weapons is a good thing."
Ex-
_____ n. "the enlargement in scope or operation"; "the stretching or unbending operation around a joint"; "an increase in length of time"
    "The _____ of the damage from the earthquake was almost *incomprehensible*."

In-

_____ adj. "existing in an extreme degree"; "marked by or expressive of great zeal, energy, determination or concentration"

"The prospective father-in-law _____ly asked about the young suitor's intentions."

Por-

_____ v. "to give an omen or anticipatory sign of; to bode"

Pre-

_____ adj. "characterized by pretension"; "making usu. unjustified or excessive claims"; "expressive of affected, unwarranted, or exaggerated importance or stature"

Hyper-

_____ n. "abnormally high blood pressure"

Hypo-

"Since his blood pressure was chronically low, the doctor *prescribed* medication for his _____."

"The _____ of a right triangle is equal to the square root of the sum of the squares of the other two legs."

Ponere" to put" or *"to place"* or *"to arrange"*

"I prefer to _____ as I wander."

_____ v. "to dispose or set firmly"; "to assume or affirm the existence of, to postulate"; "to propose an explanation, suggest"

_____ n. "a position or bearing of the body whether characteristic or assumed for a special purpose"; "the pose of a model"; "a conscious mental or outward behavioral attitude"

"She _____ as a princess to impress the handsome stranger."

Add the following prefixes:

Ap-

_____ n. "a grammatical construction in which two usu. adjacent nouns with one element serving to define the other"

Com-

"The students had to create an expository _____."

De-

"The lawyer completed the _____ of a very hostile witness."

Dis-

_____ adj. "subject to or available for disposal"; "remaining to an individual after deduction of taxes"; "designed to be used once and then thrown away"

Ex-

_____ n. "a symbol written above and to the right of a mathematical expression^2 to indicate the operation of raising to a power^2"

"The newspaper published a blistering _____ of corruption in local government."

Hydro-

_____ n. "literally to place in water"; "the growing of plants in nutrient solutions"

Im-

_____ n. "something imposed, e.g. a levy or tax"; "an excessive or uncalled for requirement or burden"

Inter-

_____ v. "to place in an intervening position"; "to intrude"; "to throw in between parts of a conversation or argument"

Juxta-

"The _____ of the two images – one of the warlord's face and the other of the atomic explosion – created an indelible impression on the viewers of his unsavory nature."

Op-

"The report from the African country said that the _____ was ready to take over control of the country."

Pre-

"The debate judge said the affirmative team presented an overwhelming _____ of evidence."

"The prefixes explained throughout this book have frequently become _____ in English."

Pro-

"The real estate developer submitted his _____ to the zoning board."

Re-

_____ n. "a place, room or container where something is deposited or stored"; "a place or region richly supplied with a natural resource"

Sub- or *sup-*

_____ n. "something that is supposed"; "hypothesis"

Un- and *im-*

_____ adj. "lacking in impressiveness"

Add *pre-*

"To _____ someone's beliefs based on their outward appearance is a clear indication of an underlying bias."

Locare – to place

"The director and producer identified the ideal _____ for their film."

_____ v. "a position or site occupied or available for occupancy or marked by some distinguishing feature"; "a tract of land designated for a particular purpose"

Add the prefixes

Al-

_____ v. "to apportion for a specific purpose or to particular persons or things, to distribute"

Bi-

_____ n. "the state or ability to be in two places at one time"

Co-

_____ v. "to set or arrange in place or position, esp. to set side by side"; "to occur in conjunction with something"

De-

"International business and trade have definitely _____ our little planet."

Dis-

"When I fell off the roof, I _____ my shoulder."

Re-

_____ v. "to locate again; to establish in a new place"

Secare – to cut, cut off, amputate

"I use a piece of round pizza to show students what a _____ looks like."

Add prefixes

Bi-

"The teacher explained that _____ a sector creates two equal sectors."

Di-

_____ v. "to separate into pieces; to expose the several parts of an animal for scientific examination"; "to analyze and interpret minutely"

Re-

_____ n. "the surgical removal of part of an organ or structure"

Inter-

_____ v. "to cut across"; "to pierce by passing through or across"; "to meet and cross at a point"

Caedre – to cut, to strike, to carve, to cut down, to wound to kill

_____ n. "a break, an interruption"; "a literary term, referring, in poetry, to a pause that occurs naturally when a line is spoken usu. a break in the flow of sound in the middle of a line of verse"; "a pause marking a rhythmic point of division in a melody"; "usu. marked by || and usually occurs at a period or comma"

Add prefixes

Circum-

_____ v. "to cut around, typically to cut off the prepuce of a male"

Con-

"The winners at the awards ceremony were asked to keep their comments _____."

In-

_____ n. "a cut or gash; a wound made esp. in surgery by incising the body"; "the act of incising or the state of being incised"

Ex-

"The _____ of my incisor was much less painful than I had imagined."

Pre-

"The lathe operator ground the widget to the _____ specifications."

Tegere – to roof over, to clothe, to protect and to conceal
_____ n. "a superficial layer or cover, usu. of a plant or animal part"
Add prefixes
_De-_

_____ v. "to discover the true character of"; "to discover or determine the existence, presence, or fact of (~ alcohol)"
Pro-

"The motto of many police departments is 'To Serve and _____.'"
_____ n. "advocacy of governmental economic protection for domestic producers through restrictions in the form of duties on foreign competitors"

Ambire – to go around
"My favorite restaurant has a very relaxing _____."

Exire – to go out
_____ n. "departure from a stage"; "a way out of an enclosed space or place"

Sequire – to follow
_____ n. "of or related to or following in sequence, serial"

Add prefixes
Con-
"Some children struggle in understanding the _____ of their actions."
Add _In-_
"His attempted heroic actions ended up being _____."
Sub-
_____ adj. "following in time, order or place"

OK, which is which? _Con-_ or _Sub-_
??? + _sequor_ usually _denotes_ a logical result of an action.
??? + _sequor_ usually _indicates_ that one thing happens after another, with no direct causal relationship.

Sedere – to sit
"His _____ lifestyle left him with weakened muscles."
_____ adj. "tending to calm, moderate or tranquilize nervousness or excitement"
"In the canyon, it's easy to see the hundreds of layers of _____ rock deposited in this former lake-bed over millions of years."
"The government still provides _____ to tobacco growers."

ANSWERS: Unit 6 Review

Con*jugation* n. "a schematic arrangement of the inflectional forms of a verb"; "a class of verbs having the same types of inflectional forms"
Conjugation is simply a way of organizing information about the mood, voice, tense, person, and number of verbs, regardless whether the language is Latin or English or any of the Romance languages.

Remember the three **MOODS** for verbs (Latin or English)???
> **Indicative** (statement or question), **Subjunctive** (what if???) and
> **Imperative** (YOU WILL DO THIS).

VOICE active – She has loved   **VOICE** passive – She has been loved
TENSE basically **present, past** and **future** with a few additional variations
PERSON refers to the subject –
> "I" 1st person, "You" 2nd person, "He, she, it" 3rd person

NUMBER either singular or plural

Facere – to make
The adjectival form of FACT is **factual** - "of or relating to facts; based on fact".
Manufacture comes from two Latin words meaning "hand" & "to make".
Adding the Latin verb for "**rotten**" to a form of *facere* gives us the English word **putrefy** or **putrefaction**.
Fabricate – v. "to invent, to create; to construct, to manufacture, esp. from diverse and standardized parts; to create or invent, to make up as in for the purpose of deception".
Another variation of *facere* describes the sense of smell.
> "My **olfactory** nerves were offended by the smell of the putrefying garbage."

Habere – to have
Habit n. "the prevailing disposition or character of a person's thoughts and feelings; mental makeup"; "a settled tendency or usual pattern of behavior"; "a behavior pattern acquired by frequent repetition"
"A place where people live" --   "The early settlers worked to establish suitable **habitation** in the wilderness."

Inhabitare – to have
> "The camp in the swamp did not look **inhabited** or even **inhabitable** for that matter."

Think negative …
> "The camp looked **uninhabited**, or even **uninhabitable**, for that matter."

Add the prefix *re-*
Rehabilitation n. "the process of restoring to a former capacity level"

Tenere – to hold, to keep fixed

Tenable [TEN uh bull] adj. "capable of being held, maintained or defended; defensible, reasonable"
"She was **tenacious** in her defense of her client."
Tenant n. "one who holds or possesses real estate"; "one who has the occupancy or temporary possession of lands or tenements of another"
Think negative ...
"When he realized his position in the argument was **untenable**, he conceded defeat."
Add the prefix _con-_
"**Containerization** has changed the way most goods are shipped between continents aboard the huge **container** ships."
Use the prefix _ab-_
"On his doctor's advice, he chose to **abstain** from alcohol."
Use the prefix _de-_
Detain   v. "to hold or keep in as if in custody; to withhold; to refrain from proceeding"
Use the prefix _main-_
Maintain   from _manu_ "hand" and _tenere_ "to hold" – v. "to keep in an existing state; to preserve from failure or decline"; "to sustain against opposition or danger, to uphold and defend"
Use the prefix _re-_
"His abnormal **retention** of fluids caused his doctor great concern."
Use the prefix _sub-_ or _sus-_
"In order to qualify for a grant, the applicant must show how they will **sustain** their project once grant funding ends."
Use the prefix _at-_
Attenuate -from _attenuare_ v. "to make thin or slender" "to lessen the amount, force, magnitude or value of"; adj. "tapering to a long slender point"

Prehendere – to lay hold of , seize, grasp
Prehension n. "act of taking hold or grasping, seizing"; "mental understanding, comprehension"
"Howler monkeys have incredibly strong **prehensile** tails."

Use the prefix _ad-_ **_Apprehendere_** "seize (upon), grasp, cling to, lay hold of; apprehend; embrace; overtake"
Apprehend v. "to arrest, seize"; "to become aware of, to perceive"; "to grasp the meaning with understanding, to understand"
"The mathematical model was challenging, but **apprehensible**."

Use the prefix *com-* **comprehendere** "to grasp"
Comprehension n. "act or action of grasping with the intellect, understanding"; "the act or process of comprising, the faculty of capability of including"

"The most **incomprehensible** thing about the world is that it is at all
comprehensible."   *Albert Einstein*

Add the prefix *in-* and turn it all negative.
Incomprehensible adj. "not able to be understood"
Make it bad by using the prefix *re-*
Reprehensible adj. "worthy of or deserving reprehension"; "culpable"
Use a variant to get "paybacks".

"Victims of domestic violence are often afraid to do anything to stop their attackers for fear of **reprisal**."

tendere "to stretch out, to extend"; "to pull tight or draw"

"The basketball player had a **tendency** to fail to follow through with his hand on his free throw shots."
Tender adj. "having a soft or yielding texture; delicate; fragile; succulent"; "immature, young"; "fond, loving; considerate, solicitous"; "gentle, mild; dear or precious".

"I gathered from the **tenor** of the note, that the newest **tenor** in the chorus had a seriously flawed **tenor** about him when it came to the ladies."

"The **tension** between the two teams was obvious once they *perceived* the **tension** of the rope in their tug of war."

"Imagine how different the American education system would be if we did not have tenure."
Tenuous [TEN you us] adj. "having little substance or strength; flimsy, weak, shaky"

Add prefixes to *tendere*
At-
Attentive adj. "mindful, observant"; "heedful of the comfort of others, solicitous"

"I plan to be an **attendee** at next year's annual vocabulary convention."
Con-
 Contender n. "one who contends"; "a competitor for a championship or high honor"
De-

"**Détente** between two superpowers armed with nuclear weapons is a good thing."
Ex-
Extension n. "the enlargement in scope or operation"; "the stretching or unbending operation around a joint"; "an increase in length of time"

"The **extent** of the damage from the earthquake was almost *incomprehensible*."
In-
Intense   adj. "existing in an extreme degree"; "marked by or expressive of great zeal, energy, determination or concentration"

"The prospective father-in-law **intentionally** asked about the young suitor's intentions."

Por-

Portend v. "to give an omen or anticipatory sign of; to bode"

Pre-

Pretentious adj. "characterized by pretension"; "making usu. unjustified or excessive claims"; "expressive of affected, unwarranted, or exaggerated importance, worth or stature"

Hyper-

Hypertension n. "abnormally high blood pressure"

Hypo-

"Since his blood pressure was chronically low, the doctor *prescribed* medication for his **hypotension**."

"The **hypotenuse** of a right triangle is equal to the square root of the sum of the squares of the other two legs."

Ponere" to put" or "to place" or "to arrange"

"I prefer to **ponder** as I wander."

Posit v. "to dispose or set firmly"; "to assume or affirm the existence of, to postulate"; "to propose an explanation, suggest"

Posture n. "a position or bearing of the body whether characteristic or assumed for a special purpose"; "the pose of a model"; "a conscious mental or outward behavioral attitude

"She **posed** as a princess to impress the handsome stranger."

Add the following prefixes:

Ap-

Apposition n. "a grammatical construction in which two usu. adjacent nouns with one element serving to define the other"

Com-

"The students had to create an expository **composition**."

De-

"The lawyer completed the **deposition** of a very hostile witness."

Dis-

Disposable adj. "subject to or available for disposal"; "remaining to an individual after deduction of taxes"; "designed to be used once and then thrown away"

Ex-

Exponent n. "a symbol written above and to the right of a mathematical expression[2] to indicate the operation of raising to a power[2]"

"The newspaper published a blistering **exposé** of corruption in local government."

Hydro-

Hydroponics n. "literally to place in water"; "the growing of plants in nutrient solutions"

Im-

Imposition n. "something imposed, e.g. a levy or tax"; "an excessive or uncalled for requirement or burden"

Inter-

Interpose v. "to place in an intervening position"; "to intrude"; "to throw in between parts of a conversation or argument"

Juxta-

"The **juxtaposition** of the two images – one of the warlord's face and the other of the atomic explosion – created an indelible impression on the viewers of his unsavory nature."

Op-

"The report from the African country said that the **opposition** was ready to take over control of the country."

Pre-

"The debate judge said the affirmative team presented an overwhelming **preponderance** of evidence."

"The prefixes explained throughout this book have frequently become **prepositions** in English."

Pro-

"The real estate developer submitted his **proposal** to the zoning board."

Re-

Repository n. "a place, room or container where something is deposited or stored"; "a place or region richly supplied with a natural resource"

Sub- or *sup-*

Supposition n. "something that is supposed"; "hypothesis"

Un- and *im-*

Unimposing adj. "lacking in impressiveness"

Add *pre-*

"To **presuppose** someone's beliefs based on their outward appearance is a clear indication of an underlying bias."

Locare – to place

"The director and producer identified the ideal **locale** for their film."

Location v. "a position or site occupied or available for occupancy or marked by some distinguishing feature"; "a tract of land designated for a particular purpose"

Add the prefixes

Al-

Allocate from *allocare* v. "to apportion for a specific purpose or to particular persons or things, to distribute"

Bi-

Bilocation n. "the state or ability to be in two places at one time"

Co-

Collocate v. "to set or arrange in place or position, esp. to set side by side"; "to occur in conjunction with something"

De-

"International business and trade have definitely **delocalized** our little planet."
Dis-

"When I fell off the roof, I **dislocated** my shoulder."
Re-

Relocate v. "to locate again; to establish in a new place"

Secare – to cut, cut off, amputate

"I use a piece of round pizza to show students what a **sector** looks like."
Add prefixes
Bi-

"The teacher explained that **bisecting** a sector creates two equal sectors."
Di-

Dissect v. "to separate into pieces; to expose the several parts of an animal for scientific examination"; "to analyze and interpret minutely"
Re-

Resection n. "the surgical removal of part of an organ or structure"
Inter-

Intersect v. "to cut across"; "to pierce by passing through or across"; "to meet and cross at a point"

Caedre – to cut, to strike, to carve, to cut down, to wound to kill

Caesura [see ZYUR uh] n. "a break, an interruption"; "a literary term, referring, in poetry, to a pause that occurs naturally when a line is spoken usu. a break in the flow of sound in the middle of a line of verse"; "a pause marking a rhythmic point of division in a melody"; "usu. marked by || and usually occurs at a period or comma"
Add prefixes
Circum-

Circumcise v. "to cut around, typically to cut off the prepuce of a male"
Con-

"The winners at the awards ceremony were asked to keep their comments **concise**."
In-

Incision n. "a cut or gash; a wound made esp. in surgery by incising the body"; "the act of incising or the state of being incised"
Ex-

"The **excision** of my incisor was much less painful than I had imagined."
Pre-

"The lathe operator ground the widget to the **precise** specifications."

Tegere – to roof over, to clothe, to protect and to conceal

Tegmen n. "a superficial layer or cover, usu. of a plant or animal part"

Add prefixes

De-

Detect v. "to discover the true character of"; "to discover or determine the existence, presence, or fact of (~ alcohol)"

Pro-

"The motto of many police departments is 'To Serve and **Protect**'."

Protectionism n. "advocacy of governmental economic protection for domestic producers through restrictions in the form of duties on foreign competitors"

Ambire – to go around

"My favorite restaurant has e very relaxing **ambience**."

Exire – to go out

Exit n. "departure from a stage"; "a way out of an enclosed space or place"

Sequire – to follow

Sequential n. "of or related to or following in sequence, serial"

Add prefixes

Con-

"Some children struggle in understanding the **consequences** of their actions."

Add *In-*

"His attempted heroic actions ended up being **inconsequential**."

Sub-

Subsequent adj. "following in time, order or place"

OK, which is which? *Con-* or *Sub-*

Con- + *sequor* usually *denotes* a logical result of an action.

Sub- + *sequor* usually *indicates* that one thing happens after another, with no direct causal relationship.

Sedere – to sit

"His **sedentary** lifestyle left him with weakened muscles."

Sedative adj. "tending to calm, moderate or tranquilize nervousness or excitement"

"In the canyon, it's easy to see the hundreds of layers of **sedimentary** rock deposited in this former lake-bed over millions of years."

"The government still provides **subsidies** to tobacco growers."

Open-ended quiz: How many words can you make with these?

Appose	**Expose**	**Oppose**	**Suppose**
Compose	**Hydroponics**	**Preponderant**	
Depose	**Impose**	**Propose**	
Dispose	**Interpose**	**Repose**	

Unit Seven
Lesson 64 – Declension of Nouns

Hopefully, now you are developing a pretty good feel for the structure of verbs in Latin. As I said earlier, you really don't need to memorize it all. However, I think this little bit of knowledge of verbs should help deepen your understanding of the Latin verbs that have migrated into English. We will be seeing more Latin nouns, adjectives and adverbs in the remaining lessons, so this lesson will provide some of the basics of DECLENSIONS. AND you don't have to memorize it – just be comfortable understanding how it works.

Just as verbs are organized into conjugations, nouns – and comparable adjectives – are organized in a somewhat similar fashion. The word "**declension**" comes from the Latin noun *declinatio* "a grammatical inflection". This comes from the verb *declinare* "to inflect or to turn aside". Declension then refers to "a class of nouns or adjectives having the same type of inflectional forms". Inflection refers to "the change of form that words undergo to mark distinctions of case, number, gender, person, tense, mood or voice". You saw many of these are traits in the previous lesson on verbs. To start, there are five declensions, cleverly labeled First through Fifth. In addition to Singular and Plural Number, each noun may have displayed itself in one of five basic Cases – Nominative, Genitive, Dative, Accusative and Ablative.

The SUBJECT of a verb is in the **NOMINATIVE** case.
  "The **man** declined to answer."
A predicate noun (PN) or a predicate adjective (PA) with various forms of the verb "to be" is also in the NOMINATIVE case.
  "She is an **audiologist**." (PN)   "He is **insensitive**." (PA)

The **GENITIVE** case was used to show possession. In English, possession is shown by an apostrophe or the word "of". Nouns in English are usually called POSSESSIVE nouns.
  "The woman's purse (The purse of the woman) was heavy."
The **GENITIVE** case was also used to *describe* or *limit* another noun.
  "He is a man *of great sensitivity*." "He withdrew part *of the money*."

The INDIRECT OBJECT of a verb was in the **DATIVE** case.
  "Mike gave a flower **to Jane**." "Mike gave **Jane** a flower."
Sometimes, translations of the indirect object used the preposition "to" and sometimes "to" was implied.English does not have a Dative case.

The DIRECT OBJECT of a transitive verb was in the **ACCUSATIVE** case.
  "William fixed the **car**."

Finally, Latin had the **ABLATIVE** case. Many prepositions that we have seen in Latin utilized the ablative case, e.g. *ab-, cum-, sine-* (without), *de-, ex- pro-*.
   "She was amazed **by** his insensitivity." "He was delighted **with** the progress."
   "He was a man **without** a country." "The bride left **from** home."
   "He was **out of** time." "The Trojan Horse was left **in front of** the gates."
Because of the endings used for the Ablative case, Romans could tell that it was the equivalent of a prepositional phrase regardless of whether or not the preposition was used. In many instances, the preposition was simply *omitted*.

In English, the **OBJECTIVE** case covers all objects, whether they are direct objects of transitive verbs or objects of a *preposition*. The exception is for use as a POSSESSIVE. **Summary**: English uses **Nominative**, **Possessive** and **Objective** cases.

So what did these declensions look like? Let's look at the First Declension with a noun all Latin students had to learn – *terra* meaning "earth".

	Singular	Plural
Nominative	*terra [ter RAH]*	*terrae*
Genitive	*terrae[ter RAY]*	*terrarum[ter RAHR room]*
Dative	*terrae*	*terris*
Accusative	*terram*	*terras*
Ablative	*terrā*	*terris*

Nouns of the First Declension are FEMALE unless they specifically denote a male. We have already seen a few First Declension nouns (e.g. *aqua, lingua)* and we will see more that have left their mark in English.
So how do you like those endings? *-a, -ae, -ae, -am, -ā   -ae, -arum, -is, -as, -is*
By reading or hearing a Latin noun, the Romans could tell its declension and how it was being used. They needed to pay close attention to endings and context.

The Second Declension has a different structure. Nouns in the Second Declension are generally masculine and have the ending *–us.* (We have already seen *amicus*.) There are some neuter nouns and they end in *-um.* Here are a few examples:

		M = Masculine				**N** = Neuter
		"man" **M**	"boy" **M**	"servant" **M**	"field" **M**	"war" **N**
SINGULAR	Nom.	*vir*	*puer*	*servus*	*ager*	*bellum*
		[VEAR]	*[pooh AIR]*	*[ser VOOS]*		
	Gen.	*viri*	*puri*	*servi*	*agri*	*belli*
	Dat.	*viro*	*puero*	*servo*	*agro*	*bello*
	Acc.	*virum*	*puerum*	*servum*	*agrum*	*bellum*
	Abl.	*viro*	*puero*	*servo*	*agro*	*bello*
PLURAL	Nom.	*viri*	*pueri*	*servi*	*agri*	*bella*
	Gen.	*virorum*	*puerorum*	*servorum*	*agrorum*	*bellorum*
	Dat.	*viris*	*pueris*	*servis*	*agris*	*bellis*
	Acc.	*viros*	*pueros*	*servos*	*agros*	*bella*
	Abl.	*viris*	*pueris*	*servis*	*agris*	*bellis*

Second Declension Endings –
Masculine nouns ending in "-r"   *-r, -i, -o, -um, -o,   -i, -orum, -is, -os, -is*
Masculine nouns ending in "-us" *-us, -i, -o, -um, -o,   -i, -orum, -is, -os, -is*
Neuter nouns ending in "-um"   *-um, -i, -o, -um, -o,   -a, -orum, -is, -os, -is*
Observe that this is why some words in English have a different ending for the plural (e.g. alumnus & alumni; curriculum & curricula)

The Third Declension has the most varied structure. Nouns in the Third Declension can be masculine and have the ending *–r* or *–us*. There are some neuter nouns and they end in *-um*. Here are a few examples:

Singular	**M** = Masculine	**F** = Feminine	**N** = Neuter	
	"father" **M**	citizen" **M or F**	"sea" **N**	"name" **N**
Nom.	*pater [PAH tair]*	*civis [SIH viss]*	*mare [MAH ray]*	*nomem*
Gen.	*patris [pah TREECE]*	*civis*	*maris*	*nominis*
Dat.	*patri*	*civi*	*mari*	*nomini*
Acc.	*patrum*	*civem*	*mare*	*nomen*
Abl.	*patre*	*cive*	*mari*	*nomine*
Plural				
Nom.	*patri*	*cives*	*maria*	*nomina*
Gen.	*patrium*	*civium*	*marium*	*nominum*
Dat.	*patribus*	*civibus*	*maribus*	*nominibus*
Acc.	*patres*	*cives*	*maria*	*nomina*
Abl.	*patribus*	*civibus*	*maribus*	*nominibus*

Third Declension Endings –
M or **F** (e.g. *mater*) ending in "-r" *-r, -is, -i, -um, -e,   -i, -ium, -ibus, -es, -ibus*
Masculine nouns ending in "-is" *-is, -is, -i, -em, -e,   -es, -ium, -ibus, -oes, -ibus*
Neuter nouns ending in "-n"   *-n, -is, -i, -n, -ne,   -na, -num, -nibus, -na, -nibus*
This is just the tip of the Third Declension iceberg. When you study Latin, you'll get to see all the other treasures available here. For now, this is plenty.

In the Fourth Declension, most nouns are Masculine and end in *–us*. The Feminine exceptions are *domus* "home" and *manus* "hand". Neuter nouns end in *–u*.

"senate" **M**		"hand" **F**		"horn" **N**	
senatus	senatus	manus	manus	cornu	cornua
senatus	senatuum	manus	manuum	cornus	cornuum
senatui	senatuibus	manui	manibus	cornu	cornibus
senatum	senatus	manum	manus	cornu	cornua
senatu	senatibus	manu	manibus	cornu	cornibus

Nouns in the Fifth Declension are Masculine and end in -es (except *dies* [de ASE] "day").

"thing" **M**		"hope" **N**	
res [RACE]	res	spes	spes
rei [RAY ee]	rerum	spei	sperum
rei	rebus	spei	spebus
rem	res	spem	spes
re	rebus	spe	spebus

Again, don't feel that you need to memorize these details. However, be sure to include your insights into Latin Declensions when you write your Reflections on this lesson.

> *I'm sure you are beginning to notice words that have migrated into English. Now that you are learning to understand the structure, we will explore more of those in upcoming lessons.*
>
> *Also, as we move forward, you should be able to utilize these words in sentences of your own creation. So, think through the meaning and make the sentence your own.*

Review: Declension, <u>Nominative</u>, Genitive or <u>Possessive</u>, Dative or Ablative or <u>Objective</u>

Unit Seven
Lesson 65
Populus = PEOPLE

This lesson will explore words about people that have evolved into English. It will give you the nominative and genitive case, as well as the gender, of the Latin words.

Man   *Vir, Viri* (m.) referred to "a man" (also a "male person, a grown man, a courageous man") and its related adjective *virilis, virile* meant "manly, male, virile; of a grown man, adult, courageous or spirited". In English, we have inherited **virile**, **virility** ("quality of being virile, manhood, masculinity"), **virilism** ("appearance of secondary male sex characteristics in a female"), **virilely** (adv.).
     The other Latin word for man was *homo, hominis* which could either refer to a specific man or person, or in a broader sense to a human or mankind. The stem *hom-* or *homo-* shows up guiding a gaggle of our words: **homo** ("any of the genus of mammals including modern humans"), **homo** ("reference to a homosexual, often disparaging"), **homophile** (fr. Greek *-philos* "lover of a man"), **homophobia** (fr. Greek *-phobos* "fearing" "irrational fear of or *aversion* to **homo**sexuality"), **homophobe** ("person with homophobia"), **homo** sapiens ("thinking man or humankind"), **hominid** ("any of the family of erect bipedal mammals *comprising* recent humans together with extinct ancestors), **hominoid**, **homicide** (fr. *homocidium* & *caedere* (remember kill?) "to kill a human being"), **homicidal** (adj.).

     Don't confuse this with the Greek root *homeo-* or *homoe-* or *homoio-* meaning "same or similar" which we will explore later.

Woman   *Mulier, mulieris* (f.) ("woman, wife, mistress") which has given us the rarely-used **muliebrity** ("femininity") and *femina, feminae* ("woman, female") which has left us **female** (n.), **feminine** (adj. fr. Latin *femeneus, -a, -um*), **femininely** (adv.), **feminineness** (n.), **femininity** (n. "effeminacy, women, womankind"), **feminism** (n. "a political, cultural, and economic movement aimed at establishing equal rights and legal protection for women"), **feminist** (n.), **feminize** (v. "to give a feminine quality to, to cause a male or castrate to take on female characteristics"), **femme fatale** (fr. the French "a *seductive* woman who lures men into dangerous or compromising situations"), **effeminate** (adj. "having feminine qualities untypical of a man, not manly in appearance or manner" or n. "an effeminate person"), **effeminacy** (n.).
     As an aside, *feminine* came from *femur* "thigh" and *feminalia* "thigh coverings".

Boy   *Puer, pueri* (m.) ("boy, child, servant, slave") and *puellis, puelli* ("little boy") give us **puerile** (adj. "juvenile, childish, silly"), **puerilely** (adv.), **puerility** (n.), and **puerilism** (n. "childish behavior, esp. as a symptom of a mental disorder").

Girl   *Puera, puerae (f.)* ("girl") and *puellula, puelullae* (f.) ("little girl") gives us no direct heritage in English. However, *virgo, virginis* (f.) ("girl of marriageable age, maiden, virgin") gives us **virgin** (n. "an absolutely chaste young woman; a person who has not had sexual intercourse"), **virginal** (adj.), **virginally**(adv.), **virginalist** (n.)

Father   *Pater, patris* (m.), stem ***pat-*** which gives us **paternal** (adj. "fatherly, like that of a father, received or inherited from one's male parent"), **paternalism** (n.), **paternalist** (adj.), **paternalistic** (adj.), **paternalistically** (adv.), **paternity** (n.), **pater noster** (Latin, "Our Father").

The other stems ***patr- patri-*** and ***patro-*** yield **patriarch** [PAY tree ark] (n. "the man who is the founder or father, the oldest male, the head of a patriarchy, a venerable old man"), **patriarchal** (adj.), **patriarchy** (n. "social organization marked by supremacy of the father"), **patriarchate** (n.), **patrician** (n. "an aristocrat"), **patriot** (n. "one who loves his or her 'fatherland' and supports its authority and interests"), **patriotic** (adj.), **patriotism** (n.), **patron** (n. "a person named, chosen or honored as a special guardian, protector or supporter), **patroness** (n.), **patronage** (n.), **patronize** (v.), **patrimony** (n. "an estate inherited from one's father"), **patrimonial** (adj.), **patrilineal** (adj. *patr-* + *linea* Latin for line "tracing descent through the paternal line"), **patricide** [PAH trih side] (n. "the murder of one's father"), **patronymic** (n. *patr* + *onyma* Greek for "name"- "a name derived from that of the father or paternal ancestor")

Mother   *Mater, matris* (f.) stems ***mat-*** which gives us **maternal** (adj. "motherly, like that of a mother, received or inherited from one's female parent"), **maternally** (adv.), **maternity** (n. "motherhood"; "a hospital facility for women before and during childbirth and for care of newborn babies")

The other stems ***matr- matri-*** and ***matro-*** yield **matriarch** (n. "the woman who is the founder or mother, the oldest female, the head of a matriarchy, a venerable old woman"), **matriarchal** (adj.), **matriarchy** (n. "social organization marked by supremacy of the mother"), **matriarchate** (n.), **matron** (n. "a married woman, usu. marked by dignified maturity or social distinction"), **matronly** (adj.), **matrimony** (n. "marriage, the union of a man and a woman as husband and wife"), **matrimonial** (adj.), **matrilineal** (adj. "tracing descent through the maternal line"), **matricide** (n. "the murder of one's mother"), **matrix** (n. "something within or something from which something else originates, develops or takes form"), **matronymic** (n. "a name derived from that of the mother or maternal ancestor"), **mater familias** (Latin "a woman who is the head of a household")

WHEW! That's just for four terms. From the review list on the following page, make sure you feel good that you can **explain the terms** and know how to **use them** in a sentence.

Now, **REFLECT** on how all of these words have evolved into contemporary English, especially the blending of Latin and Greek roots with contemporary endings.

REVIEW:

virile

virility

virilism

virilely

hominid

hominoid

homicide

homicidal

homo

homosexual

homosexuality

homophobia

-phobos

Homophobe

Homophile

-philos

homo sapiens

muliebrity

female

feminine

femininely

feminineness

femininity

feminize

feminism

femme fatale

effeminate (adj. or n.)

effeminacy

puerile

puerilely

puerility

puerilism

virgin

virginal

virginally

virginalist

paternal

paternalism

paternalist

paternalistic

paternalistically

paternity

pater noster

patronymic

onyma

patriarch

patriarchal

patriarchy

patriarchate

patrician

patriot

patriotic

patriotism

patron

patroness

patronage

patronize

patrimony

patrimonial

patrilineal

linea

patricide

maternal

maternally

maternity

matriarch

matriarchal

matriarchy

matriarchate

matron

matronly

matrimony

matrimonial

matrilineal

matricide

matrix

mater familias

matronymic

Consider **writing a paragraph** or two utilizing a number of these words and others that you have incorporated into your vocabulary.

Unit Seven
Lesson 66
Populi Plures – More People

Let's look at some more words, where they came from and what they have given us.

Family   *familia* gives us **family** "a group of individuals living under one roof, typically of common ancestry" and the adjectives **familial** & **familiar** which in turn yield the verb **familiarize** and the noun **familiarity**. It also passes along the difficult to pronounce adverb form **familiarly** and its noun form **familiarness**.
The other Latin word for family is *gens, gentis* which offers us **gentile** (n. or adj. "of or related to non-Jewish persons; heathen or pagan") and **gentle** (adj. "belonging to a family of high social station, honorable, distinguished") and the noun **gentility**.

Son *filius* and **Daughter** *filia* provide English the word **filial** (adj. "of or relating to or befitting a son or daughter") and **filiation** (n. "the filial relationship of a son to his father"). You can also add a prefix *ad-* or *a-* to get **affiliate** (v. "to associate as a member" or n. "an affiliated person or organization". You can also go negative with *dis-* and get **disaffiliate** (v. "to disassociate or terminate an affiliation").
Vide: **affiliated affiliating affiliation disaffiliation unaffiliated**

Baby   *infans, infantis* from *in- + fans* "to speak", so literally "incapable of speech", giving us ***infant*** which means "a child in the first period of life".
Vide: ***infancy infantile infanticide infantilism infantry***

Grandson   *nepos* leaves us the English noun **nepotism** which means "favoritism based on kinship" and its adjectival form **nepotistic**.

Teacher   *magister -tri* gives us **magisterial** (adj. "having the characteristics of a master or teacher") and **magistrate** "an official entrusted with the administration of laws". Another Latin term for teacher was *doctor, doctoris* from *docere* "to teach" giving us **doctor** meaning "a learned or authoritative teacher". One may earn a **doctorate,** the degree title or rank of a doctor. The noun **doctrine** means "something that is taught, dogma" and is related to **doctrinal** and **doctrinaire.** The other Latin term is *praeceptor, praeceptoris* which gives us **preceptor** meaning "teacher, tutor, the headmaster of a school" who may make a **precept**, "a command or principle intended as a general rule of action; a law".
Vide: **magistrial magistrature preceptory preceptorial preceptive**
One root of teaching is from *instruire, instructum* which gives us **instruct, instructor, instruction, and instructive**

Student   *studens, studentis* from *studere* "to study" giving us **student** meaning "a scholar, a learner, one who attends a school".

181

When one completes the course of studies one becomes a ...

Graduate   and depending on gender and number, in English it becomes **alum**nus (one male graduate), **alumni** (male graduates or graduates in general), **alum**na (one female graduate), **alum**nae (female graduates)

Principal   *Principalis –is -e* as a noun is "the person who is the primary teacher and administrator of a school" and as an adjective is "the main, most important, consequential, or influential".

Leader   *dux, ducis* comes from our old friend *ducere* "to lead" and all the words we saw previously.

Senator   *senator* "a member of the senate" -- then and now.

Citizen   *civis* and *civicus* and *civilis* give us **civic** "of or related to a citizen, a city, citizenship or civil affairs" and **civil** "of or related to the state or its citizenry; polite, courteous, gallant; related to the general public as opposed to military or religious affairs".
   Vide: **Citizenship civilize civilized civilization civilian civilly uncivil**

Neighbor *vicinus* and **Neighborhood** *vicuas* or *vicinia* give us **vicinity** (n. "surrounding area or district; proximity; neighborhood"). Vide: **vicinage vicinal**

Doctor   *medicus* provides English a wide range of terms, starting with **medic** (n. "one engaged in medical work or study").
   Vide: **medical medicine medicate medication medicinal Medicare**

Nurse   *nutrix, nutricis* and *nutrire* "to nurse" have given English **nutritious**, (adj. "nourishing"), **nutrition**, (n. "nourishment"), **nutriment**, (n. "something that nourishes or promotes growth"), **nutritionist**, (n.), **nutritive**, (adj.), **nutritionally**, (adv.).

People   *populus* **populace** "the common people", **population** "the whole number of inhabitants in a country or region", **populate, populous, popular, populist** "member of a political party claiming to represent the common people", etc.

BTW there is another Latin word that means "nourishing". If you have heard the phrase "**Alma Mater**" referring to the college or university where one first earned a degree, then you know that it means "nourishing mother".

Reflect: How have the words related to people impacted your active vocabulary? Consider writing a story about people utilizing some of the terms summarized on the next page.

Review

family
familial
familiarize
familiarity
familiarly
familiarness

gentile
gentle
gentility

filial
filiation
affiliate
disaffiliate
affiliated
affiliating
affiliation
disaffiliation
unaffiliated
infant
infancy
infantile
infanticide
infantilism
infantry

nepotism
nepotistic

magisterial
magistrate
magistial

magistrature

doctor
doctorate
doctrine
doctrinal
doctrinaire

preceptor
precept
preceptory
preceptorial
preceptive

instruct
instructor
instruction
instructive

student

alumnus
alumni
alumna
alumnae

Citizen
Citizenship
civic
civil
civilize
civilized

civilization
civilian
civilly
vicinity
vicinage
vicinal

medic
medical
medicine
medicate
medication
medicinal
Medicare

nutritious
nutrition
nutriment
nutritionist
nutritive
nutritionally

Alma Mater

populus
populace
population
populate
populous
popular
populist

Unit Seven
Lesson 67
Loci – PLACES

It's time to take a closer look at how Latin words describing **places** migrated into English. Previously, you learned about the verb *locare* meaning "to place". The noun form is *locus, loci* which meant "place or location" or "point" in math.

Earth   *terra* left us a variety of alternates based on its stem **ter**:
territory n. "geographical area belonging to a government" (adj. **terri**torial, n. **terri**torialism); **terr**estrial (adj. "of or related to the earth; mundane in scope or character; prosaic"); **terr**ain (alt. **terr**ane) n. "a geographical area, a piece of land, ground"; **terr**ace n. "a colonnaded porch or promenade"; "a relatively flat paved or planted area adjacent to a building"; **terr**arium "a usu. transparent container for keeping or raising plants; often a mini habitat or environment"; **terr**aqueous (from *terra + aqua*) "consisting of land and water"; **terr**ier n. "literally an 'earth dog'; any of the small dogs used by hunters to dig for small underground game"; **terr**ine (alt. spelling tureen) n. "earthenware dish in which food is cooked and served"; **terra** n. "any of the light colored highland areas on the surface of the moon or a planet".   Some terms have retained their Latin as they became part of English: *Terra firma* "dry land or solid ground"; *Terra cotta* "brownish-orange glazed or unglazed fired clay used for architectural purposes"; *Terra incognita* "unknown territory, an unexplored country or field of knowledge"

World   *mundus* gave us one of my favorite words, **mundane** "characteristic of the world; practical, transitory and ordinary; commonplace"

Sky   *caelum, caeli* changed the *ae* to *e* and left us **celestial** "suggesting heaven or divinity; relating to the sky or the visible heavens"; another Latin term was *aether* which borrowed from the Greek and evolved into English as **ether** "the rarified element formerly believed to fill the upper regions of space; the heavens"; its adjectival form is **ethereal** "related to the regions beyond the earth; celestial, heavenly, unworldly, spiritual; lacking material substance"
          Vide: **ether**ealize **ether**ealization **ether**eally

Sun   *sol, solis* (from its Greek origin in *helios)* has shined its light on our adjective **solar** "of or relating to the sun, esp. as effecting the earth; produced or operated by the action of the sun's light or heat"   **solar**ium "a glass enclosed porch or room for 'gathering' the sun's heat or rays"   **solar**ize v. **solar**ization n.

Planet *stella* and **Star** *stella* or *astrum* obviously passes along **stellar,** an adjective "of or relating to the stars, composed of stars, astral; also relating to a film or theatre star; principal, leading; outstanding (~ student)". Scientists also use the adjective

stellate to describe "something resembling a star, e.g. a shape". **Astronomers** studying stars would be lost with their **astral** insights into paths of celestial asteroids which they track using **astrometry** and **astrophotography** based on the principles of **astrophysics** . Comparably, an **astronaut** (fr. *aster* + *nauta* "sailor") would be ineffective without a clear understanding of **astronautics.** Likewise, **astrologists** would not be able to practice **astrology** without "divining the supposed influences of the stars and planets on human affairs and terrestrial events by their positions and *aspects*".

Back on earth, we might find ourselves in the ...
Country   *patria, patriae* which as you probably intuited came from *pater* and gave us "our country, our fatherland" and the wealth of associated words from the previous lesson (e.g. **patriot**). However, the Latin *fines, finium* is loosely connected to our **finite** "having definite or definable limits" and its antonym **infinite** "without limits". BUT, if you "go out in the country" you are likely to find a farmer working in the *ager, agri, agrorum* "field", from which we inherit **agrarian** "of or related to the fields and their tenure; organized to support agricultural efforts", n. **agrarianism.** When you combine the stem **agri-** with *cultura* "cultivation", English gets **agriculture**. This combines with several other words to give us **agribusiness, agroforestry, agrochemical, agroindustrial, agronomy.**
BTW, the Greeks are very possessive of their roots (in this case, *agr-*) so don't be surprised if they show up wanting some acknowledgement of their contribution.

Well, when I include this much corn, you can definitely tell we are in the ...
Countryside   *rus, ruris* "open land" which looks suspiciously like the roots of our word **rural**, "of or relating to the country, country people or life, or agriculture", and the noun **ruralist** "one who lives in the country". There is one more related term, but that will have to come in the next lesson after *urbs*.

Got your feet on the ground with these places? Then it's time for Reflection and ...
Review:

territory	*Terra firma*	astronomers	agrarian
territorial	*Terra cotta*	astral	agrarianism
territorialism)	*Terra incognita*	astrometry	*agri-*
terrestrial	mundane	astrophotography	agriculture
terrain (terrane)	celestial	astrophysics	agribusiness
terrace	ether	astronaut	agroforestry
terrarium	ethereal	astronautics	agrochemical
terrier	etherealize	astrologists	agroindustrial
terrine	etherealization	astrology	agronomy
(or tureen)	ethereally		rural
terra	stellar	finite	ruralist
	stellate	infinite	

Unit Seven
Lesson 68
Loci plures – MORE PLACES

Before we leave the country, let's go to the ...

Village   *vicus & pagus* where we are likely to meet a **villager** *vicanus & paganus*. From these roots, we derive the noun **vicinity** "the quality or state of being near, proximity; a surrounding area or district, neighborhood" adj. **vicinal** "related to a limited district, local" and n. **vicinage** "a neighborhood or surrounding district".
A **pagan** is "a heathen, a follower of a polytheistic (many gods) religion; one who has little or no religion and who delights in *sensual* pleasures and material goods." The adjectival form is **paganish** and the noun representing the way of life is **paganism**.

City   *urbs urbis*   adj. **urban** "of, relating to, or characteristic of a city";
v. **urbanize** n. **urbanization** n. **urbanite** n.   **urbanist** adj.   **urbanistic**
n. **urbanism** n. **urbanology** n. **urbanologist**
urbane "notably polite or finished in manner, polished; suave" n. **urbanity**
         Suburb "an outlying part of a city; a smaller community adjacent to or within commuting distance of a larger city"; adj. **suburban**, n. **suburbanite**
n. **suburbia**, v. **suburbanize** n. **suburbanization**

Now, here is the rarely used combination word left over from **rural** – **rurb**an "relating to or constituting an area which is chiefly residential, but where some farming is carried on"
Next, take a *visit* to the ...
Farm   *rustica* or *ager, agri* where you will meet the **Farmer** *agricola*
Rustica actually comes from *rus* which meant "open land". **Rustic** can be an adjective "suitable for the country, rural; lacking in social graces or polish" or a noun "an inhabitant of a rural area; an unsophisticated rural person". "To go to reside in the country" employs the verb **rusticate**. Vide: **rustical rustication rusticator**

You don't have to live on a farm to have a ...
Garden   *hortus* which leaves us **horticulture** "the science and art of growing fruits, vegetables, flowers or ornamental plants"
         Vide: **horticultural horticulturalist horticulturally**

You can also go for a walk in the ...
Forest or **woods**   *silva* or *sylva* gives us **silva** or **sylva** "the forest trees of a region or country" and **silvan** or **sylvan** as the adjectival form "living or located in the woods or forest; wooded".

To get there, you would have probably taken a ...

Road   *via* yields **via** a preposition meaning "by way of" and when combined with our old friend *ducere* gives us **viaduct.** *(Remember previously we saw the* **aqueduct**?*)* Another Latin word for road was *iter, itineris* "road, route, march or journey". From this, English has derived **itinerary** "the route or journey or the proposed outline of one; a travel diary or guidebook". The word **itinerant** as an adjective describes "traveling from place to place; covering a circuit" and as a noun refers to "a person traveling from place to place". There is even the verb **itinerate** if you choose to employ that approach.

On your journey, you may have to cross a ...

River   *flumen* which has given us **flume** "an inclined channel for conveying water; a ravine or gorge with a stream running through it". Latin also used *fluvius* for river and it has left geologists and hydrologists the adjective **fluvial** "related to living in a river; produced by the action of a stream". They have graciously agreed to let us use the word also.

The river runs through the ravine or gorge or ...

Valley   *vallis, -is* obviously led to **valley** and its diminutive friend **vale.**

Beyond the valley is the ...

Mountain   *mons, montis* Geologists also lay claim to **montane,** an adjective describing "the biogeographic zone of relatively cool moist upland slopes below timberline dominated by large coniferous trees." Somewhere along the line, English added a "u" and gave us the noun **mountain** "a landmass that projects conspicuously above its surroundings and is higher than a hill". From that comes the adjective **mountainous**, the noun **mountaineer** "a native or inhabitant of a mountainous region; one who climbs mountains", and even the noun **mountaintop**.

> *"The day I climbed the mountain peak, I found the peace of mind I seek.*
> *From there the big things look so small. The little things are not at all."*

Review:

vicinity	urbanology	rustical	itinerary
vicinal	urbanologist	rustication	itinerant
vicinage	urbane	rusticator	itinerate
pagan	urbanity	horticulture	flume
paganish	suburb	horticultural	fluvial
paganism	suburban	horticulturalist	valley
urban	suburbanite	horticulturally	vale
urbanize	suburbia,	silva	montane
urbanization	suburbanize	sylva	mountain
urbanite	suburbanization	silvan	mountainous
urbanist	*rur*ban	sylvan	mountaineer
urbanistic	rustic	via	mountaintop
urbanism	rusticate	viaduct	

Unit Seven
Lesson 69
Quoque loci plures – Even MORE PLACES

Popular people prefer places – like buildings.

Building   *aedificium* or *aedificatio* Again, the *ae* in Latin morphed to *e* taking us to **edifice** "a building, esp. a large or massive structure". The related Latin verb was *aedificare* (observe the embedded variant of *facere* "to make") which originally meant "to instruct or to improve spiritually OR to erect a house". From this we get **edify** "to build, to lift up, to establish, to instruct and improve in moral and religious knowledge" and the associated noun **edification**.

Like today, Romans had to go to a …
Workplace   fabrica, -ae which gives us **fabric** "structure, building; also an underlying structure or framework (e.g. the ~ of society". The verb form is **fabricate** "to construct, to *manufacture*; to make up, to invent"; the noun for the process is **fabrication** and for the person who does the action **fabricant.** The other Latin word was *officina, -ae* (a combination of *opus* "work" and *facere* "to make or to do" which has given us **office** "a place where a particular kind of business is transacted; the place in which a professional *conducts* business".

Usually, before you go to work you go to …
School   *ludus* (for boys, elementary school) from which we get **ludic** "playful, characterized by play" and one of my favorites, **ludicrous** "amusing or laughable through obvious absurdity, incongruity, exaggeration or eccentricity; meriting derisive laughter or scorn as absurdly inept, false or foolish; syn. Laughable, HA!"   *gymnasium* "the center for athletic practice" which now refers to "the center for athletic practice" hmmm?   There was also the *schola* "a school for men, followers of a system/teacher/subject" (e.g. when I was in college I was in the *schola cantorum* a "school of singers" or specialized chorus). You can imagine that we get **scholar, scholarship, scholastic, school, scholasticism, scholasticate** "college level school for those preparing for life in a religious order". However, *collegium, collegii* was a special **college** for training priests. Now we have **college** "a building used for an educational or religious purpose", with the person attending being known as a **collegian**. There is also **collegium** "a group in which each member has approximately equal authority", which explains **collegial** & **collegiality** & **collegiate** "designed for or characteristic of college students".
University   *universitas, universitatis* is "an institution of higher learning providing facilities for teaching and research and authorized to grant academic degrees."   *Academia, Academiae* originally referred to the grove near Athens where Plato taught but has since given us **academy** "a private high school where specialized subjects are taught".

We also have the adjective **academic** (e.g. ~ year or ~ freedom), the person (noun) **academician** and **academe** or **academia** "the community or world of academic life." My caution to you – watch out for those academia nuts. (LOL)

People had choices for **Church.**   *templum, templi* gave us **temple** "an *edifice* for religious exercises; a building for Mormon sacred ordinances; a local lodge for a fraternal order". *ecclesia, ecclesiae* has left us **ecclesia** "church", **ecclesial**, **ecclesiastical**, **ecclesiasticism**, **ecclesiology**. Also, when you see the stems ***ecclesi-*** & ***ecclesio-,*** understand that the word is related to "church". From its original meaning as a court of justice or public forum, ***basilica,*** *basilicae* is now a Roman Catholic church given higher privileges. The ***Cathedral*** *cathedralis* housed the "chair or throne of the bishop", hence something that is ***ex cathedra*** comes from the highest local authority.

Senate   *senatus* **Senate house**   *curia* Sorry, but even though we may sometimes wonder about what goes on there, *curia* does not yield curious.

Country house   *villa* Place a gathering of villas in proximity and you get a village.

House   *domus* (f.) or *domicilium* leave us **domicile** n. "a dwelling place, a residence", adj. **domestic** "relating to the household of the family; devoted to home duties and pleasures; indigenous"; v. **domesticate** "to adapt an animal or plant for life with humans". Another word for house was *aedificium* which we saw earlier.

Room   *cella* **cell** and **cellular** or *cubiculum* **cubicle** or ***conclave*** "a private meeting room or secret meeting place" or *spatium* **space, spatial** or *locus* (that place we saw previously).

Bedroom   *cubiculum* (as above)

Kitchen   *culina* leaves us **culinary** "of or related to the kitchen or cooking" and **culinarian** a noun meaning "chef or cook".

Study   *studium*   was obviously the room where a **student** went to **study.**

Review:

edifice	scholastic	academe	domicile
edify	school	academia	domestic
edification	scholasticism	temple	domesticate
fabric	scholasticate	ecclesia	cell
fabricate	college	ecclesial	cellular
fabrication	collegian	ecclesiastical	cubicle
fabricant	collegium	ecclesiasticism	*conclave*
office	collegial	ecclesiology	space
ludic	collegiality	*ecclesi-*	spatial
ludicrous	collegiate	*ecclesio-*	culinary
gymnasium	university	Senate	culinarian
schola cantorum	academy	*curia*	study
scholar	academic	*villa*	
scholarship	academician		

Unit Seven
Lesson 70
Adiectiones – Adjectives

Adjectives in Latin were declined in a similar but simpler fashion compared with nouns, in that feminine adjectives used the first declension format and masculine or neuter adjectives followed the second declension format. So if you see the Latin word for "high or deep" *altus, alta, altum* observe that *alta* (f.) would be used to modify feminine nouns, *altus* for masculine nouns, and *altum* for neuter nouns. When you see a word given ending in *–us,* know that the feminine and neuter forms are lurking silently nearby. In Latin, the adjective (from *adiacere* "to lie near") followed the noun it modified.

Meus, mea, meum – **mea culpa** "through **my** fault" to acknowledge an error
      Tuus – your   *Suus* – his, hers, its
Observe the following adjectives that surface frequently in English, often as a prefix.
 bonus- good - **bene**diction "good speaking or a blessing"; **bene**factor "one who does good for another"; **bene**ficent [be NIH fi sunt] "performing acts of kindness and charity"; **bene**fit "something that promotes well-being"; **bene**volent (+ *volens* "wishing") "wishing well" (but NOT **A** WISHING WELL, OK?).
malus- bad, badly, abnormal, inadequate- **mal**ediction "speaking badly of another; a curse"; **mal**edict "accursed"; **mal**efactor "one who commits an offense of the law; an evil-doer"; **mal**eficence [mal EF ih sense]"act of committing harm or evil"; **mal**feasance [mal FEE sense]"misconduct by a public official" ; **mal**adjusted "lacking harmony with one's environment"; **mal**adroit [mal uh draw] "awkward"; **mal**aprop[mal uh PROP] "unintentionally humorous misuse of a word"; **mal**apropos [mal ah pro PO] "in an inappropriate or inopportune way"; **mal**content "one who bears a grudge from a sense of grievance"; **mal**evolent (+ *volens* "wishing") "wishing evil or ill will; an unkind spirit".

 multi Many or Multiple or Much – **multiple, multilingual, multicultural, multitudinous, multiplication, multiplier, multiplicand**, etc.
 pauci Few -- **paucity** "smallness of number, fewness; smallness of quantity, dearth" – "They suffered from a paucity of opportunities." (Antonym: plethora)

amicus Friendly – **amicable,** "characterized by friendly good will, peaceable"; **amiable** "generally agreeable; being friendly, sociable and congenial"
 inimicus Unfriendly – **inimical** "being *adverse* often by reason of *malevolence*"

 longus Long – **long, e**l**ongate** (**elongated**) "make (or made) longer"; **longitude,** "an imaginary line extending from pole to pole; a meridian (from Latin *meri* "middle" + *dies* "day")"; **longitudinal; longanimity** (+ *animus* "soul") "a disposition to bear injuries patiently; forbearance" *brevis* Short – **brevity** "shortness of duration; shortness of conciseness of expression"

latus Wide or Side – **lateral** "extending from side to side"; **latitude** "imaginary horizontal lines circling the earth starting with the equator; freedom of action or choice"; **lats** "slang term for *latissimi dorsi*, meaning 'broadest muscle of the back'"

novus New – **novel** "new, not resembling something known or seen before"; **novice** "beginner; a person *admitted* into probationary membership in a religious community"; **renovate** "to make new again";

antiquus Old – **antique** "a relic or object of ancient times"; **antiquity** "ancient times, esp. those before the middle ages"

senex, senis Old (for people) *senior* Older – **senior** "a person older than another; a person with higher standing or rank"

vetus Old (experienced) – **veteran** "a person of long experience in some occupation or skill"

aequus Equal – **equal** "like in quantity, nature or status"; **equalize** "to make equal; to compensate for"; **equable** "uniform, marked by lack of variation or **inequality**"; **equate** "to make equal, to equalize"; **equity** "justice according to natural law; freedom from bias or favoritism"; **equanimity** "evenness of mind, right disposition, balanced"; **equivocal** (+ *vocare)* "subject to two or more interpretations and often used to confuse"; **equivocate** "to use equivocal language with the intent to deceive"; **equilateral** "having all sides equal"; **equidistant** (+ *distare* to stand apart) "equally distant"; **equivalence** "a state of balance between two objects"; **equinox** "lit. equal nights; one of the two times a year (spring & fall) when day and night are the same length"; etc.   Vide: **unequivocal**

dissimilis Unequal – **dissimilar** "unlike"; **dissimulate** (+ *simulare* "to simulate") "to hide under a false appearance"; **dissimilitude** "lack of resemblance"

Are you getting the feeling that there are multiple options based on Latin roots and stems?   REVIEW:

mea culpa	*mal*adjusted	paucity	inequality
bonus-	*mal*adroit	amicable	<u>equ</u>ate
bene<u>diction</u>	*mal*aprop	amiable	<u>equ</u>ity
bene<u>fact</u>or	*mal*apropos	inimical	<u>equ</u>animity
bene<u>fic</u>ent	*mal*content	brevity	<u>equ</u>ivocal
bene<u>fi</u>t	*mal*evolent	longitudinal	<u>equ</u>ivocate
*bene*volent	multiple	<u>long</u>animity	<u>equ</u>idistant
malus-	multilingual	<u>lateral</u>	<u>equ</u>ivalence
male<u>diction</u>	multicultural	<u>latitude</u>	<u>equ</u>inox
male<u>dict</u>	multitudinous	<u>lats</u>	unequivocal
male<u>fact</u>or	multiplication	<u>equal</u>	dissimilar
male<u>fic</u>ence	multiplier	<u>equ</u>alize	dissimulate
mal<u>f</u>easance	multiplicand	<u>equ</u>able	dissimilitude

Unit Seven

Lesson 71
Numeri – Numbers and MORE

Here is a reference chart for Latin numbers, cardinal and <u>ord</u>inal (by order).

Latin <u>Cardinal</u> numbers	Latin <u>Ordinal</u> numbers
One 1 - unus, una, unum	First 1st *primus (-a, -um)*
Two 2 - duo, duae, duo	Second 2nd *secundus, alter*
Three 3 - tres, tres, tria	Third 3rd *tertius*
Four 4 - quattuor	Fourth 4th *quartus*
Five 5 - quinque	Fifth 5th *quintus*
Six 6 - sex	Sixth 6th *sextus*
Seven 7 - septem	Seventh 7th *septimus*
Eight 8 - octo	Eighth 8th *octavus*
Nine 9 - novem	Ninth 9th *nonus*
Ten 10 - decem	Tenth 10th *decimus*
Eleven 11 - undecim	Eleventh 11th *undecimus*
Twelve 12 - duodecim	Twelfth 12th *duodecimus*
Thirteen 13 - tredecim	Thirteenth 13th *tertius decimus*
Fourteen 14 - quattuordecim	Fourteenth 14th *quartus decimus*
Fifteen 15 - quindecim	Fifteenth 15th *quintus decimus*
Sixteen 16 - sedecim	Sixteenth 16th *sextus decimus*
Seventeen 17 - septendecim	Seventeenth 17th *septimus decimus*
Eighteen 18 - duodeviginti	Eighteenth 18th *duodevice(n)simus*,
Nineteen 19 - undeviginti	Nineteenth 19th *undevice(n)simus*
Twenty 20 - viginti	Twentieth 20th *vice(n)simus*
Twenty one 21 - viginti unus	Twenty first 21st. *unus et vice(n)simus*
Thirty 30 triginta	Thirtieth 30th *trice(n)simus* or *trigesimus*
Forty 40 - quadraginta	Fortieth 40th *quadrage(n)simus*
Fifty 50 - quinquaginta	Fiftieth 50th *quinquage(n)simus*
Sixty 60 - sexaginta	Sixtieth 60th *sexage(n)simus*
Seventy 70 - septuaginta	Seventieth 70th *septuage(n)simus*
Eighty 80 - octoginta	Eightieth 80th *octoge(n)simus*
Ninety 90 - nonaginta	Ninetieth 90th *nonage(n)simus*
One Hundred 100 - centum	One hundredth 100th *cente(n)simus*
Two hundred 200 - ducenti, -ae, -a	Two hundredth 200th *ducente(n)simus*
300 - trecenti, -ae, -a	300th *trecentensimus*
400 - quadrigenti, +	400th *quadringentensimus*
500 - quingenti, +	500th *quingentensimus*
600 - sescenti, +	600th *sescentensimus*
700 - septingenti, +	700th *septingentensimus*
800 - octingenti, octingentae, octingenta	800th *octingentensimus*
900 - nongenti, nongentae, nongenta	900th *nongentensimus*
One thousand 1000 - mille	One Thousandth 1000th *millensimus*
Two thousand 2000 - duo milia	Two thousandths 2000th *bis millensimus*

OK, you don't have to memorize the numbers ... unless you really want to.
Numbers generally behave like adjectives ("There is **one** thing I really like." "This is her **first** birthday."), but depending on the context and structure of the sentence, they may act like a noun ("She is the **one**." "His birthday is on the **first**.") or even a pronoun ("**Twelve** were found alive.").
Adjectives need to agree with the noun they modify in number and gender.
The only singular number is ONE; all others are plural.

Let's lay in some Greek numbers for comparison. ***Observe*** the word in parentheses.

eis, mia, ev; (mono)- - 1
duo; dis (di-) - 2
treis, tria; tris (tri-) - 3
tettares, tettara; terakis (tetra-) - 4
pente; pentakis (penta-) - 5
hex (hexa-) - 6
hepta (hepta-) - 7
octô (octa-) - 8
ennea - 9
deca (deca-) - 10

endeca - 11
dodeca - 12
treiskaideca (trideca-) - 13
tettares kai deca - 14
pentekaideca - 15
hekkaideca - 16
heptakaideca - 17
oktôkaideca - 18
enneakaideca - 19
eicosi (icosa-) - 20
hecaton - 100

What words do we use to measure the passage of time from year to year?
Think Latin ROOT and Stems-, along with the *–ennial* or *–enniel* ending.

Uni	**annual** (every year – fr. *anuus* "annual")
Bi- duo-	**biennial** (occurring every two years),
Tri-	**triennial** (occurring every three years),
Quadri- Quart-	**quadriennial** (occurring every four years)
Quinque- Quint-	**quinquenniel** (occurring every five years)
Sex-	**sexenniel** (occurring every six years)
Sept-	**septenniel** (occurring every seven years)
Oct-	**octenniel** (occurring every eight years)
Nonus- Novem-	**novenniel** (occurring every nine years)
Deca- Dec- De-	**decenniel** (occurring every ten years)

Even though the Greeks had a chronological head start on developing mathematical insights, their verbal numbering was quite cumbersome. As the Romans refined their math, they applied their numeric prefixes, many of which have stuck with us today.

The **decimal numeral system** (also called base ten or occasionally denary) is most frequently used in modern civilization. It is based on the number 10 (*decim*).
Decimal notation often refers to the base-10 positional notation based on powers of ten.

Think of how it works with mathematical exponents (e.g. 10 x 10 = 10^2 = 100   or 10 x 10 x 10 = 10^3 = 1,000). The ending typically is -illion. (THINK: ex + ponere)
  A (million), billion 10^9, trillion 10^{12}, gradrillion 10^{15}, quintillion 10^{18}, sextillion, septillion, octillion, nonillion, decillion 10^{33} (10 + 33 zeroes)

Now try the much simpler number of people in a musical ensemble (after 3, -tet).
  Soloist, duet, trio, quartet, quintet, sextet, septet, octet, etc.

Think about the ordinal relationships or ranks (typically ending with –ary).
  Primary (of the first rank)
  Secondary (of the second rank) or binary
  Tertiary (of the third rank) or trinary
  Quaternary, quinary or quinquenary, senary or sexenary, septanary, octanary, nonary, denary

How about the number of sides (-laterals) on a shape or in an agreement?
  Unilateral, bilateral, trilateral, quadrilateral, quinquelateral, ... octilateral

How about the number of angles on a shape? CAUTION:
  Triangle (triangular), fr. Latin quadrangle (quadrangular) – now switch back to the Greek prefixes – pentangle, hexangle, heptangle, octangle, etc.
        Why? Take it up with the ancient Greeks and Romans.

Take a look at these terms that utilize Greek numeric prefixes:
  Triangle (a polygon with 3 angles and sides), tetragon (a polygon of four angles and sides), pentagon, hexagon, heptagon, octagon, enneagon, etc. (BTW, polygons with more sides are referred to as n-gons, with n referring to the number of sides.)

  Tetrahedron (a 3D figure called a polyhedron that has four faces), pentahedron, hexahedron, heptahedron, octahedron, enneahedron, decahedron, etc.

  Biathlete (athlete who competes in two events), triathelete, tetrathlete, pentathlete, decathlete ...   Vide: biathlon, triathlon, etc.

  Tetrameter (+ metron "measure" – a line of verse consisting of five metrical feet), pentameter, hexameter, heptameter, octameter, decameter

  Pentagram (penta + gram "line"), hexagram, heptagram, octagram, etc.

  Monarchy (ruler - one person), diarchy, triarchy, tetrarchy, pentarchy, hexarchy, heptarchy, etc.

The Greek words in bold (in parentheses on page 193) are the ones typically pre-fixed to words in English, such as the following sample terms:
monocracy (government by one person), **monocle** (one lens), **monocular** (effecting one eye), mono**theism** (one god), **monochromatic** (one color), **monotone, monogamy** (state of being married to one person), **monogram** (sign of identity unique to one's initials), **monopoly** (exclusive ownership by one), **mono**syllabic (one syllable), **tetrapod** (animal with two pairs of limbs), **tetrachloride** (a chloride containing four atoms of chlorine, etc.

Observe these words based on the Latin numeric prefixes:
Unicycle, unicameral (legislature with one chamber or house), **unicorn, uniform, unidimensional, unique, biannual** (occurring two times in a year);
bicameral, bicentennial (200th anniversary), **bicycle** (vehicle with two wheels in tandem), **bifocal** (two focal lengths), **bigamy** (marriage to two people at the same time), **bigamist** (*a larga fog ina Italy*, or a person married to two people at the same time), *bilingual* (able to use two languages with *equal* fluency), **biped** (two feet), **bicuspid** (a tooth with two cusps), etc.

> *Caution:* there is also a Greek prefix *bio-* or *bi-* meaning life (e.g. *bio*logy). Watch the context to determine the meaning. More on this later.

Triangulate, tri-cornered, tricuspid, tricycle, trident (a 3 pronged spear), **triceratops** (+ Gr. *keras* "horn" + *ops* "face" – "large dinosaur with three horns), etc.

> *Caution:* there is also a Greek prefix *hepat-* or *hepato-* meaning "liver" (e.g. *hepa*tectomy "*excision* of the liver"). Watch the context to determine the meaning.

Some times, it's hard to tell the exact origin, or even harder to care. **The key is for you to be able to look at any word, then identify the root word or stem and affixes (pre- and suf-) connected to the stem.**

Review: no words, just parts. Which combinations work together for you?

Uni **1 L.**	*mono*- 1	*-illion*
Bi- duo- **2 L.**	*di- or dy* - 2	*-tet*
Tri- **3 L.**	*tri*- 3	*-ary*
Quadri- Quart- **4 L.**	*tetra*- 4	*-gon*
Quinque- Quint- **5 L.**	*penta*- 5	*-hedron*
Sex- **6 L.**	*hexa*- 6	*-meter*
Sept- **7 L.**	*hepta*- 7	*-gram*
Oct- **8 L.**	*octa*- 8	*-ennial*
Nonus- Novem- **9 L.**	*ennea* - 9	*-angle*
Deca- Dec- **10 L.**	*deca*- 10	*-lateral*
		-archy
		-cracy
		-ped

Unit Seven

Lesson 72
Mensura – MEASUREMENT & MATH

Well, now that we have all these cool numbers, how can we use them?
You can measure length (**longitudo, -onis**), width (**amplitudo, -onis; latitudo, -onis**),
as well as height or depth (**altitudo, -onis**). Vide: <u>longitude</u>, <u>amplitude</u>, <u>altitude</u>
You can find out how short (**brevis, -e**) or tall (**altus, -a, -um; excelsus, -a, -um;
procerus, -a, -um**); high (**altus**) or low (**abiectus, -a, -um; demissus**).
   Vide: <u>brief</u>, <u>altimeter</u>, <u>abject</u> "sunk to a low state, as in 'abject poverty'",
<u>demit</u>, <u>demission</u> "resignation, abdication".

With your knowledge of numeric stems, you can measure time (**tempus, -oris**) by
the hour (**hora, -ae**), minute [MIN it] "1/60th of an hour" (**minutus**), second "1/60th of
a minute" or the second sexagesimal (60 part division) of an hour (**secundus**).
Vide: <u>temporary</u>, <u>tempo</u>, <u>temporal</u>, <u>minute</u> [my NYUTE], <u>minutia</u> [mih NU shia] "the
small stuff we're not supposed to sweat"

You can also measure longer periods of time, such as a day (**dies, diei**). The Romans
didn't really have a specific term for "week", but **septimana** (or seven days) comes
close. Month (**mensis, -is**) and a six month period (**sex + mensis**) gives us **semester**.
   Vide: **menses, menstrual, menstruation, menopause**
Previously, we saw year (**annus, -i**); here are some its related terms (**annual,
annually, annualize, annuity**). A key unit of the Roman military included 100 soldiers
who were led by a **centurion**. This evolved to our **century**, or period of 100 years.

This lays a solid foundation for working mathematically. I bet you can figure out
these terms: **addere, subtrahare, multiplicare et** (and) **dividere. Adding, subtracting,
multiplying** and **dividing** are all the essential ingredients in **arithmetic** (fr. Gr.
arithmein "to count" fr. *arithmos* "number") "a branch of mathematics that deals
with real, non-negative numbers and their operations".

Mathematical **operations** (fr. L. *operare* "to work" fr. L. *opus, opera* "work") "any of
the various mathematical processes (e.g. addition)".

You also have heard of **algebra** (fr. Arabic *al-jabr* "the reduction") "a generalization
of arithmetic in which letters representing numbers are combined according to the
rules of arithmetic". Students of algebra should be able to:
- Understand patterns, relations and **functions** (e.g. "a variable that depends
  on and varies with another")
- Represent and **analyze** (fr. G. *analyein* "to break up") mathematical
  situations and structures using algebraic symbols

- Use mathematical models to represent and understand **quantitative** (fr. L. *quantitas* "quantity" – "involving the measurement of quantity or amount") relationships
- ***Analyze*** change in various contexts

Remember all the multi-sided (or should I say ***multilateral***) shape names from the last lesson? You know – the *–gons* and *–hedrons*? That is all part of **geometry** (fr. Gr. *geo* "earth" + *metria* "to measure") "the branch of mathematics that deals with measurements, properties and relationships of points, line, angles, surfaces and solids", with **mathematics** (fr. Gr. *mathemat* or *mathema* "learning or mathematics" fr. *mathenein* "to learn, which is akin to pay attention") "the science of numbers and their operations, interrelations, combinations, generalizations and abstractions, as well as of space configurations".

In geometry, among other goals students should be able to:
- Analyze characteristics and properties of two- and three-dimensional geometric shapes (*-gons* and *–hedrons*) and develop mathematical **arguments** (fr. L. *arguere* "a reason given in proof or rebuttal") about geometric relationships
- Use ***visualization*** (the process of seeing how some process works), spatial (fr. L. *spatium* "space") reasoning, and geometric modeling to solve problems

longitude	menses	dividing
amplitude	menstrual	arithmetic
altitude	menstruation	operations
brief	menopause	algebra
altimeter	semester	analyze
abject	annual	quantitative
demit	annually	*multilateral*
demission	annualize	geometry
temporary	annuity	mathematics
tempo	century	arguments
temporal	adding	
minute	subtracting	
minutia	multiplying	

Unit Seven
Lesson 73
Mensura Plura – More MEASUREMENT & MATH

If you put two Greek words together (*trigonon* "triangle" + *metria* "measure"), you get **trigonometry,** "the study of right triangles". We have previously worked with terms that are relevant to this and other aspects of math. From *sectare*, we get *bisect* "to cut in two", *intersect* "to cut across", **secant** "a straight line cutting a curve at two or more points" and **cosecant** "a trigonometric function that for an acute angle is the ratio of the *hypotenuse* of a right *triangle* of which the angle is considered part and the leg opposite of the angle". Then, you get to have more fun with **sine** and **cosine**, which offer variations on that ratio theme.

Excuse me for a moment while I go off on a **tangent** (fr. L. *tangere* "to gently touch") "a single point where a straight lines touches to circumference of a circle"; ("diverge from the current topic") with **circumference** (fr. L. *circum* "around" + *ferre* "to carry or bear") "the perimeter of a circle; the external boundary of a figure; periphery", with **perimeter** (fr. Gr. *peri* "all around , near, enclosing" + *metria*) "the boundary of a closed plane figure", with **boundary** (fr. L. *bindere* "to bind") "something that fixes a limit".

After studying *trig* (the affectionate name for trigonometry), you may study **calculus**. This comes from the Roman transportation system … ??? Yes, that's correct – from their taxicabs. The story goes that the drivers (or peddlers, if you will) had to have some way to keep track of the distance traveled. So they attached a small device to drop a pebble (**calculus**) into a cup after a certain number of rotations of their tire. In this way they could **calculate** the fare. Now, calculus comes in two flavors – **differential** calculus and **integral** calculus. Just as geometry is the study of shapes, calculus is the study of change, specifically rates of change.

In your mathematical meanderings, you may run across **polynomials** (fr. Gr. *poly* "many" + L. *nomen* & Gr. *onoma* "name") "a mathematical expression of one or more algebraic terms", or even **binomials** or **trinomials**.

You will probably encounter a **parabola** (fr. G. *parabole* "a comparison") – "a plane curve generated by a point moving so that its distance from a fixed point I equal to its distance from a fixed line". Vide: **parabolic curve**

Without yielding to **hyperbole** [high PUR bo lee] (fr. Gr. *hyper-* + *ballein* "to throw") "extravagant exaggeration (e.g. "running 90 miles an hour"), I imagine you will encounter **hyperbola** or even a **hyperbolic** curve, "a plane curve generated by a point so moving that the difference of the distances from two fixed points is a constant".

You might even encounter the Greek symbol **π** (sometimes written *pi*). **π** is "a mathematical constant whose value is the ratio of any circle's circumference to its diameter". It is found by *dividing* 22 by 7. The *dividend* is a number that never ends or repeats beginning with 3.141592653589793... which is usually shortened to 3.1416 or 3.14.

Math fans celebrate **π** on 3/14 (March 14th).

BTW, don't let the terms scare you away from math. It's just a secret language until you understand it. *Mathenein* and ENJOY!

Also – what did you learn in this lesson?

trigonometry	*peri-*	parabola
bisect	perimeter	parabolic curve
intersect	boundary	
hypotenuse	calculus	hyperbole
triangle	calculate	hyperbola
sine	differential	hyperbolic
cosine	integral	Pi **π**
tangent		
	polynomials	
circum-	binomials	
circumference	trinomials	

Unit Seven
Lesson 74
Greek & Latin Stems

Greek and Latin offer us numerous stems that show up in English.

prot- proto- (G.) 1st **prototype** "original model on which something is patterned"; "code *prescribing* strict adherence to etiquette"
        Vide: **prototypical, protohistory, protohuman, protoplast**

omni- (L.) all **omniscient** "knowing all things"; **omnipotent** "having virtually unlimited power or influence; can do all things"; **omnificent** "unlimited in creative power"
        Vide: **omnidirectional, omnipresent, omnibus**

pan- (G.) all **panorama** "unobstructed view of an area in all directions"; **panacea** "a remedy for all ills or difficulties; a cure-all"; **pandemic** (*pan + demos* "the people") "illness or disease spreading across a wide area and effecting a high percentage of the people"; **Pandemonium** (*pan + daimon* "evil spirit, devil") "hell in Milton's *Paradise Lost*"; no caps "a wild uproar, tumult"
        Vide: **Pan-American**

Now, it's time for just HALF the story …

semi- (L.) half **semi aquatic** "growing equally well in or adjacent to water"; or twice **semiannual** "occurring every six months or twice a year"; **semiquaver** "1/16th note"
        Vide: **semiautomatic, semiconductor, semidarkness, semiformal**

demi- (L.) half of **demitasse** "a small cup of black coffee"; **demigod** "mythological being with more power than a mere mortal"; **demisemiquaver** "1/32nd note"

hemi- (G.) half **hemisphere** "half of a celestial sphere"; **hemiplegia** "total or partial paralysis of one side of the body"; **hemidemisemiquaver** "1/64th note"

If you want to talk about BOTH sides … well, sometimes I do and sometimes I don't…

ambi- ambo- (G.) both **ambivalence** "simultaneous and contradictory feelings (e.g. attraction and repulsion) toward an object, person or action"; **ambivert** "having the characteristics of both and *introvert* and an *extrovert*"

amph- amphi- (G.) on both sides **amphitheatre** "a very large auditorium"; **amphibology** "a sentence or phrase (e.g. 'Nothing is good enough for you') susceptible to more than one interpretation"

Speaking of phrases, "All things being equal" comes from …

equi- equa- (L.) equally **equiangular** "equal angles"; **equanimity** "evenness of mind, esp. under stress; right disposition; balanced"; again **equilateral**

Some things are really **small** …

micro- (G.) small, *minūte* **microflora** "minūte plants, invisible to the naked eye"; **microeconomics** "study of economics in terms of individual areas of activity, e.g. household finances"

Vide: **microphone, microscope, microbiology, micrometer**, etc.

mini- (L.) small, miniature **minibus** "a small bus or van"

Vide: **miniseries, miniskirt, minicamp, minimax** (yes, really...)

milli- (L.) 1/1000th of a unit **millisecond** "one thousandth of a second"

Vide: **milliliter, milligram, millivolt**

Some things are really **big** …

macro- (G.) large or long **macroeconomics** "a study of economics in terms of whole systems"; **macroscopic** "large enough to be observed by the naked eye"

maxi- (L.) extra large or extra long **maximal** "being an upper limit; complete"

Vide: **maximum, maximin** (*that's right **maximin** – look it up*)

Review:

prot- proto-	Pandemonium	*ambi- ambo-*	*mini-*
prototype	pandemonium	ambivalence	minibus
protocol	Pan-American	ambivert	miniseries
prototypical		*amph- amphi-*	miniskirt
protohistory	*semi-*	amphitheatre	minicamp
protohuman	semiaquatic	amphibology	minimax
protoplast	semiannual		*milli-*
	semiautomatic	*equi- equa-*	millisecond
omni-	semiconductor	equiangular	milliliter
omniscient	semidarkness	equanimity	milligram
omnipotent	semiformal		millivolt
omnificent	semiquaver	*micro-*	
omnidirectional	*demi-*	microflora	*macro-*
omnipresent	demitasse "	microeconomics	macroeconomics
omnibus	demigod	microphone	macroscopic
	demisemiquaver	microscope	*maxi-*
pan-	*hemi-*	microbiology	maximal
panorma	hemisphere	micrometer	maximum
panacea "	hemiplegia		maximin
pandemic	hemidemisemiquaver		

Unit Seven
Lesson 75
More Greek & Latin Stems

Some times, there are **many** …
mult- multi- (L.) many **multiplex** a complex that houses multiple movie theatres"
   Vide: **multinational, multilevel, multitalented, multiply, multivitamin**, etc.
poly- (G.) many **polyhedron** "a solid formed by many plane faces"
   Vide: **polysyllabic, polytechnic, polypropylene**, etc.

Some times, it's the **whole** thing …
hol- holo- (G.) whole, total **hologram** "a 3 dimensional image created by laser"

… or just **sounds** or **seems** like it.
hom- homo- (G.) same, similar, alike **homonym** "two or more words spelled or pronounced alike but different in meaning"; **homology** "similarity often attributed to common origin"; **homogeneous** "of uniform composition or structure throughout"
sym- syn- sys- (G.) same **synonym** "two or more words that have the same or similar meanings"; **symmetry** "balanced proportions (e.g. *bilateral* or radial ~)"; **symbiosis** "the intimate living together of two *dissimilar* organisms in a mutually beneficial relationship; if both organisms benefit, it is called *mutualism*; a **symbiotic** relationship"
is- iso- (G.) equal, similar, alike **isomorphic** "being of identical or similar form"; **isometrics** "exercising of muscle groups using resistance"; **isosceles** (*iso* + *skelos* "leg")"a triangle having two equal sides"
similis- (L.) similar, alike **similar** "having characteristics in common; strictly comparable"; **verisimilar** "having the appearance of truth"
   Vide: **similarly, similarity, similitude, verisimilitude, dissimilar**

Try putting several stems together:
soph- (G.) wise, clever
-moros (G.) foolish   **sophomore** "wise fool"
biblio- (L.) book
-theca (L.) case, covering bibliotheca = library

If …
morph- (G.) means "having a form"
-morph -morphic -morphous (G.) having a form
Then …
Amorphic means "without form"
Polymorphous means "lit. 'many forms'; having, assuming or occurring in various forms, characters or styles"

Previously, you learned that in Latin …

> *bene-* (L.) good and *male-* (L.) bad   evil

In Greek …

> *eu-* (G.) good and *mis-* (G.) wrong, bad

So, **euphoria** means "a feeling of well being or elation"; **eulogy** normally delivers "good words or high praise at a funeral"; **euphemism** (+ *pheme* "speech or word") "the substitution of (good words) an agreeable or inoffensive expression for one that may offend or suggest something unpleasant"; **eugenics** "a branch of science that deals with improvement of hereditary qualities of a race or breed"

Mis- yields a **plethora** ("abundance, excess superfluity, profusion") of words in its role as prefix.

Miscellaneous "consisting of *diverse* things or members, heterogeneous"; **miscreant** "one who behaves criminally or viciously; infidel, heretic"; **misdemeanor** "a crime less serious than a felony, a misdeed (bad deed)"

You can **mis**interpret, **mis**pronounce, **mis**communicate, **mis**handle, **mis**lead, **mis**read, **mis**construe, **mis**place, **mis**translate, **mis**utilize, *mis*transcribe or be **mis**taken, **mis**understood, **mis**chievous, or just plain **mis**erable. Did I miss any?

> Vide: next lesson …

Time to see something beautiful –

kalei- (G.) *kalos* "beautiful" yields **kaleidoscope** "an instrument containing loose bits of colored material reflected in an endless variety of images"

But it might be *pseudo-* (G.) false   **pseudonym** or …

-let small, diminutive   **star**let ank**let**

mult- multi-	**syn**onym	*biblio-*	**mis**creant
multiplex	**sym**metry	*-theca*	**mis**demeanor
multinational	**sym**biosis	*morph-*	**mis**interpret
multilevel	**sym**biotic	*-morph*	**mis**pronounce
multitalented	*is- iso-*	*-morphic*	**mis**communicate
multiply	**iso**morphic	*-morphous*	**mis**handle
multivitamin	**iso**metrics	a**morph**ic	**mis**lead
poly-	**iso**sceles	**poly**morphous	**mis**construe
polyhedron	*similis-*	*bene-*	**mis**place
polysyllabic	**simil**ar	*male-*	**mis**read
polytechnic	**veri**similar	*eu-*	**mis**translate
polypropylene	**simil**arly	*mis-*	**mis**utilize
hol- holo-	**simil**arity	**eu**phoria	*mis*transcribe
hologram	**simil**itude	**eu**logy	**mis**taken
hom- homo-	**veri**similitude	**eu**phemism	**mis**understood
homonym	**dissimil**ar	**eu**genics	**mis**chievous
homology	*soph-*	*mis-*	**mis**erable
homogeneous	*-moros*	**plethora**	**kale**idoscope
sym- syn- sys-	**soph**omore	**mis**cellaneous	

Unit Seven

Lesson 76
Even More Greek & Latin Stems

I have mentioned previously that stems can be quite similar in appearance but with significant differences in meaning. One such example is the Greek word *misein* "to hate". The stem is *miso-* and shows up in the following words in English.

Misogamy (*miso + gamy* "marriage") [mih SOG uh mee] "the hatred of marriage".
Misogamist "a person who hates marriage"

Misogyny (*miso + gyne* "woman or queen") [mih SAGH uh nee] "hatred of women"
Misogynist "a person who hates women"

Misanthropy (*miso + anthropo* "human being") "hatred of mankind"
Misanthrope "the person who mistrusts or hates mankind"

I agree that it is *bad* to *hate*. Just observe the context to understand the difference.

Let's look at some terms that show up about nature. Use the skills you have been accumulating about roots, stems and affixes.

ge- geo- (G.) earth **geometry, geology** "science that deals with the history of the earth, esp. as recorded in rocks"**, geodesic** "shortest line between two points on a given plane; geodetic", **geode** "a nodule of stone with a cavity filled with crystals", **geography** "science that deals with the description of the features of the earth's surface", **geohydrology, geocentric, geophysics, geomorphology** (observe the three related roots within this word), etc.

bio- (G.) life **biology, biochemistry, biodegradable, biogeography, biohazard, biosynthesis, biotechnology, bionomics,** etc.

helio- (G.) sun **heliograph, heliometer, heliotrope** (+ *trop* "to turn"), **helium,** etc.

sol- (L.) sun (as before) **solar, solarium** "room for gathering sun", **solarize,** etc.

selen- (G.) moon **selenite, selenium** "nonmetallic element, atomic # 34", **selenocentric, selenology,** etc.

luna- (L.) moon **lunar, lunate** "crescent shaped", **lunacy** "intermittent insanity once attributed to phases of the moon" *hydr- hydro-* (G.) water **hydro**logy, **hydrogen** (+ *gene* "born of") "the lightest, simplest element, atomic #1; water is generated by its combustion", **hydro**meter, **hydro**lysis, **hydroponics** "growing of plants in nutrient solution instead of soil", **hydro**meter, **hydro**morphic, **hydro**thermal, **hydro**sphere, etc.

aqua- (L.) water **aqua** "a light bluish green color", **aquarium, aquaculture, aquanaut** (+ *nauta* "sailor"), ***aqueduct*, aqueous, aquatic,** etc.

lith- lithic- (G.) stone **lith**ology "the study of rocks", **lithium** "element, atomic #3", **lith**ography "printing process", **lithosphere** "outer part of solid earth, remember *terra firma ?*", **lithic,** etc.

phyto- -phyte (G.) plant **lithophyte** "a plant that grows on rock", **phytochemistry** "the chemistry of plants", **phytopathogen** "an organism parasitic on a plant host, e.g. mistletoe", **phytotoxic** "toxic to plants", etc.

phon- phono- -phony (G.) sound **phonograph, phonology** "science of sound", **phono**cardiogram (fr. G. *kardio* "heart"), **symphony,** etc.

photo- (G.) light **photometry, photogenic, photon** "a unit of measurement of light", **photographic, photojournalism, photolithography, photogrammetry,** etc.

pyro- (G.) fire **pyrotechnic** "firework", **pyrogenic** "born of or produced by fire", **pyrometer, pyrophoric** "igniting spontaneously", etc.

electr- electro- (L.) **electricity, electrify, electrocrdiogram, electrode, electrocute, electrodynamics, electrodynamometer, electrolysis, electron, electronics,** etc.

dyn- dyna- (G.) power **dynamo, dynamometer, dynamics, dynamite,** etc.
rheo- (G.) flow, current **rheostat, rheology, rheometer,** etc.

Review the summary of the words from this lesson on the following page. As you are doing this, begin to look at suffixes and see which stems will work with them. For example, how many words can you think of that could end with -**METER**?

miso-	sol-	lith- lithic-	electr- electro-
Misogamy	solar	lithology	electricity
Misogamist	solarium	lithium	electrify
Misogyny	solarize	lithography	electrocrdiogram
Misogynist	selen-	lithosphere	electrode
Misanthrope	selenite	lithic, etc.	electrocute
Misanthropy	selenium		electrodynamics
	selenocentric	phyto-	electrodynamo-
ge- geo-	selenology	-phyte	meter
geometry		lithophyte	electrolysis
geology	luna-	phytochemistry	electron
geode	lunar	phytopathogen	electronics
geodesic	lunate	phytotoxic	
geodgraphy	lunacy		dyn- dyna-
geohydrology		phon- phono-	dynamo
geocentric	hydr- hydro-	-phony	dynamometer
geophysics	hydrology	Phonograph	dynamics
geomorphology	hydrogen	phonology	dynamite
	hydrometer	phonocardiogram	
bio-	hydrolysis	symphony	rheo-
biology	hydroponics		rheostat
biochemistry	hydrometer	photo-	rheology
biodegradable	hydromorphic	photometry	rheometer
biogeography	hydrothermal	photogenic	
biohazard	hydrosphere	photon	
biosynthesis		photographic	
biotechnology	aqua-	photojournalism	
bionomics	aqua	photolithography	
	aquarium	photogrammetry	
helio-	aquaculture		
heliograph	aquanaut	pyro-	
heliometer	aqueduct	pyrotechnic	
heliotrope	aqueous	pyrogenic	
helium	aquatic	pyrometer	
		pyrophoric	

Recognizing these words when you see them is great!
Being able to explain them and use them correctly in a sentence is even better!!

Unit Seven
Lesson 77
Loves & Hates, Manias & Phobias, OH MY

People are all unique, and sometimes it is their Loves & Hates, Manias & Phobias that create that uniqueness. These affixes from the Greek will help you identify their characteristics.

-phobe (G.) person who is excessively fearful

-phobia (G.) abnormal fear

-mania (G.) a mental disorder or wild enthusiasm for …

-maniac (G.) person with a mental disorder or wild enthusiasm for …

mis- miso- (G.) hating or hater

-philia (G.) friendly feeling towards; abnormal liking for …

-philiac (G.) a person with a friendly feeling towards or abnormal liking for …

phil- philo- (G.) lover of; loving; having a strong liking for …

-phil -philo (G.) lover of; loving; having a strong liking for …

First, add a few new words:

Acr- acro- (G.) height	*Claus- claust-* (L.) closed space, cloister
Agor- agoro- (G.) a gathering place; the marketplace in ancient Greece	*Franc-* French
	Gyn- woman
Anglo- English	*Klept-* (G.) stealing, theft
Arachn- (G.) spider	*Megal-* or *megalo-* (G.) large, of giant size, grandiose
Aritmo- arithmetic	*Nykt-* (G.) night
Astr- astro- (G.) star, heavens, outer space; *astra-* lightning	*Ophidio-* (G.) snake
	Techno- technology

Add these to words you have previously learned and explain the following terms:

acrophobia	kleptomaniac
agoraphobia	megalomaniac
Anglophile	misogynist
aquaphobe	misanthrope
aquaphobia	nyctophobia
arachniphobia	ophidiophobia
astrophile	pedophile
astraphobia	pyromaniac
blbllophile	pyromania
claustrophobia	pyrophobia
Francophile	technophile
homophobia	technophobia
hydrophobia	triskaidekaphobia

The answers are on the next page in case you need help.

Solutions:

Fear of heights (*acra-*)
Fear of crowds or open spaces (*agora-*)
Love of things English (*Angl-*)
Fear of water (*aqua-*)
Person with a fear of water (*aqua-*)
Abnormal fear of spiders (*arachn-*)
Star lover (*astro-*)
Fear of lightning and thunderstorms (*astra-*)
Lover of books (*biblio-*)
Fear of closed spaces (*claust-*)
Someone with a strong affinity for France or French culture (*Franc-*)
Fear of homosexuals (*hom-*)
Fear of water (*aqua-*)

Person with a persistent neurotic impulse to steal (*klept-*)
Person with an exaggerated sense of self (*megalo-*)
Hater of women (gy*n*-)
Hater of mankind (anthropo-)
Fear of darkness (*nykt-*)
Fear of snakes (*ophidio-*)
Pervert who is attracted to children (*ped-*)
Person with a persistent neurotic impulse to start fires (*pyro-*)
A persistent neurotic impulse to start fires (*pyro-*)
Fear of fire (*pyro-*)
Person comfortable with and loving to use technology (*techno-*)
Fear of technology (*tech-*)
Abnormal fear of the number thirteen (*triskaideca*)

Unit Seven

Lesson 78
Additional Prefixes & Roots

Here are more prefixes that should help you in your understanding of the new words you encounter every day. You should have a solid foundation to draw on for understanding these words. If you can't figure out the meaning from the roots, stems and affixes, look it up in a dictionary or on-line.

anti- against	**antibiotic, anti-apartheid, antibacterial**
ante- in front of	**anteroom, antebellum, ante mortem** (+ *mors* "death")
dia- through, between	**diagonal, diameter, dialogue**
retro- backward	**retrofit, retrograde, retroactive**
infra- (L.) below, lower than	**infrared, infrastructure, infrasonic**
endo- within	**endodontic, endometriosis, endophyte**
epi- on the outside	**epidermis, epilogue, epiphyte**
exo- outside of	**exodermis, exodontist, exoskeleton**
peri- beyond around	**perimeter, perihelion, pericardium**
para- by the side of	**paraprofessional, paradox, parabaloid,**
tele- at a distance; the end	**telekinesis, television, teleology**

-nym name	**homonym, synonym, antonym, pseudonym**
-oid resembling	**humanoid, asteroid, hyperboloid**
-osis action, process, disease	**hypnosis, osmosis, osteoporosis**
-otic of action, process, condition	**symbiotic, antibiotic, probiotic**
idio- idiot (G.) one's own personal	**idiosyncrasy, idiomorphic, idiopathic**
-eer person who does or makes something	**engineer, buccaneer** (expensive corn)

ethno- (G.) race	**ethno, ethnicity, ethnographer**
paleo- (G.) ancient	**paleontologist, Paleolithic, paleogeography**
anthro- anthropo- (G.) man	**anthropologist, anthropomorphic, anthropometry**
-gamy (G.) marriage	**monogamy, bigamy, polygamy, misogamy**
vice- (L.) one who takes the place of	**vice-admiral, vice-chancellor, vice president**

See if you can match these words and meanings (*answers in the Review*)

biped	a) Instrument for viewing beautiful images
dialog or dialogue	b) Instrument to measure power
dynamo	c) Conversation between two persons, oral or written
dynamometer	d) A forceful, energetic individual; a generator
kaleidoscope	e) Animal with two feet

209

narcolepsy	f) Branch of medicine for correction of skeletal deformities
ornithology	g) Condition characterized by *brief* attacks of deep sleep
orthopedics	h) One who helps a professional
paraprofessional	i) Study of birds
philosopher	j) A scholar, a thinker; a lover of wisdom

photometry	k) Branch of medicine dealing with mental disorders
psychiatry	l) Branch of science for measurement of intensity of light
rheostat	m) Examination of the nose
rhinoscopy	n) Instrument for measuring flow or current
selenocentric	o) Moon-centered

REVIEW:

anti-
antibiotic
anti-apartheid
antibacterial
ante-
anteroom
antebellum
ante mortem
dia-
diagonal
diameter
dialogue
retro-
retrofit
retrograde
retroactive
infra-
infrared
infrastructure
infrasonic
endo-
endodontics
endometriosis
endophyte
epi-
epidermis
epilogue
epiphyte

exo-
exodermis
exodontics
exoskeleton
peri-
perimeter
perihelion
pericardium
para-
paraprofessional
paradox
parabaloid
tele-
telekenesis
television
teleology
-nym
homonym
synonym
antonym
pseudonym
-oid
humanoid
asteroid
hyperboloid
-otic
symbiotic
antibiotic
probiotic

idio- idiot
idiosyncrasy
idiomorphic
idiopathic
-eer
engineer
buccaneer

ethno-
ethno
ethnocity
ethnographer
paleo-
paleontologist
paleolithic
paleogeography
anthro- anthropo-
anthropologist
anthropomorphic
anthropometry
-gamy
monogamy
bigamy
polygamy
misogamy

vice-
vice-admiral
vicechancellor
vice president

biped e)
dialog dialogue c)
dynamo b)
dynamometer d)
kaleidoscope a)

narcolepsy g)
ornithology i)
orthopedics f)
paraprofessional h)
philosopher j)

photometry l)
psychiatry k)
rheostat n)
rhinoscopy m)
selenocentric o)

Unit Seven
Lesson 79
Body parts

"Parts is Parts"
Based on your reservoir of developing verbal knowledge, think of the words you can
make from these body parts. (*Suggestions in the Review*)

Body *somata- (G.) corpus-* (L.)

Head *caput (L.)*

Heart *cardi- cardio- (G.)*

Lung *pneumo- (G.) pulmo- (L.)*

Mind *psyche- psycho- (G.)*
     mens, mentis (L.)

Nerves *neur- neuro- (G.)*

Ear *oto- (G.) aura- (L.)*

Eye *ophthmal- (G.) oculo- (L.)*

Nose *rhino- (g.) nasus (L.)*

Mouth *stoma- (G.) os, oris (L.)*

Bone *osteo- (G.) os- ossis- (L.)*

Blood *hemo- (G.) sanguis- (L.)*

Skin *dermis- (G.) cutis- (L.)*

Foot *-pod (G.) -ped (L.)*

Woman *gyn- (G.) mulier- (l.)*

Midwife *obstetric- (L.)*

Children *pedi- -pedics (G.)*

Protein *prote- proteo- (G.)*

Vein *phleb- phlebo- (G.)*

Fatty *lipo- -lip (G.)*

Sleep *narco- (G.)*

How about these bodily conditions or related actions?

genos (G.) natus- (L.) birth

-itis (G.) disease, inflammation

-ectomy (G.) removal

-iatry (fr. G. *iatron* "doctor") treatment

-lysis (G.) destruction, dissolving, loosening

-lepsy (G.) fit, attack

orth- ortho- (G.) straight

-scope (G.) skopein instrument for viewing

-stat (G.) instrument for reflecting movement

Review
somata- **somatology, somatotype, somatotropin**

corpus- **corporal, corporeal, corporate, corps, corpse**

caput- **capital, capricious, decapitation**

cardi- cardio- **cardiac, pericardial, tachycardia**

pneumo- **pneumonia, pneumograph, pneumonectomy, pneumotology**

pulmo- **pulmonary, pulmonate, cardiopulmonary**

psyche- psycho- **psychology, psychiatry, psychotic, psychosis, psychosomatic**

neur- neuro- **neurology, neuritis, neurotic, neurotoxin, neurogenic**

oto- **otitis, otocyst, otolithic, otoscope, otolaryngology**

aura- **aural, aurally**

ophthmal- **ophthmologist, ophthalmia, ophthalmoscope**
oculo- **ocular, oculist, ocularist, oculomotor, oculus**
rhino- **rhinitis, rhinoplasty, rhinoscopy, rhinovirus**
nasus **nasal, nasality, nasogastric, nasopharyngeal**
stoma- **stoma, stomatitis >> stomach**
os, oris **oral, orate, oration, oratory**
osteo- **osteal, osteitis, osteocyte, osteogenesis, osteopathy**
os- **osseus, ossification**
hemo- **hemostat, hemocyte, hemoglobin, hemolysis, hemophilliac, hemorrhage, hemorrhoid**
sanguis- **sanguine, sanguineous, sanguinary**
dermis- **dermatitis, dermatosis, dermatologist, epidermis, endodermis**
cutis- **cutis, cuticle**
prote- proteo- **protein, proteinaceous, proteinuria**
phleb- phlebo- **phlebology, phlebitis, phlebotomy, phlebotomist**
lipo- -lip **lipid, lipogenesis, lipotropic, liposuction**
pedi- -pedics **pediatrics, pediatrician, pedophile**

genos- **gene, genetic, genesis, genus, osteogenesis**
natus- **native, nation, nativity, nationalism**
-itis **otitis, neuritis, dermatitis, rhinitis**
-ectomy **appendectomy, tonsillectomy, mastectomy**
-iatry **psychiatry, podiatry**
-lysis **paralysis, analysis, electrolysis**
-lepsy **narcolepsy, epilepsy**
orth- ortho- **orthopedic, orthography, orthodontist, orthotics**

-scope **periscope, endoscopy, colonoscopy, oscilloscope**
-stat **hemostat, rheostat, thermostat**

Assignment:
This is a great time for reflection!
What are you learning about how all these roots and stems work together?

Consider writing a short story about a **hypochondriac** (*hypo + chondros* "cartilege")
who has ailments in a variety of different body parts as a way of using your increasing
knowledge.

Unit Seven
Lesson 80
Words of Wisdom in action

See how much of this short essay makes sense. If you need more explanation, the definitions follow.

"Reversal of Fortune"

Rich seemed to have lived a charmed life.

His parents were professionals and earned a very good living. His mother was an ophthalmologist and his father an orthodontist. They lived to make sure that he had the best of everything and they succeeded. Unfortunately, they left him a legacy of entitlement, to which he adapted quite easily. He assumed that lIfe owed him the best and he enthusiastically pursued a sensual, epicurean lifestyle to accomplish that aspect of what he considered his teleonomy. His appetite for the best food and drink was insatiable. He was quite gregarious and earned a reputation as a party boy, describing himself as "selfish, arrogant, supercilious, annoying, impulsive, self righteous, loquacious and vociferous in his dealings with the hoi polloi." He prided himself on being able to callously obfuscate every nebulous situation with his clever wit and charm. His only dealing with the "plebeians" was to tease those fawning sycophants into thinking that they might curry some of his favor. Behind his back they viewed his pusillanimous behavior for what it was, while maintaining their own obsequious appearances and disguising their acrimony towards him with their low-class idioms.

When his parents were killed in the crash of their private plane, he inherited their fortune. If his lifestyle had been somewhat less extravagant, this should have satisfied his needs and wishes for a lifetime. However, his egregious, fatal error was his unabated, conspicuous consumption. After a scant two years, his wealth dissipated leaving him impoverished, his name in disrepute. All of his still affluent friends deserted him, ascribing his calamitous fall from fortune to his own making.

This reversal of fortune forced him to rethink his way of life. He began to realize that his desultory approach, meandering from one selfish, meaningless expenditure to another with total disregard of others, was not working. He began to really see and appreciate the "little people" whom he had previously held in such disdain. His newly-found clairvoyance and astuteness helped him develop a spirit of altruism he had never experienced. He determined that this iteration of his life would be different. He vowed that if he were ever to regain his prior station, he would be much more munificent. His newfound abstemious life allowed him to be more genuinely animated, as well as generous. He found himself associating with exciting, vivacious people who didn't have to fawn over him for his wealth. He found gracious and pleasant people to be more ubiquitous than he had ever realized. He didn't have to live surreptitiously or vicariously; he could have his own genuine personal experiences in full view of his newly found world.

Abstemious "marked by restraint, esp. In the consumption of food or alcohol"

Acrimonious adj. (fr. L. *acer* "sharp") "caustic or biting in feeling, language or manner"

Altruistic (fr. L. alter "another") "unselfish regard for the welfare of others over that of self"

Animated (fr. L. *animus, -a* "spirit") "filled with life or spirit"

Calamitous adj. "a state of deep distress or misery caused by major misfortune or loss; an extraordinarily grave event marked by great loss and lasting distress and affliction; disaster"

Clairvoyant adj. (*clair* "clear" + *voyant* "seeing") "able to perceive matters not present to the senses"

Desultory adj. (fr. a Roman story describing a circus rider who jumps from one moving horse to another) "marked by a lack of a definite plan, regularity or purpose; not connected with the main subject; sluggish"

Disdain n. (fr. *dignare* "to deign") "a feeling of contempt for what is beneath one; scorn"

Egregious "conspicuously bad; flagrant (an ~ mistake)"

Entitlement "birthright"

Epicurean (fr. followers of Epicurus) "possessing discriminating taste, esp. in food or wine"

Gregarious (fr. L. *grex* "flock") "social, tending to associate with others of one's kind; sociable"

Hoi polloi n. (fr. G. an expression meaning "the many" or "the majority") "used in English to denote 'the masses' or 'the people', usually in a derogatory sense"

Idiom n. (fr. L. *idioma* "individual peculiarity of language"; fr. *idio-* "one's own, personal, separate, distinct") "language peculiar to a people, or to a district, a region or a class; dialect"

Iteration (fr. *iter* – road, route, or journey) "the act of repeating a process usually with the aim of approaching a desired goal. Each repetition of the process is also called an 'iteration', and the results of one iteration are used as the starting point for the next iteration."

Legacy (fr. L. *legatus*) "a gift by will of money or other inheritance"

Meander "to wander, to follow a winding or intricate course; a turn or the winding of a stream"

Munificent adj. (fr. L. *munus* "service or gift") "very liberal in giving or bestowing, lavish; characterized by great generosity"

Nebulous adj. (fr. *nephos* "cloud of dust in interstellar space") "indistinct, vague, not clear"

Obfuscate (fr. L.*ob-* + *fuscus* "dark brown") "to darken, to make obscure, to confuse"

Obsequious adj. "marked by or exhibiting a fawning attentiveness; subservient"

Plebeians n. (fr. L. *plebs* "common people") "the common people; crude or coarse"

Pusillanimous adj. (fr. L *pusillus* "small boy" + *animus* "spirit") "lacking courage and resolution; marked by contemptible timidity"

Satiated (fr. L. *satis* "enough") satiable insatiable satisfied

Supercilious (lit. nose "above the eyebrow") "coolly and patronizingly haughty, arrogant"

Surreptitious "done, made or acquired by stealth; clandestine"

Sycophant n. (fr. G. *sykophantes* "slanderer, swindler") "a servile, self-seeking flatterer; syn. Parasite"

Teleonomy n. (fr. G. *telos* "end" + *nomos* "sum of knowledge on a subject") "the quality of apparent purposefulness in living organisms that derives from their evolutionary adaptation"

Ubiquitous adj. (fr. L. *ubi* "where") "existing everywhere at the same time; omnipresent"

Vicarious (fr. L. vicis "change, stead") "experienced or realized through imaginative or sympathetic participation in the experience of another"

Vivacious (fr. L. vivax "long-lived") "lively in temper, conduct or spirit; lively"

Vociferous "uttered loudly; marked by or given to vehement incessant outcry"

As you move forward, consider writing your own descriptive essay, incorporating some of the words from this book that you have integrated into your active vocabulary.

Words of Wisdom

Four Minutes a Day to a Richer and More Powerful Vocabulary

INDEX

Words are identified by Unit and Lesson (e.g. 6-48 = Unit 6, Lesson 48)

219

magistrial 7-66
magistrate 7-66
magistrature 7-66
maintain 6-48
maintainability 6-48
maintainable 6-48
maintained 6-48
maintenance 6-48
maladjusted 7-70
maladroit 7-70
malaprop 7-70
malapropos 7-70
malcontent 7-70
male- 7-75
maledict 7-70
malediction 7-70
malefactor 7-70
maleficence 7-70
malevolent 7-70
malfeasance 7-70
malus- 7-70
man 7-65
-mania 7-77
-maniac 7-77
Manias, Phobias 7-77
Manu 6-48
manufacture 6-46
manufactured 6-46
manufacturer 6-46
manufacturing 6-46
mastectomy 7-79
mater familias 7-65
maternal 7-65
maternally 7-65
maternity 7-65
mathematics 7-72
matriarch 7-65
matriarchal 7-65
matriarchate 7-65
matriarchy 7-65
matricide 7-65
matrilineal 7-65
matrimonial 7-65
matrimony 7-65
matrix 7-65
matron 7-65
matronly 7-65
matronymic 7-65
maxi- 7-74
maximal 7-74
maximin 7-74
maximum 7-74
mea culpa 7-70
meander 7-80
medic 7-66
medical 7-66
Medicare 7-66

medicate 7-66
medication 7-66
medicinal 7-66
medicine 7-66
megal- 7-77
megalo- 7-77
megalomaniac 7-77
menopause 7-72
menses 7-72
menstrual 7-72
menstruation 7-72
Mensura 7-72
Mensura Plura 7-73
meta- or *met-* 5-37
Metacognition 5-37
Metacognitive 5-37
-meter 7-71
micro- 7-74
microbiology 7-74
microeconomics 7-74
microflora 7-74
micrometer 7-74
microphone 7-74
microscope 7-74
milli- 7-74
milligram 7-74
milliliter 7-74
millisecond 7-74
millivolt 7-74
mini- 7-74
minibus 7-74
minicamp 7-74
minimax 7-74
miniseries 7-74
miniskirt 7-74
minute 7-72
minutia 7-72
mis- 7-75
mis- 7-75
misanthrope 7-76
misanthropy 7-76
miscellaneous 7-75
mischievous 7-75
miscommunicate 7-75
misconstrue 7-75
miscreant 7-75
misdemeanor 7-75
miserable 7-75
mishandle 7-75
misinterpret 7-75
mislead 7-75
misogamist 7-76
misogamy 7-76
misogynist 7-76
misogyny 7-76
misplace 7-75

mispronounce 7-75
misread 7-75
missile (adj.) 4-8
missile (n.) 2-8
missileer 2-8
missileman 2-8
missilery 2-8
missiology 2-8
mission 2-8
missionaries 2-8
missionary 2-8
missioned 2-8
missioning 2-8
missionize 2-8
missionizer 2-8
missive 2-8
mistaken 7-75
mistranscribe 7-75
mistranslate 7-75
misunderstood 7-75
misutilize 7-75
Mittere 2: 8-13
Mittimus 2-8
monarchy 7-71
mono- 1 Gr. 7-71
monochromatic 7-71
monocle 7-71
monocracy 7-71
monocular 7-71
monogamy 7-71
monogamy 7-78
monogram 7-71
monopoly 7-71
monosyllabic 7-71
monotheism 7-71
monotone 7-71
montane 7-68
-moros 7-75
-morph 7-75
morph- 7-75
-morphic 7-75
-morphous 7-75
mountain 7-68
mountaineer 7-68
mountainous 7-68
mountaintop 7-68
muliebrity 7-65
mult- multi- 7-75
multicultural 7-70
multilateral 7-72
multilevel 7-75
multilingual 7-70
multilingual 4-31
multinational 7-75
multiple 7-70
multiplex 7-75
multiplicand 7-70

multiplication 7-70
multiplier 7-70
multiply 7-75
multiplying 7-72
multitalented 7-75
multitudinous 7-70
multivitamin 7-75
mundane 7-67
munificent 7-80
narcolepsy 7-79
narcolepsy 7-78
nasal 7-79
nasality 7-79
nasogastric 7-79
nasopharyngeal 7-79
nasus 7-79
nasus 7-79
nation 7-79
nationalism 7-79
native 7 79
nativity 7-79
natus- 7-79
natus- 7-79
nebulous 7-80
nepotism 7-66
nepotistic 7-66
neur- 7-79
neur- neuro- 7-79
neuritis 7-79
neuritis 7-79
neuro- 7-79
neurogenic 7-79
neurology 7-79
neurotic 7-79
neurotoxin 7-79
n-gons 7-71
Nominative 7-64
nonary 7-79
noncommittal 2-9
nonillion 7-71
nonlinguistic 4-31
nonsense 5-39
non-sense 5-39
nonsensical 5-39
nonsensically 5-39
Nonus- L. 7-71
Noscere 4-34
Nota Bene 4-34
notable 4-34
notably 4-34
Notare 4-34
notary 4-34
notate 4-34
notation 4-34
note 4-34
notice 4-34
noticeable 4-34

223

List of resources

Borror, Donald J. **Dictionary of Root Words and Combining Forms** Mayfield Publishing CO.: Mountain View, CA 1960

.. **Family Word Finder** Reader's Digest Association, Inc.: Plesasntville, NY, 1975

Freundlich, Charles I. **Review Text in First Year Latin** Amsco School Publications: New York, NY, 1958

Funk, Wilfred & Lewis, Norman **30 Days to a More Powerful Vocabulary** Pocket Books: New York, 1969

Garrison, Webb **Why You Say It** Rutledge Hill Press: Nashville, TN, 1992

Handford, S A & Herberg, Mary **Langenscheidt Pocket Latin Dictionary** Langenscheidt: Berlin & Munich, 1966

.. **Merriam-Webster's Collegiate Dictionary** Merriam-Webster, Inc.: Springfield, MA 1993

Shorrock, Robert & Butterfield, David **Latin Dictionary** Penguin Books: New York, NY 2007

.. **Webster's Encyclopedic Unabridged Dictionary of the English Language** Gramercy Books: New York, 1996

Hartsell, Jonathon **Let's Have a Word or Two** Lexicom Products: Austin, TX 1996

Internet resources

About	http://about.com/
Ancient History	http://ancienthistory.about.com/
Answers	http://www.answers.com/
Ashburnham Westminster Regional School District	http://www.awrsd.org/
Ask	http://www.ask.com/
Ask Kids	http://www.askkids.com/
Ask Reference	http://ask.reference.com/information
BBC	http://news.bbc.co.uk/
Bing	http://www.bing.com/
Brainy Quote	http://www.brainyquote.com/
Dictionary.com	http://dictionary.reference.com/
Dictionary.net	http://www.dictionary.net/
EdWeb Portal	http://edweb.fdu.edu/welcome/
Encyclopedia 2, the Free Dictionary	http://encyclopedia2.thefreedictionary.com/
ETS	http://www.ets.org/portal/
FacePunch	http://www.facepunch.com/
Fun Trivia	http://www.funtrivia.com/
Google	http://www.google.com
Investor Words	http://www.investorwords.com/
Latin Dictionary and Grammar Aide	http://www.nd.edu/~archives/latin.htm
Lycos	http://www.angelfire.lycos.com/
Merriam-Webster	http://www.merriam-webster.com/dictionary/
Metacrawler	http://www.metacrawler.com/
Phrontistery	http://phrontistery.info/
Synonym	http://www.synonym.com/synonyms/
True Knowledge	http://www.trueknowledge.com/
University of Ottawa	http://www.uottawa.ca/academics/index.html
Webster's On-Line Dictionary	http://www.websters-online-dictionary.org/
Wiktionary	http://en.wiktionary.org/wiki/Wiktionary:Main_Page
Wikipedia	http://en.wikipedia.org/wiki/Main_Page
Word Reference	http://www.wordreference.com/
Yahoo	http://answers.yahoo.com/
Your Dictionary	http://www.yourdictionary.com/

Fresh Perspectives is not responsible for the content of the external websites.

www.MorePowerfulWords.com

Other Books & Courses available from FRESH PERSPECTIVES

Using "Words Of Wisdom" to Enhance Writing and Technology Skills

Using MS Office & Internet Resources to Enhance Elementary Mathematics

Using MS Office & Internet Resources to Enhance Elementary Science

Using MS Office to Enhance Student Higher Order Thinking Skills

Integrating MS Office Applications for the Classroom Teacher

Grant Writing Workshop

(For Windows 2007 or 2003)

Introduction to Microsoft Word for Teachers

Intermediate Microsoft Word for Teachers

Advanced Microsoft Word for Teachers

Introduction to Microsoft Excel for Teachers

Intermediate Microsoft Excel for Teachers

Advanced Microsoft Excel for Teachers

Introduction to Microsoft Excel for Teachers

Intermediate Microsoft Excel for Teachers

Advanced Microsoft Excel for Teachers

Introduction to Microsoft Publisher for Teachers

Creating Your First Website

Technology Boot Camp (MS Office Intro level courses)

Contact freshper@gmail.com for details or further information about presentations, books, courses or graduate credit

www.MorePowerfulWords.com

www.fresh-perspectives.biz